HISTORIC TEXTS AND INTERPRETERS IN BIBLICAL SCHOLARSHIP

General Editor:
Professor J. W. Rogerson (Sheffield)

Consultant Editors:
Professor C. K. Barrett (Durham)
Professor R. Smend (Göttingen)

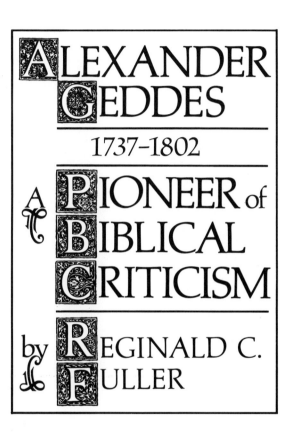

ALEXANDER
GEDDES

1737–1802

A PIONEER of
BIBLICAL
CRITICISM

by REGINALD C.
FULLER

The Almond Press · 1984

HISTORIC TEXTS AND INTERPRETERS
IN BIBLICAL SCHOLARSHIP, 3

British Library Cataloguing in Publication Data:

Fuller, Reginald C.
    Alexander Geddes, 1737-1802.—(Historic
    texts and interpreters in Biblical
    Scholarship, ISSN 0263-1199; 3)
    1. Geddes, Alexander 2. Biblical scholars
    —Great Britain—Biography
    I. Title   II. Series
    220.6'092'4   BS501.G4

    ISBN 0-907459-26-9
    ISBN 0-907459-27-7 Pbk

ISSN 0263-1199

Published by
The Almond Press
P.O. Box 208
Sheffield S10 5DW
England

Printed in Great Britain by
Dotesios (Printers) Ltd
Bradford-on-Avon, Wiltshire
1984

TABLE OF CONTENTS

GENERAL EDITOR'S PREFACE

It is fifteen years since Reginald Fuller was awarded a Cambridge doctorate for his thesis "Dr Alexander Geddes: A Forerunner of Biblical Criticism". That so many years have elapsed between the presentation of the thesis and its publication as a book in a revised form, is in no way the fault of the author. Previous attempts at publication ran into difficulties, mainly financial. In one case a famous German publishing house felt unable to proceed, despite the strongest recommendations from eminent continental scholars.

The non-publication of the thesis has deprived the scholarly world of permanent and easy access to a study of the highest quality, based upon most painstaking research, whose subject is a man who occupies an almost unique place in the history of biblical criticism. Of course, the thesis has always been available for consultation in the normal manner, and it is a tribute both to Dr Fuller's work and to the significance of Alexander Geddes that the thesis has been used not only by biblical scholars, but by English Literature scholars such as Elinor Shaffer in her *'Kubla Khan' and The Fall of Jerusalem*. It is to be hoped that publication of the thesis will make it known to a much wider readership.

Inevitably, a thesis prepared so long ago cannot expect to remain unaffected by later scholarly work. For the most part, Dr Fuller's thesis has not dated, simply because nobody else has researched the life of Geddes so minutely; nor is anyone ever likely to. However, in the case of parts of the material contained in chapters six and seven, where Dr Geddes's place in the history of biblical criticism is considered, there have been advances in knowledge, for some of which the present writer is responsible. In particular, in my *Myth in Old Testament Interpretation* (1974), I discussed fully the anthropological and philosophical assumptions behind the use of the concept of myth in the late 18th and early 19th centuries. I argued that there was a more radical discontinuity between de Wette and his contemporaries than was assumed in the standard literature which Dr Fuller studied so carefully, and whose results he presented so lucidly. In my view, de Wette's work from his earliest writings onwards owes much more to the philosophy of J. F. Fries than has been previously recognised, and his very sophisticated position is to be distinguished, on the one hand, from that of G. L. Bauer and J. P. Gabler, and on the other from that of

D. F. Strauss. I am not sure that I could agree with Dr Fuller's statement on p. 110 that 'had Geddes continued his research he would in all likelihood have reached very much the same position as de Wette'.

These remarks are not written in order to detract in any way from the great merits of Dr Fuller's work, but simply to indicate to the reader some more recent developments in criticism. A considerable amount of revision was carried out by the author prior to his departure for Africa in 1972, but since his return to England his commitments have precluded further detailed attention to the work.

The editors of the series *Historic Texts and Interpreters* are convinced that it is their duty to delay publication no longer.

J. W. Rogerson
The University of Sheffield

FOREWORD

Among eighteenth century British scholars, wrote T. K. Cheyne, there are but three "who appear to have shown any talent or inclination for a criticism of the Old Testament which is not merely concerned with various readings of the text—Bishop Warburton, Bishop Lowth and Dr Alexander Geddes; and of these the only one who can properly be called a founder of criticism is the third".[1] This estimate of Geddes's place in the history of biblical criticism has been endorsed and indeed developed in more recent times by Professor J. G. Macgregor of Los Angeles. 'Geddes,' he observes, 'was incontestably a man of great learning and independence of mind and his work as a pioneer of modern biblical scholarship is of the greatest historical importance.'[2]

It is therefore a matter calling for some consideration that the details of his work should be largely unknown to many scholars at the present day. Indeed his very name is usually quoted only in connection with the Fragment Hypothesis of Pentateuchal Composition which he initiated but which was mainly developed by Johann Severin Vater. The attention of the present writer was drawn to Geddes when engaged on a study of Roman Catholics and the Bible since the Reformation.

If Geddes has indeed the significance which a careful study of his work implies, how does one explain the neglect which appears to have been his lot? One may suggest a number of reasons. In the first place, he never completed his translation of the Bible and published only one volume of his Critical Remarks on the text, though much more was promised. Secondly, and more significantly, scholars in Britain were, on the whole, not receptive of the ideas which he sought to propagate and were antagonized by the forceful and exaggerated way in which he put them forward. It was mainly this opposition which led to the oblivion which many of his critics promised him. It is the aim of the present writer to show that the subsequent neglect has been undeserved.

The very circumstances which led to his being almost forgotten could in fact be adduced as a reason for singling him out today. For it was his courage, not unmixed with rashness, that impelled him to question the existing attitude to the inspired character of the sacred books of the Bible at a time when such a line of inquiry was widely regarded as tantamount to heresy. Geddes stood almost alone in his endeavours to introduce principles of literary and historical criticism into Bible study in Britain.[3]

His comparison of the Hebrew historians with Homer and Herodotus or his explanation of the Garden of Eden and the Fall of Man as mythical would hardly cause surprise today. But the long and hard-fought struggle against 'The Doctrine' (as S. T. Coleridge called it) of absolute and universal inspiration has been almost forgotten. In this struggle Geddes played a part, though victory was long delayed and he did not live to see it.

But Geddes has an additional claim on our interest. He was one of the few scholars in Britain who thought it important to learn German and make contact with German biblical scholars. After the founding of Göttingen University, many Free Churchmen had gone there from Britain; but their interests were mainly literary. Geddes learnt German specifically to enable him to read the abundant literature on biblical criticism which was being produced in that country and so introduce it, as far as he could, into Britain. If his efforts did not meet with much response this was not for want of trying; his failure should be ascribed to the existing British conservatism in Bible study.

No up-to-date biography of Geddes exists nor any detailed study of his critical work. Apart from articles in various periodicals, modern writers have been content to allocate a few lines or paragraphs to Geddes in studies and histories of biblical criticism.

The present study, an edited version of a dissertation originally submitted to the University of Cambridge for the Degree of Doctor of Philosophy, makes full use of the relevant eighteenth century literature, both British, French and German, including contemporary periodicals. In addition to this, the writer was fortunate in being able to avail himself of a large quantity of hitherto unpublished material, mostly letters written by or to Geddes. Only a small proportion of these letters and writings is concerned with biblical matters; nevertheless the material is of value in the work of recreating a picture of the man, especially in view of the obscurity into which he had fallen. At the same time, it is not the purpose of this study to give a full biography of Dr Geddes, but to describe and evaluate his biblical criticism, above all his literary and historical criticsm in which lies any originality he may possess. In accord with this aim, his poetical and other religious productions are referred to only in passing, and his Bible translation is considered only in connection with his criticism. Geddes himself, as the inscription on his tombstone indicates, wished to be known as a Bible translator, but, even apart from the fact that he did not complete his task, it is safe to say that any title to fame he may have lies elsewhere. His views on a vernacular liturgy, the election of bishops and relations between the churches are surprisingly modern, though mixed with many exaggerations.[4] But it is as a biblical critic that Geddes claims our attention here and in pursuing this study of his work it has seemed useful to include a description of the German critical school of the late eighteenth and early nineteenth centuries with a special consideration of such great scholars as Lessing, Heyne, Eichhorn and de Wette. Britain's ties with Germany in the intellectual sphere are of longer standing than perhaps generally realised and the University of Göttingen, founded in 1737 by the Elector of Hanover, George II of England, figures largely in the following pages as the home of many of Geddes's fellow scholars and, in some cases, friends.

It would be difficult to enumerate all those who have been of assistance in the writing of this work. I may be allowed to recall with gratitude the late Rev. W. J. Anderson, Curator of the Scottish Catholic Archives and his successor, Mgr David McRoberts; Mr Colin A. McLaren, Archivist and Keeper of Manuscripts, Aberdeen University; Dr Siegfried Joost, Oberbibliotheksrat of the University of Heidelberg; Professor Leslie F. Chard of the University of Cincinatti; Mr F. G. Pullen, former Librarian of Oscott College, Birmingham; Mr F. G. Emmison, Archivist, and Miss Nancy Briggs of the Essex County Record Office, Chelmsford; Miss Elizabeth Poyser, Archivist at Archbishop's House, Westminster. All of these have been of material assistance to me in the necessary research. I must also thank Mrs Elizabeth Tucker and Miss Valerie Scammell for valuable help in the preparation and typing of the work. I am especially grateful to Professor Nineham and to Dr Ernst Bammel, who were my Supervisors at Cambridge, for their guidance, advice and encouragement and to the Staff of the University Library for unfailing co-operation. Lastly, a word of thanks to Lord Petre of Ingatestone Hall, Essex and to Mr Peter Maxwell Stuart of Traquair House, Peebles, for their kind permission to reproduce paintings and photographs and for the interest they have shown in my attempt to draw Dr Geddes out of the obscurity in which he has rested for so long.

Reginald C. Fuller

ALEXANDER GEDDES

CHAPTER ONE

EARLY INFLUENCES

Under the date 26 February 1802, Bishop John Douglass, at his residence in London, wrote in his diary: 'This morning also died at his lodgings Alexander Geddes, the pensioner of the late Lord Petre and author of an unfinished translation of the Bible, replete with irreligious and heterodox reflections. He died under ecclesiastical censure.'[1] In harmony with their bishop's views and actions most of the Roman Catholic clergy in London had long since severed all connection with the unorthodox biblical critic. Certainly the majority of his co-religionists, both lay and clerical, besides many of other faiths, were of the opinion that Bishop Douglass's attitude was no more than Geddes had merited by his actions and writings. Others felt that he had been punished too severely. A few saw what he was consciously aiming at in his biblical criticism and gave him support and friendship without necessarily agreeing with all his conclusions.

The obituary in the *Gentleman's Magazine* had this to say about him: 'This libertine. . . is removed after having been permitted for a season, to concur with the Author of all Evil in exercising the faith and patience of the Saints.'[2] And a bishop of the Established Church pronounced the following not long after Geddes's death: 'Of those who, professing the Faith, have yet laboured to do it most essential injury and whom charity itself can hardly exculpate from the charge of wilfully endeavouring to bring it into contempt, none perhaps appears in a more disgraceful light than a distinguished Divine of the Romish Church patronized in this country by some persons little aware of his designs. This Writer applied the whole weight of his learning and talents to an artful attack upon the Divine Authority of the Scriptures. . . had the Writer lived to complete his design it is impossible to say how much Revealed Religion might have suffered. But happily his efforts (highly as they have been extolled by Critics of similar principles with his own) have not obtained a very extensive circulation and as it has pleased God to remove him before his labours were nearly completed, we may trust that not all the unmerited commendations of his infidel encomiasts will be able to rescue his work from speedy oblivion.'[3]

The *Monthly Review* took a rather different line: 'It will be the opinion of many that Dr Geddes evinced more intrepidity than judgment and that in discharging the office of Commentator he has taken too great liberties with the Sacred Scriptures. Against this charge we cannot altogether defend him but he seems to have been betrayed into this error by observing how much superstitious reverence for the Jewish Scriptures and the belief in their Inspiration have enervated the hand of criticism and prevented their elucidation.' After affirming that in the long run nothing but good can come from the scientific criticism of the Scriptures the reviewer continued: 'We are persuaded that if there had been more *Geddeses* there would have been fewer infidels; that the Old Testament would have been perused and studied with more profit had it been fairly appreciated and that Revelation would have been a gainer by disclaiming all absurd and ridiculous demands on our Faith. . . It is impossible that a Commentator of the above complexion can be generally acceptable—and so perilous an attempt must necessarily be attended with many failures; but by this kind of examination truth is likely to be benefited and the text of Scripture to be purified and explained.'[4]

On the whole however the attitude taken in the above review was shared by only a small minority. The prevailing post-Revolution attitude in Britain towards the literary and historical criticism of the Bible, then strongly developing in Germany, was one of absolute or near-absolute rejection and Dr Van Mildert's forecast that Geddes would be forgotten has very nearly been fulfilled. Even if Geddes had put forward his views with studied moderation it is unlikely that the result would have been very different or that scholars of note in Britain would have approved, at least in public. The tide of opinion was running too strongly in the other direction.

The circumstances of Geddes's life were unusual. Born in the Highlands of Scotland, he began his education in a remote glen, continued his training for the priesthood in Paris, the centre of culture, exercised his ministry for some years in Scotland and spent the remaining twenty years or so in London as a prominent biblical scholar. The aim of this first chapter will be to outline the circumstances of his early life and pastoral ministry which contributed to his formation as a Bible translator and critic of considerable reputation.

EARLY EDUCATION, 1744-1758

'The parish of Rathven,' wrote the Rev. James Stothert,[5] extends about ten miles along the southern shore of the Moray Firth, from the neighbourhood of Cullen, westwards to a little brook called the Burn of Tynet which divides it from the parish of Bellie. Its southern boundary lies in the vicinity of Keith. This parish includes the greater part of the rural district or barony known as the Enzie of Banff, a tract of country very celebrated in the history of Catholicity in Scotland for at least two centuries. The majority of the population has always professed the ancient religion, of which many traditions still linger among them.'[6] That so many remained Catholics[7] was due very largely to the fact that the Gordons, who owned most of the country around, were themselves Roman Catholics until 1728 when, on the death of the second Duke, his children were brought up in the Episcopal Church by their mother.[8]

Alexander Geddes, the son of a small tenant farmer at Arradowl, on the borders of the Gordon estates, was born on 4 September 1737 at a time when Roman Catholics, although discriminated against in various ways, were not being actively persecuted. This was particularly true in the Highlands where the clan system established definite limits to what the government could do in the way of enforcing its will. His parents were good practising Catholics. In the circumstances of the time, full commitment was required and it would have been almost unthinkable to call oneself a Catholic and not to practise and fuflil the obligations of one's faith. Yet together with this unambiguous allegiance, his parents regularly used and were greatly attached to the Common or Vulgar Version of the Bible, i.e. the Authorized (or King James) Version. 'Although my parents were Roman Catholics,' wrote Geddes, 'they were not bigots; and the Bible was the principal book in their scanty library. They taught me to read it with reverence and attention; and before I had reached my eleventh year, I knew all its history by heart.'[9] Geddes wrote that in 1790 and allowing for a certain mellowing of perspective after forty years there appears to be no good reason for doubting its substantial accuracy. Though it could hardly have been typical of Roman Catholics at that time, it is probable that, at least among Lowland Scots, regular Bible reading was not uncommon. It would have taken place at the time of family worship when the head of the family would not only conduct the prayers and lead the psalm singing but read a portion of the Bible as well. In such families as these the Bible would almost certainly have been the common version because it was both cheaper in price and more readily available.[10] It would however be idle to suggest that the majority of Catholics had ever acquired the habit of regular Bible reading.

The only official Catholic Bible in English was the Rheims-Douay version, originally published in the years 1582 (New Testament) and 1609-10 (Old Testament). But the translation had never been popular or widespread at any time, partly because its language was stiff and grating, being a very literal translation from the Latin, partly because it was too expensive, being published in three large volumes.[11] It may further be taken for granted that if these Bibles were scarce in England they were even more scarce in Scotland where half the population would have been unable to read English anyway.

In later years, when he had grown more critical of the Church, Dr Geddes described the situation in characteristic fashion. 'The greater part of the R. Catholics of Great Britain and Ireland might be said to be without a Bible. The Common National Version they would not use, because (forsooth), it was the work of Heretics; and because, as they pretended, it was unfairly translated; and also because several Books, which the Council of Trent had decreed to be Canonical, were either entirely omitted in the editions of the Common Version or accounted Apocryphal. . . Precluded thus from the use of the Common Version, they had no alternative, for more than a century, but to put up with a barbarous Translation, made at Rheims and Douay, from an uncorrected copy of the Latin Vulgate; accompanied with virulent Annotations against the Protestant Religion and manifestly calculated to support a system, not of genuine Catholicity, but of trans-alpine Popery.'[12]

Eventually in 1749-50 Dr Challoner, Vicar Apostolic of the London District, completed a revision of the whole Bible and omitted most of the controversial notes, substituting a number of his own, more doctrinal in character and less controversial.[13] About the year 1750, Bishop Smith, Vicar Apostolic, was doing his best to distribute copies of Challoner's New Testament to his people in Scotland, in difficult conditions, following the rebellion of 1745.[14]

By the middle of the eighteenth century the Common Version of the Bible had become a part of the British heritage and the standard by which all others were judged; and this to such an extent that any notable deviation from it had small chance of gaining a wide public. To make his version acceptable Challoner had revised it in the direction of the Common Version but Geddes did not account this a virtue. He himself had long since abandoned any idea of using that version as a standard for his own. Furthermore Dr Challoner's version was based, like its predecessors, on the Latin, and, though Challoner had stripped it of nearly all its polemical notes, 'yet still in those which he retained or altered, the spirit of theologic system is but too visible.'[15]

In 1744, the youthful Alexander, then aged seven, joined a small group of boys from the locality, sons of both lairds and their tenants, who were receiving elementary schooling from a Mr James Shearer, tutor to the sons of Mr Gordon, laird of Cairnfield. It appears that Shearer was a student of King's College, Aberdeen, and probably undertook some teaching in order to defray his University expenses.[16] During the troubled period of the Rising of 1745, young Geddes had various teachers, last of whom was the local priest, Mr Alexander Godsman,[17] who came to Preshome, a village near the Burn of Tynet, in 1748. His companions in study were his cousins John Geddes,[18] two years his

senior, and John Reid, both of whom had been in the earlier group
taught by Mr Shearer. Under Mr Godsman's direction the boys began to
learn Latin and French, apart from other subjects. All three were
destined to become priests and one, John Geddes, a bishop. No doubt
here too, as his education already began to take an ecclesiastical turn,
Alexander made his first nodding acquaintance with the Vulgate Latin
Bible. During these early years he had also the privilege of guidance
from another priest, one who looked upon him almost as his own son.
James Grant had been thrown into prison at Inverness after the Rising
of 1745 and had spent two years there in chains. His brother eventually
managed to obtain his release and he returned, broken in health, to his
native Enzie. After spending some time at his brother's home to regain
his health, he was put in charge of the Catholics of Rathven parish in
1748. He remained there until his consecration as Bishop in 1755.[19]
Thus, from 1747 when he was released from prison until 1751 when
Alexander Geddes went to Scalan, the two would have been constantly
together and their later correspondence is abundant testimony to the
affection which each had for the other. It is not fanciful to suggest that
Mr Grant probably had a good deal to do with Geddes's decision to offer
himself as a candidate for the priesthood.

In 1751, when Alexander was fourteen years old, he went to a small
local school at Scalan which served in those times as a minor seminary.
The place was in the Braes of Glenlivet, a remote valley nearly forty
miles south of Elgin and specially chosen for its seclusion in view of
persecution.[20] A wide range of subjects was taught, though the
emphasis was always on piety and religious formation rather than on
intellectual brilliance. Besides Latin, Greek and even Hebrew were
taught if a pupil showed any aptitude and the older students embarked
on studies which would now be carried out in the major seminary.[21] It
was here that Geddes made his first real acquaintance with the Latin
Bible. 'When I had acquired a sufficient knowledge of Latin, the Vulgate was put into my hands, which I was afterwards to study more
minutely, as being the text book of our schools and colleges. And now
it was that I perceived a considerable difference between it and the
English translation' (the Common Version). 'The latter appeared to me
rugged, constrained and even obscure where the former was smooth,
easy and intelligible. . .' It appears however, that Geddes did not begin
either Greek or Hebrew at Scalan or at least that he did not get very far,
if he began at all. '. . . in 1762,' he wrote (i.e. four years after arrival in
Paris), 'I began to read the originals. . .'[22]

Apart from the difficulties arising from religious and political conditions there were other drawbacks. The valley in which the college was
situated was one of the most sunless of Scotland.[23] Geddes preserved

no tender recollections of Scalan and appears never to have referred to his stay there except on one occasion, to his cousin Bishop John Geddes, in 1784. The bishop had written informing him that a reorganisation was in progress at Scalan. 'I am glad,' replied Alexander, 'to learn that improvements are making at Scalan—I will not add your epithet "beloved" for I cordially hate it. It was there I first lost my health and ruined an excellent constitution.'[24]

Geddes remained at Scalan until he was twenty-one and that probably meant without any considerable break. In those days school holidays were not so regular or so long as today, and in any case boys at minor seminaries (which is really what Scalan was) did not normally go home at all during their course there. This long stay at Scalan would suggest (for he was an intelligent youth) that Alexander was already well launched on his studies for the priesthood by the time he left there for Paris. There were indeed a few students who completed their studies and were ordained at Scalan. But the facilities there were necessarily meagre and it was customary to spend a number of years at one of the Scots colleges abroad, at Douay, Paris, Madrid or Rome. Geddes was destined to continue his studies at the Scots College, Paris, and in the autumn of 1758 he set sail for France as his cousin John had done for Rome a few years previously. The weather was rough and Geddes became ill on the voyage. In consequence of the need for convalescence on landing he did not reach Paris until December. The Rev. Mr Duthie, his superior at Scalan, was his companion on the journey as he had just been appointed Prefect of Studies at the Paris College. While Alexander was studying in Paris, his brother Andrew John set off for Germany and entered the Scottish Abbey of St James at Würzburg where, as a Benedictine monk, he spent the rest of his life.[25]

PARIS, 1758-1764

When Geddes reached Paris in 1758 he found a very sharp contrast with his previous environment. From the remote fastness of a Highland glen he now stepped into one of the acknowledged centres of the intellectual life of the civilized world. In the middle of the eighteenth century the Enlightenment was at its height. Reason must investigate and explain everything. The tendency was to get away from authoritarian ecclesiasticism and supernatural religion and to emphasise the capacity of man's rational faculty to discover truth. It was not however abstract reasoning which interested the *philosophes*—the men of the Enlightenment. They had a distrust of philosophical systems and the fitting of facts into any ready-made pattern. It was reason operating on experience which was capable of reaching truth.[26] They liked to be thought of as philosophers in the Socratic rather than the systematic sense. Two points in particular made a great impression on Geddes. The *philosophes* had a confidence in the perfectibility of human nature which could be seen as a reaction against the pessimism of some of the Reformers. In the second place, their antipathy to organised religion was clearly influenced by the earlier wars of religion. This had an effect on Geddes which was visible in his later years.

By the time of Geddes's departure from Paris, the current of new thought seemed to be carrying all before it.[27] D'Alembert spoke of the spirit of discovery spreading like a river in flood which had burst its banks.[28] Meanwhile the Church closed its ranks and tried to retain what influence it could without compromising in any way with the new thought.[29] William Cole wrote this account: 'To such a pass were these philosophers arrived, as not only in their writings to fall foul of all Revelation but also in private companies to ridicule the religion of their country; insomuch that the Religious Orders could not pass the streets without being pointed at and turned into ridicule for the singularity of their several habits—in the very same manner that the two last Whitehall Evening Posts (I write this May 31st 1766) have contained each a long letter to ridicule the dress of the English clergy. . . For it is the selfsame principle that animates the enemies of the Church in both kingdoms. . . To such a pitch of assurance was the French philosophy risen that I was told by Mr Walpole, on observing to him the few regular clergy one saw in the streets of Paris, that they had orders from their superiors to keep more within their cloisters not to give offence to their enemies by their too open appearance in the world and their ridicule had had this effect that many of the younger monks of St Germain and other convents had actually petitioned the Parlement for leave to quit their religious habit. The men who take the lead in their several, busy and factious parliaments—if we may judge of all by the specimens we have of many of them—are of too philosophical a turn to allow that Reason is only a handmaid of Revelation. In short, the present situation of France has much the appearance of being soon the theatre of a civil war.'[30] This was the world in which Geddes spent six years training to be a priest among a people who appeared very largely to regard the clergy as belonging to an obscurantist past. Admittedly, those who thought like the *philosophes* constituted but a minority; they were nevertheless a highly vocal minority. They possessed moreover a high degree of literacy and Geddes, attending as he did the University of Paris, would have been in close contact with them. The effect on him was considerable, even though it took time to mature. Yet he never lost his sense of allegiance to the Church, whatever other people might think of him and however far outside the pale they might regard him. If Geddes attacked the Church, he was attacking, like Voltaire, the Church as he saw it and as it presented itself to the world in the eighteenth century. Similarly, Geddes's criticisms were those of an Erasmus rather than a Gibbon. He criticised not so much the truth itself as the way it was presented.[31] At least that is how he would have explained his conduct and what he was conscious of doing. Others might have difficulty in seeing it his way. 'Ecrasez l'infame' are words which are not recorded in Geddes's works though they might well serve as a summary of certain of his later writings. Whatever the sincerity in Voltaire's words, 'Vous pensez bien que je ne parle que de la superstition, car pour la religion je l'aime et la respecte comme vous,'[32] Geddes would have endorsed them wholeheartedly as applying to himself.

The Collège des Ecossais to which Geddes came in 1758 was of ancient origin, tracing its history to a foundation near Paris by the Bishop of Moray in 1325. Its original purpose was to provide for poor Scots students at the University of Paris. With the change of religion in the sixteenth century it was refounded in Paris itself and given over to the training of priests for Scotland. Queen Mary Stuart provided it with endowments and the exiled Archbishop James Beaton of Glasgow gave his own house in the rue des Amandiers as premises for the College.[33] In 1662 a house in the rue Fossés St Victor was acquired and the College established there.[34] Finally Letters Patent of Louis XIV confirming the establishment were issued in 1688. The College was to be connected with the University of Paris and enjoy all the rights and privileges of colleges so attached to the University.[35] The Prior of the Carthusians in Paris was to be the ecclesiastical superior; there were also a Principal in charge of the College and a Procurator, both to be natives of Scotland. By privilege these two officials were also French subjects. Evidently the Scottish bishops were to have no say at all in the conduct of the College, except such as any well-disposed Principal was inclined to concede — but it is well to remember that at the time the arrangement was made there were no Scottish bishops.[36]

It was a time of spiritual renewal in the French Church and during the twenty years 1640-1660 no less than four seminaries were opened in Paris alone, namely, the Oratoire, St Sulpice (founded by M. Olier), St Nicholas du Chardonnet (begun by Père Bourdoise) and the Collège des Bons Enfants (refounded by St Vincent de Paul).[37] Not all these colleges gave lectures. There were many houses in Paris which were no more than halls of residence for students attending courses at the Sorbonne (the divinity school), or other Faculties of the University of Paris.[38] The Scots College itself was a hall of residence and its students attended lectures elsewhere but it is not easy to determine exactly where. Apparently it was a matter for the Prefect of Studies to settle, and not all the students would go to the same place. Some would go to the Sorbonne, others to the Collège de Navarre or to St Nicholas du Chardonnet. Later in their course the students might spend some time at the Oratorian house of Notre Dame des Vertus, to the north east of Paris. Geddes began his studies at the Collège de Navarre where he studied Rhetoric under Professor Vicaire and, it seems, [39] soon became head of his class. In his second year instead of Natural Philosophy he was recommended to start theology under Buré and de Saurent in the same college. Meanwhile he kept up his Latin and Greek and modern languages. Later in his studies he took up Hebrew under the direction of Prof. de L'Advocat at the Sorbonne, the first holder of the chair of Hebrew recently founded by the Duc d'Orléans. He made such good progress that his professor was anxious for him to remain in Paris and pursue an academic career but this invitation he was not in a position to accept. Geddes claimed later that it was in Paris that he first conceived the idea of translating the Bible into English. [40]

The Scots College was hardly an intellectual centre. Apart from housing the students, it was, after 1688, also a centre of Jacobite activity and the Principal of the College, Mr Lewis Innes, was chaplain to the exiled Stuarts at the Court of St Germain. This necessitated his absence from the College for long periods. Moreover the doors of the College were always open to any Scotsman passing through Paris, regardless of his religion or politics, and many a Scotsman made use of this freely dispensed hospitality. David Hume visited it more than once. Not long after his arrival in Paris, 1763, Hume obtained permission from Principal Gordon to inspect the College archives. He wrote, 'I have here met with a prodigious historical curiosity, the Memoirs of King James II in fourteen volumes, all wrote with his own hand and kept in the Scots College.' [41] When Hume visited the College Geddes was within a year of his ordination to the priesthood and the completion of his course. It is tempting to think that he may have met and conversed with Hume but this is improbable. Hume as a distinguished visitor would have dined at the high table and been entertained afterwards by the Principal. In the library however there would have at least been common ground, and the possibility of a meeting cannot be altogether excluded.

Students on their way to Rome from Scotland would stop at the College en route and be well entertained, besides having their expenses for the journey paid by the College. It was, too, an important centre of information and the bishops' agent there frequently had to inform Rome of the circumstances of the Church in Scotland and the hardships endured by the missionaries. The agent was normally the Procurator of the College and he was the channel by which subsidies from the Congregation *de Propaganda Fide* reached Scotland. Money belonging to the

Scottish mission was also invested in Paris and managed by the Procurator.

The spirit of Gallicanism was still very much alive at the end of the seventeenth century. This showed itself particularly in the discussions between Church and State on the question of the appointment of bishops and other higher ecclesiastics, and was epitomized at an assembly of the clergy in 1682. At this the bishops and deputies present declared what they held to be their rights and formulated them in four articles, severely curtailing the powers of the Pope over the French Church.

The Scots College, Paris, owed its remarkable independence to the situation just described and in this respect must have contrasted strangely with the general atmosphere of the Scots College, Rome. The Paris College was as unlike a seminary on the Tridentine model as it was possible to be, but as long as it was under the judicious direction of its earlier Principals the bishops had little to complain about. An abrupt and unwelcome change however took place with the appointment of Mr John Gordon of Auchentoul as Principal in 1752. He made it clear, not only that the College was not a seminary but that it was independent both in name and in fact of the Scottish bishops. Difficulties in the relationship of Principal with the bishops arose almost at once. It will be noticed that just about this time Alexander Geddes arrived at the College and he spent the entire six years of his residence there under the direction of Mr Gordon. What disturbed the Scottish bishops even more than their lack of control, was the defective training, as they saw it, 'of the young ecclesiastics which deprived the missions of many promising students and too often resulted in their open defection from religion on their return to their own country.'[42] The bishops remonstrated but with no result and they had no alternative but to leave the College alone or cause an open rupture. Bishop Hay, assistant to Bishop Grant, Vicar Apostolic of the Lowland District, had himself been educated in the Scots College, Rome. He thought it wrong that the Paris College should be independent of the bishops in this way. So also did the Congregation *de Propaganda Fide.* But no outside person or body had any power or jurisdiction in France and nothing could be done. No Visitation of the College was ever made, (except of course by the ecclesiastical superior, the Prior of the Carthusians) because no such thing could take place without royal permission and that was never granted. Nearly a quarter of a century later Geddes wrote: 'We English Catholics, although sufficiently unfortunate in other respects, were at least lucky in this: that between us and Rome lay the great kingdom of France. The Gallican Church, or rather the University of Paris, supported by the French Parliaments, was long a strong bulwark against the irruption of

Romish opinions among us. But for this intermediate barrier we should all have been Bellarminites, Parsonites, Knottites, not English Catholics. But under the shelter of the Gallican liberties, and by adopting Gallican maxims, we saved ourselves from the imputation of many errours; and were hence enabled to carry on a more rational controversy with our Protestant brethren.'[43]

Besides its Gallican tendencies, the Scots College, Paris, had at various times during the eighteenth century shown sympathy towards Jansenism and the Jansenists. The condemnation of Pasquier Quesnel in the Bull *Unigenitus* (1713) was such an occasion. Cardinal de Noailles, Archbishop of Paris, who refused either to promulgate or to accept the condemnation, was a frequent and welcome visitor at the Scots College where he was often referred to as 'Good Mr Noble'. The historian Thomas Innes, brother of Principal Lewis Innes, and archivist at the College, was inclined at times to say violent things about *Unigenitus* or the 'Onlybegotten' as he called it, but he was prudent enough to confine his remarks to private letters.[44] Cardinal de Noailles after receiving his red hat at the Consistory of 1700 never returned to Rome till his death in 1729. The French Church seemed on the brink of schism.

The College openly read and used the *Bible de Mons*, a Jansenist publication printed and published by Elzevier of Amsterdam, though with the false imprint of 'Mons' on the title page for security reasons. A sumptuously bound copy of the Montpellier Catechism was also a valued possession of the College and is still extant.[45] Probably not many of the students were greatly influenced by these tendencies, but some undoubtedly were; and this was the occasion for Cardinal Lercari to make inquiries in the College to discover which Scots students and priests had Jansenist sympathies and showed reluctance to sign the anti-Jansenist Formula.[46]

Rome's policy towards the Jansenists during the eighteenth century fluctuated considerably. If its opposition could not always be effective in France itself, no effort was spared to pursue an anti-Jansenist policy in Scotland. Every priest who came to work in Scotland was required to sign an anti-Jansenist Formula and those priests who had been trained at the Scots College, Paris, were often suspected of disloyalty by that very fact, even when no definite evidence was forthcoming.[47] Some of this suspicion was no doubt born of the inevitable rivalry between priests educated in Rome and those trained elsewhere, especially Paris. Accusations of disloyalty were easy to make but often hard to refute. Even Bishop Smith had to complain of opposition to himself on this account on the part of his brother priests. The anti-Jansenist Formula was originally presented to and signed by the Scottish clergy in 1733. In 1770 at the normal clergy meeting it was rewritten and signed once more by them.[48] The remaining blank space under the text and first signatures was gradually filled in during the succeeding twenty years, so that no one can say precisely when any given signature was affixed. Geddes was certainly asked to sign in 1770. He refused and requested further time to think it over. In March 1771 Bishop Grant wrote to him complaining that he had had many months to consider it and still had not signed.[49] In his reply Geddes apologized for the delay in signing but explained that he should be fully convinced before doing so. Writing of himself in the third person he said: 'If ever he can bring himself to abjure the Catechism of Montpellier in all its editions (*edita et edenda*) he means to abjure it in good earnest—or if he is permitted to subscribe it (the Formula) with limitations he intends making these limitations a part of his subscription.' He stressed that the delay did not in any sense indicate a criticism of or disloyalty to his bishop. He went on: 'Whatever turn the affair takes and whatever be his last resolution, he will always retain the utmost sincere friendship and unfeigned regard for his best benefactor, earliest patron and most tender parent.'[50]

It is not easy to explain Geddes's reluctance to sign the Formula except on the general grounds of allegiance to his Alma Mater in Paris and an indisposition to obey episcopal authority, which he had acquired there. Doctrinally he could hardly be said to be a Jansenist at all; and this is how it appeared to Geddes himself. Writing many years later to his cousin, Bishop John Geddes, he said, 'The opposition of Thomas Innes and others to the Bull *Unigenitus*, especially before it was so universally received, did them honour—and though I am far, very far from being a Jansenist, I would, most probably oppose, myself, another such indefinite Bull... though I firmly hope and believe such would hardly ever be issued again.'[51] The return to a more primitive and scriptural Christianity which Jansenism claimed to be attempting certainly had its attractions for Geddes, but its rigorist discipline and Calvinistic doctrine on grace and predestination, not to mention other tenets, would have found no answering response and acceptance on his part. On the contrary his ingrained dislike of organised religion, his restiveness under authority, and his rationalism, tended to show that he had been more strongly influenced by the French *philosophes* and leaders of the Enlightenment.

One prominent feature of Jansenism Geddes did absorb—an appreciation of Holy Scripture. The Counter-reformation had steadily resisted any suggestion that the scriptures should be read by everybody, even as a desirable objective, let alone a necessary one. The translators of the Rheims-Douay Bible had been quite clear about this. They brought out their translation, they said, not because of any misguided notion that the scriptures should be in the hands of all, but because there were many Protestant vernacular versions in circulation. It therefore became necessary for Catholics to have one too, so that the true interpretation of scripture might be ascertained and heretics refuted.[52]

A special feature of Jansenist spirituality was the personal reading of the Bible; and they so far approached the Protestant point of view as to claim that it was something that everyone should do as a necessary part of the spiritual life. However, this attitude to the Bible, was intermingled with a great deal of interpretation of the scriptures which was directed to the proving of doctrines frankly Calvinistic in tone and unacceptable to the Catholic Church. This is at least part of the reason for including in the Bull *Unigenitus* condemned propositions about Bible reading which today would pass almost without comment.[53] Thus proposition 79: 'It is useful and necessary in every age and place for every kind of person, to study and know the spirit, piety and mysteries of Sacred Scripture'. Of this and suchlike one might say that it sounds a little exaggerated but it is difficult to think of propositions of this kind as qualifying for solemn condemnation by the Holy See. Moreover their presence in the list was bound to convey the impression that the Church was still in favour of keeping the scriptures from the body of the faithful. In the absence of any positive statements to the contrary it is hard to see what other conclusion could be drawn. Geddes was very conscious of this. Years later his thoughts crystallized on the subject. Writing to his cousin the bishop, he said: 'The Scripture, as you observe, is ours. But you must allow that we have on many occasions used improper means to vindicate a fair claim. When the generality of our divines industriously vilified the originals to raise the authority of a translation, when they affirmed that the Vulgate was the only authentic text on which the Hebrew and Greek were to be emended, when they cried down all vernacular versions, and contrary to the practice of the primitive Christians, prohibited the use of them, did they consult the real interest of religion or the honour of Scripture? The Scripture is the great Charter of the Catholic Church—why should she be afraid to have it universally known? Did ever an Ambassador strive to smother his own credentials? The Scriptures may be abused and wrested by the ignorance or rather the malice of the reader to his own perdition. But were the Fathers of the first six centuries ignorant any more than we? Yet they never thought of forbidding the use of them. They were extremely careful to explain them to the people, but never dreamed of taking them out of their hands. St Jerom, who bitterly complains that in his time every old woman had become a Bible interpreter does not propose as a remedy to forbid even old women to read the Bible. Has such a prohibition, introduced only in the worst ages of the Church and (if we will speak the truth) from interested motives, been of any real service to religion? I believe quite the contrary. . .'[54]

Writing again to his cousin the following year on the same subject, Geddes took the argument a stage further: 'It was not till after the clergy themselves had got plunged into the most deplorable ignorance of the S[acred] Books that they began to think of shutting them up from the laity, and very little more attention to discharge their own duty would have easily prevented all the danger which they pretended would attend a contrary measure. The most specious and most powerful argument which modern sectarists have employed and still employ to support their heresy is precisely derived from that restraint. "If the religion of the Romanists,' say they, "were agreeable to Scripture—that Scripture which they allow to be the Word of God—why are they so careful to prevent you from looking into it? And why in the name of heaven is it locked up in languages you do not understand?" Truly, my friend, we may here exclaim, *'Pudet hoc potuisse dici et non potuisse refelli'*. In good truth the best refutation we can make is to translate the Scriptures for the use of the people and take as much pains to explain them in their genuine sense as our adversaries take to pervert them to a spurious one.'[55] But these developments of Geddes's thought were still in the future. In Paris, his mind had not yet turned to consider such problems, though the seed, no doubt, had been sown.

MINISTRY, 1764-1780

On his return to Scotland after ordination, Geddes spent some months in Dundee on pastoral work. Then, for reasons unknown, he was appointed to Traquair House, Peebles, home of the Earl and Countess of Traquaire, John and Christian Stuart, a leading Catholic family. Also in residence was their son Charles, Lord Linton, then a young man of nineteen and later to become a close friend of Geddes. Lastly, there was the Dowager Countess of Traquaire, a very devout and religious person and a good friend of Bishop George Hay who received her into the Catholic Church in 1771. Hay was also a convert and of very strict principles. He was likewise highly gifted and of good family. He had studied for the priesthood in Rome in an atmosphere far removed from that of Paris. We need feel no surprise therefore that Lady Traquaire did not at all approve of Geddes with his free and easy ideas and lack of respect for Rome. In 1768 Lady Traquaire asked Hay, as Geddes's ecclesiastical superior, to remove him on account of various imprudences.

After a short return visit to Paris, he was appointed in 1769 to the charge of the Mission at Auchinhalrig, a small village on the Gordon estates, near his birthplace, vacated by the death of the previous incumbent, Mr Godsman. The place was in a clearing near the edge of the forest which surrounded Gordon Castle and about half-way between the small town of Fochabers in front of the Castle gates and the little chapel of Tynet beyond the fringe of the forest. Geddes had charge also of Fochabers and the Tynet chapel and, during his time there, was busy building chapels at Auchinhalrig and Fochabers and restoring the chapel at Tynet built by his predecessor, Mr Godsman.

The next eleven years were spent away from scripture studies[57] and Geddes threw himself wholeheartedly into the pastoral work allotted to him. He got on well with everyone around him, regardless of religion or social distinction. With his Paris education, vivacious personality, exceptional intelligence and ready wit, he was a welcome guest in the houses of the nobility, who were, for the most part, Episcopalian. Chief among these were the Duke and Duchess of Gordon, and Geddes enjoyed their friendship for many years.[58] In addition, he was on good terms with the local ministers whether Episcopalian or of the Established Kirk, and often visited them. In those days and in that locality there was a good deal of contact of this kind though the same was not necessarily true of all parts of Scotland.

With all his pastoral and social activity Geddes managed to fit in only the minimum of literary work, which consisted mostly of poetry to which he was strongly inclined, and religious essays, called forth by the circumstances of the moment. Writing to Charles Cruikshank, a fellow priest, on 23 October 1772, Geddes remarked that he was all skin and bone from stomach disorders and would like a holiday. 'I have not poetized for some months: only my own Elegy, by starts, in case no other body should take the trouble. When it is finished I will send it to Mr Hay. Alas, the Muses themselves in my present situation afford no solace. The verses on Campbell's sermon have been lying ready for the press since midsummer but I expect your and Mr Hay's sentiments as to the propriety of publishing them.' The library which he had used for his biblical work at Traquair had no counterpart in his new surroundings. Geddes became acquainted with a number of professors at Aberdeen, but as that city was over fifty miles away by road his contacts were only occasional. His particular friend was Dr James Beattie, professor of Moral Philosophy at Marischal College, which at that time was a university separate from King's College. The basis of their friendship was not a common liberal tendency, for Beattie did not share such views.[59] It was rather the generous nature of 'the warm-hearted Scot' as Beattie was called, and, even more, their common love and gift for poetry. Geddes was also well-known to Dr George Campbell, Principal of Marischal College since 1759; a man of wide culture, extensive learning and balanced judgment, though rather conservative in outlook—a characteristic typical of the university as a whole.

After some years at Auchinhalrig, Geddes discovered a further reason for writing poetry. He had never been able to live and manage the financial affairs of his mission within the meagre allowance he received.[60] He ran heavily into debt; though it must be said that much of this was incurred in building or repairing chapels. In 1779 he went to London to see to the publication of his *Select Satires* of Horace, translated into English verse. This earned him a very useful £100.[61] But Geddes also made good use of the visit to become acquainted with the 'beau monde'. Old Lord Traquaire died in this year at his Paris residence and his son, Charles, now thirty-three years of age succeeded to the title. Charles, who had married Mary Ravenscroft six years previously, was at this moment in London, and was able to introduce Geddes to his friends. It was probably on this occasion that he first met his future patron, Lord Petre. Besides meeting the nobility, Geddes went round the various Embassy chapels in the metropolis, preaching and otherwise exercising his ministry. With the passing of the Catholic Relief Bill in this year, preaching by Roman Catholics had been made legal, with the result that it had become a very popular activity. But Geddes had a poor opinion of the English as preachers. While he was in London, the possibility of his becoming a chaplain attached to one of the Embassy chapels was evidently in his thoughts, as is clear from his correspondence with his friend, John Reid.

The publication of his *Select Satires* did more than earn money. It was the immediate cause of his obtaining the degree of LL.D. at Aberdeen, for which he was proposed by Dr George Campbell, principal of Marischal College, Dr James Beattie and others.[62] He received the degree from King's College on 20 May 1780 and from Marischal College probably the same month.[63] This degree undoubtedly served him in good stead later when he came to London. It gave him a standing in the eyes of the *literati* to whom he was to owe so much.

His departure from Auchinhalrig came about largely because of his inability to manage his financial affairs but also because, with his liberal Paris training, much of Geddes's social activity was considered by his bishop, George Hay, to be indiscreet and even dangerous. The situation was aggravated by the total dissimilarity of their temperaments.[64] The dispute came to a head when Geddes attended a service in an Episcopalian chapel at the invitation of the Earl of Findlater, in order to hear a Mr Nichols preach.[65] By means of rebukes and veiled threats Bishop Hay contrived to bring about Geddes's resignation, but even then did not offer him an alternative post or take any practical steps to provide him with means of support. Strangely enough, Geddes received his LL.D. at Aberdeen at the precise moment of his leaving his home in the Enzie to seek a livelihood further south. For some months he stayed

with friends in Aberdeen and Edinburgh. Much of this time was spent
with Charles and Mary Traquaire, now his closest friends, either at Traquair House, Peebles, or at their house in Edinburgh, Ramsay Lodge.[66]
In the early months of 1781, Geddes heard of the possibility of his
obtaining a post as chaplain at one of the Embassy Chapels in London
and began to make his preparations to settle in the metropolis. He
travelled south in May 1781 at the moment when his cousin John
Geddes was coming north to take up his post as assistant to Bishop Hay,
after ten successful years as rector of the Scots College in Spain. From
this time begins the voluminous correspondence between the two
cousins which continued for ten years and constitutes a unique
source of information for this period in their lives.

Even now however Geddes had no clear idea of permanently remaining in London and still cherished the hope that his quarrel with Hay
might be healed, thus opening the way to his return to his native
Scotland.[67]

CHAPTER TWO

PREPARING TO TRANSLATE THE BIBLE:
GEDDES'S TEXTUAL CRITICISM

It is one of the ironies of fate that had Geddes been a man more readily amenable to authority and his bishop less of a stickler for the letter of the law, he would in all probability never have written a line of his translation of the Bible. It was Geddes's quarrel with his bishop and subsequent migration to London that provided the circumstances which alone made possible his later work on the Bible. Had he remained at peace with his bishop it is probable that he would have been known, if indeed he were known at all, as a minor Scottish poet and a classical scholar of moderate attainments.

When Geddes reached London about the end of May 1781,[1] he quickly found a lodging in Maddox Street and a livelihood as chaplain at the nearby Imperial Chapel in Portman Square. 'I am at length fairly settled down in London,' he wrote to his friend John Reid, priest at Preshome in Banff, 'and enrolled among the Imperial chaplains but don't know yet if I shall like it or not,'[2] Geddes lost no time in renewing his contacts with the literati and members of the nobility whom he had met on his previous visit in 1779. Among the latter he particularly singled out Lord Petre, to whom he had been introduced by the Duchess of Gordon and it was then that he learnt for the first time about Lord Petre's desire to provide for English Catholics a satisfactory revision of the Challoner Bible.[3]

Geddes's term of office as chaplain was of unexpectedly short duration. Before the end of 1781[4] the chapel was closed on the Emperor's orders and Geddes found himself without a livelihood. It was fortunate indeed that he now acquired the patronage of Lord Petre. Writing to his cousin Bishop Geddes he said, 'when I last wrote to you, I think I told you that Lord Petre had desired me not to think of leaving London. He has since transmitted me from Bath a part of his views in wishing me to remain here. A new edition of the Bible for the use of British Catholics is deemed so necessary that we cannot be long without it. His Lordship wishes me to revise and correct the Doway and Chaloner's translations and add such notes and illustrations as are needful to make it as compleat as possible. This I have undertaken and his Lordship is to be at the whole expense of this edition which is to be executed on the most elegant plan. You have frequently wished to see the talents of your friend applied to an object becoming his character. He is now on the point of engaging in one altogether so. . . . You will receive in after weeks a printed *Idea*[5] of this work for your remarks and observations.'[6]

The bishops, however, unlike Lord Petre, suspected that Geddes's revision might be more thorough than they had a mind for and decided to bring out one of their own. An important result of this unexpected turn of events was that Geddes abandoned his intention to revise the Douay-Challoner Bible and decided to make an entirely new translation from the original languages. He had only agreed in the first place, he said, to revise the Challoner Bible, out of deference to the bishops, but now that they claimed that version as their own property he felt himself 'totally dispensed from raking in their rubbish for materials which I can find elsewhere with much less trouble.'[7] With characteristic energy he now gave himself entirely to the preparation of plans for such a translation and to make a lengthy examination of manuscripts wherever they might be available. At the same time he started to write his *Prospectus of a New Translation of the Bible*. 'I am preparing at broken hours my large *Prospectus* which will differ in some ways from the *Idea*. I am now determined to translate from the originals, as I find it impossible to make a tolerable one from the Vulgate. I mean with regard chiefly to the Old Testament. . .'[8]

Geddes submitted his project to Dr Robert Lowth, Bishop of London, and received from him both approval of his plans and an invitation to his house.[9] By the autumn of 1782 Geddes was hard at work: 'I am now labouring like a galley slave and seldom spend less than ten hours a day in my little Museum. I cannot indeed boast that I make great progress. The Pentateuch teems with difficulties yet the road seems to grow smoother as I proceed and I hope to get to the end of my first journey about Candlemas next. . .'[10] Two months later he was able to say that he had got as far as the Book of Numbers, the fourth chapter.[11]

Geddes was now making the acquaintance of prominent biblical scholars among whom he regarded Dr Benjamin Kennicott with particular veneration. With thirty years work behind him spent on the study of Hebrew manuscripts culminating in the publication of his Hebrew Bible in 1776 and 1780, Kennicott had reached the height of his reputation when Geddes first met him. Unfortunately the acquaintance was to be of short duration. Kennicott died two years later. After a European tour in the company of a young gentleman named Howell during the summer of 1783, Geddes returned with renewed vigour. 'Here I am my dear friend,' he wrote to his cousin, 'after having traversed nine different countries and seen everything in them worth seeing. . . My Bible runs constantly in my head and I am every night drowned in

Greek and Hebrew.'[12] After a visit, with Mr Howell, to Scotland, Geddes returned to London in September and now began to acquaint himself with the biblical literature of foreign countries. He spoke with enthusiasm of the taste for biblical learning which was spreading rapidly. 'In Germany almost every man of learning is an Orientalist. In short, Sacred Criticism is everywhere the predominant study of the learned of all communions who seem to vie with one another which shall do most towards restoring the Scriptures to their primitive purity or as near to it as possible. I know you are acquainted with the Spanish king's librarian. Will you find out some method of introducing me to him so that we may correspond? I have some thoughts of writing to De Rossi and F. Fabricy but know not well how to go about it. You who understand Italian modes do give me your best counsel.'[13] Having recently been in Germany Geddes decided that to keep abreast of much of the best literature on the Bible it was essential to know German. 'So many excellent remarks on the scriptures have been lately published in the German language that I have come to the resolution of learning it. An hour a day for six months will, I think, make me master of it, I mean, as to understanding it perfectly, for that is all I want.'[14] Although a generation had already passed since German scholars began to write in their native language rather than in Latin, there were remarkably few in England who had made any attempt to learn that language and eminent scholars openly confessed their ignorance of German in a way that surprises the modern student.

Bishop Lowth of London warmly encouraged Geddes to continue with his Bible project and introduced him to the Archbishop of Canterbury. 'My plan is daily acquiring some new patron among persons of all denominations from the Archbishop of Canterbury downwards to the Dissenter. The good old Bishop of London has advised me to publish an ample *Prospectus* which I am now preparing for the Press and it will probably make its appearance about the beginning of next year. The presuppositions that were raised against it, chiefly by Bishop Hay's secret manoeuvres are dying fast away.'[15] Geddes spent many hours at the British Museum: 'After poring daily for six hours together over musty manuscripts at the British Museum I have very little inclination to sit down... My new *Prospectus* is fairly written out for the Press... Bishop Lowth has done me the honour to read it over and gave it his most flattering approbation... Through Bishop Lowth's means I have free access to all the repositories in the British Museum and he has engaged to procure me the perusal of the Lambeth MSS which are not communicated without a special order from the Archbishop of Canterbury.'[16] A few weeks later he was able to describe his new routine. 'A long walk to Lambeth every morning and another back to dinner keeps my spirits and appetite in good order. I have a room for myself at the Palace and one of the Archbishop's chaplains to pay me constant attention and to bring from the Library every book or manuscript I want, with pens, ink and paper to use at discretion. This is truly liberal. . .It will take most of the summer to examine the Lambeth manuscripts and I shall have abundance of work to digest my discoveries.'[17]

In the autumn of that year, 1785, Geddes visited Glasgow in order to collate the manuscripts in the University College—the one of most interest to him being the Glasgow Octateuch.

'I began to collate my MS on Friday and find that instead of five chapters which I had calculated as my daily task I can with ease do seven or eight. . . Besides the Octateuch which I am collating there are several other curious manuscripts in the College library of some of which I will take a particular notice.' [18] The Octateuch in question was a fifteenth century manuscript codex containing the Septuagint Greek version of the first eight books of the Bible. It is a specially fine codex and is now in the University Library at Glasgow. Bound into the volume at the beginning is an introduction to the codex written by Dr Alexander Geddes and filling ten octavo pages. Evidently he composed this during his stay in 1785. An unexpected result of the visit was his decision to print the *Prospectus* there instead of in London and he came to an agreement with Mr Foulis for that purpose. The warmth of Geddes's reception in Glasgow may have had something to do with this decision: 'I have been feasted in rotation by all the professors yet in town who seem to vie with one another in shewing me civility.'[19] The work finally appeared in the early days of January the following year. Geddes arrived back in London in February and wrote to his cousin, 'I believe some little curs are threatening to bark but they will hardly bite. Lord Petre had before my arrival presented a few copies to some of the first literary men of the kingdom who were much pleased with it and my bookseller tells me that it will have a pretty rapid sale.'[20] Later he was able to add: 'Principal Campbell has written to a friend of his concerning it in the strongest terms of approbation. I have received from Oxford the most encouraging compliments. . . Mr Bradley has also favoured me with his excellent MS observations and promises me when he returns to Oxford a complete new version of Jeremiah. . . By contrast Dr Gillies of Glasgow thinks it a most dangerous book as it will make Protestants look too favourably on Catholicism. . .'[21]

In this work which was more widely commended by the world of learning than any other of his writings, Geddes discussed the reasons which made a new translation necessary, and in so doing he produced in effect a comprehensive introduction to the whole art of Bible translation. He dealt at length with the original languages of the Bible, giving the history of their use in this connection, the causes of corruption in the text and the means of emending it, accounts of the principal versions, both ancient and modern, and lastly, in great detail, the qualities of a good translation and translator.

The remainder of this chapter will be devoted to a consideration of Geddes's work on textual criticism, mainly as set out in the *Prospectus,* together with the views of other scholars. Other parts of the *Prospectus* do not here directly concern us. Not surprisingly, since he wrote as a Roman Catholic, Geddes gives the Vulgate lengthy treatment, not only because of its importance in Roman Catholic tradition, but also to explain why he had decided not to make it the basis of his translation. Apart from faulty texts there were faulty translations, though the former defect was worse. 'But still the greatest imperfection of St Jerome's version arises from his too great confidence in his Jewish guides and his being prepossessed with an idea that the Hebrew copies were then absolutely faultless.'[22] Geddes returned to this theme from time to time. Textual criticism had advanced so rapidly that it made translation from the original absolutely necesssary. To do otherwise, he held, was to cope with two sets of errors in place of one: those in the original text and those proper to the translation. But to get a good translation from the originals it was necessary to carry out a great work of collating the manuscripts. The scriptures were indeed divine but that did not mean that they had been miraculously preserved from error and transcribed by inspired men.[23]

The imperfect state of the Hebrew text, which today is taken for granted, was by no means obvious to scholars in Geddes's time, notwithstanding the rapidly accumulating evidence—and the issue was hotly debated by the opposing sides, with inevitable exaggerations. Geddes's desire to destroy the persistent notion of the inviolable Hebrew text amounted almost to an obsession and pervades all his work. It is worth while therefore to give his views at some length. From the publication of the first printed Hebrew Bible, he said, the notion had persisted that the text was exact and complete in every respect and that somehow God had guaranteed words, letters and even punctuation. The idea came from the Jews and was consequent on the unification and stabilization of the text carried out by the rabbis over many centuries but especially by the Massoretes when the vowel points were introduced. The very fact that the work had taken so long surely pointed, suggested Geddes, to the existence of a variety of readings among which it was hard to make a choice. Yet the tradition had grown up that not only the unpointed text but even the points themselves dated back to the time of Moses and partook of his inspiration. Later, this view was modified and it was claimed that the points dated only from the time of Ezra. The important thing was that they should date from a time when

Hebrew was a spoken language, otherwise their accuracy would be suspect. 'Thus they produced an artificial creation. Through their rabbinical prejudices they appretiated the manuscript that was to serve as an archetype for the impression. The Massora was to those text-torturers the bed of Procrustes, to the exact length and breadth of which every word was to be fitted with the greatest precision and this pretended standard being once established as infallible, all posterior editions were judged to be accurate or erroneous only insofar as they agreed or disagreed with it.'[24] In an age when textual criticism had not been thought of and when ideas on inspiration were of the most literal kind, this attitude to the Massoretic text occasioned no surprise. In fact the Reformation gave it a new impetus.

'The Protestants,' wrote Geddes, 'on separating from the communion of Rome seem to have thought that they could not get at too great a distance. Finding it convenient to appeal from the decisions of a living assembly to the dead letter of scripture, they considered themselves as under a necessity of maintaining that the Scripture text was not only incorrupted but even incorruptible; and as the Massoretic system favoured this hypothesis, they adopted it without hesitation and defended it with more pertinacity than even the Jews themselves. To recede from it in the smallest degree was, they imagined, to open a door for Popery, by overturning this fundamental article of Protestantism "that the Scripture alone is a sufficient and infallible rule of faith".'[25] And this attitude, argued Geddes, was not yet dead. Why was there so little critical work done on the Hebrew text, especially when one considered the abundance of scholarly research carried out on classical literature? Was it because the Bible was considered of less importance? Or that the editors were ignorant or careless? By no means, he argued. It was due to this exaggerated respect for the views of Jewish rabbis, regarded as masters of the Hebrew language and alone competent to decide these questions.[26]

But with the coming of the seventeenth century the situation began to change. Geddes regarded Louis Cappel—the man who had shown that the vowel points were of recent origin—as the 'Founder of this new Academy'.[27] Cappel had demonstrated not only that Hebrew was a dead language at the time of the invention of the points but also that the Massoretic text, far from being uniform, was full of innumerable variants, even in the printed editions.[28] This disclosure however was so opposed to the views of his fellow-Calvinists that he could not find a publisher among those of his own faith for his great work *Critica Sacra*. It was eventually produced in Paris in a sumptuous edition in 1650 through the good offices of his son, who had meanwhile become a Roman Catholic. It appears however that some changes were made in the text presumably to suit Roman Catholic taste, which by no means pleased the author. This was the work which Geddes regarded as a landmark in textual criticism; and he lavished praise on it. Geddes maintained that Roman Catholics on the whole formed a sounder judgment on the state of the Hebrew text than the generality of Protestants. But 'whether it was always a sincere love for the truth or sometimes an excessive partiality for the Vulgate Version that made them so clearsighted and keen in discovering the faults of the original, I will not take upon me to determine.'[29] But they erred, said Geddes, in the opposite direction; for, having found that the Hebrew text was faulty in some places where the Vulgate was not, they concluded that the latter was everywhere preferable to the former. The decree of the Council of Trent strengthened their belief, though this could only be through a misunderstanding of the meaning of the decree. But the ruling that all public vernacular versions must be made from the Vulgate Latin undoubtedly fostered the impression that that version was to be regarded as superior to the original Hebrew and Greek. Geddes was fond of referring to the 'vulgar Papist' who relied on his infallible Church and the 'vulgar Protestant' who relied on his infallible Bible; and he was of the opinion that the bulk of Christians fell into one or other of these groups. There was however a small number of 'curious and learned men' who had thoroughly examined the motives of their religious belief. It was to such men as these that one looked for real progress in biblical science and these could be found in every religion.[30]

Jean Morin, the French Oratorian, who first published the text of the recently discovered *Samaritan Pentateuch*, was enthusiastic for its importance as a source of emendation for the Hebrew text.[31] The greater frequency of the *scriptio plena* in the Samaritan Pentateuch he took to be a sign of greater antiquity and he concluded that the text represented an earlier form than the Massoretic and consequently should be preferred. Morin's enthusiasm was contagious. Geddes tended to follow him and to accord to the Samaritan Pentateuch an authority which subsequent investigations should have warned him was excessive. There had been no lack of more prudent judgments. Thus, Richard Simon typically refused to be carried away by Morin's enthusiasm and was always of the opinion that on the whole the Samaritan Pentateuch was less authentic than the Massoretic Text. In fact he went further: he accused Morin of bias against the Massoretic Text, in his assertion that the Samaritan Pentateuch, the Septuagint and even the Vulgate were more accurate in those passages where they differed from the Massoretic Text. In so doing, Simon declared, Morin thought he was rendering a service to the Church by thus exalting the versions approved through long usage. But he did not take note of the fact that in authorizing the ancient version of the Septuagint and the new translation of St Jerome, the Church never presumed to condemn the Hebrew text or accuse the Jews of corrupting it.[32]

Ignoring Simon's warning, Geddes wrote: 'The Samaritan Scripture, as far as it goes, for it contains only the Pentateuch, must appear to everyone who examines it with any degree of attention and void of rabbinical prepossessions, a far more faithful representative of the prototype than any Massoretic copy at this day extant.'[33] This forthright expression of opinion seems to have surprised Johann David Michaelis, professor at Göttingen, for in reviewing Geddes's book, he wrote, 'Geddes prefers the Samaritan Pentateuch presumably without knowing the arguments against.'[34] Geddes persisted in this point of view and in his translation constantly preferred the Samaritan Pentateuch reading to the Massoretic Text.[35]

It was Houbigant, the last of the great pre-Revolution Oratorian biblical scholars that attracted most of Geddes's attention and praise, with the exceptions only of Drs Kennicott and Lowth. His life work, the massive Hebrew Bible together with *apparatus criticus* and a Latin translation, appeared in 1753, just before Geddes went to Paris, so that we should be justified in assuming that it figured largely in his biblical studies. Houbigant printed the unpointed Hebrew text, sharing as he did the contemporary suspicion of the Massoretic pointing. The Hebrew text he used was that of Van der Hooght (1705). There was an abundant *apparatus criticus* containing variants drawn chiefly from the Samaritan Pentateuch and ancient versions and in addition a number of conjectural emendations. Apart from the Samaritan Pentateuch only twelve Hebrew MSS were cited (three in the Royal Library and nine at the Oratoire) and even they were not systematically used. Not infrequently they appeared to be employed only when they supported a reading from an ancient version without enough other evidence; but even more alarming was the lavish introduction of conjectural emendation. Fortunately Houbigant did not put these into the Hebrew text itself; but he did put them into his Latin translation—a fact that diminished the value of that work notwithstanding the elegant Latin in which it was phrased. Not only did Houbigant furnish more evidence of the defective nature of the Massoretic text—as for example that the first Hebrew Bibles were printed from late and faulty manuscripts,[36] but he accused the Jews of cutting out the vowel letters as and when the vowel points were introduced. This last accusation was repeated by Geddes. 'The invention of vowel points, by rendering the genuine vocalic elements quiescent, gave frequently occasion to throw them out as useless and that very thing which was absurdly looked upon at the chief preservative of the sacred text from future errors largely contributed to make it still more erroneous.'[37]

In his *Prospectus*, Geddes was enthusiastic about the work of Houbigant. 'To shake off these (rabbinical prejudices) entirely and to open a new and rational career to the biblical critic was reserved for Houbigant,' he wrote, and after referring to his plan for a corrected edition of the Hebrew text together with a new Latin translation, added: 'With what ingenuity and judgment he had executed the great design is well known to those who have perused this work. Nothing can exceed the purity, simplicity, perspicuity and energy of his translation... The clamours that have been raised against him are the clamours of illiberal prejudice or of partiality to a system which he had turned to ridicule.'[38] Few today however would thus dismiss the strictures made by eminent contemporary scholars, British and German, as 'the clamours of illiberal prejudice'. Most present-day scholars, while freely recognising Houbigant's vast learning and his great contribution to biblical science, would agree with the criticism that he went much too far in his devaluation of the Hebrew text and in his conjectural emendation.[39]

Houbigant began the collation of MSS but never got very far. The real work was undertaken by Dr Benjamin Kennicott about the time when Houbigant was publishing his Hebrew Bible, and to this colossal task the Oxford scholar devoted the rest of his life. The undertaking was initiated in 1751 and Kennicott emphasized in his writings the absolute necessity for such a work.[40] He said that unless we were prepared to admit that mistakes could creep into the copying of Hebrew manuscripts as much as any others, there was serious danger of these errors being perpetuated in the printed editions.[41] At this stage an admission of the possibility of error was about all that Kennicott could reasonably expect. It would be long before a real critical knowledge of the manuscripts was attained. There were few however that would even concede that the work was necessary.[42] Kennicott met with persistent opposition throughout his work. The text, said his opponents, was inviolable. 'This notion,' he replied, 'though it should be in fact utterly indefensible may require some considerable attention... because those who ventured formerly to controvert it were deemed heretics of the most dangerous kind: because subscription to the truth of this notion is still rigidly required from candidates for Holy Orders in some other countries; and because the denial of it, in this our land of light and liberty, has been urged by some divines as a proof at least of Deism and lately represented as a crime so replete with public evil as to call for public censure.'[43]

Geddes, who fully endorsed Kennicott's complaint, pointed out that their opponents had several times shifted the ground of their defence. Having conceded that the authority of the text was rabbinical and not divine they argued that the wonderful uniformity of all the Hebrew manuscripts and their perfect agreement with the printed text pointed unmistakably to the integrity of the latter. But 'when by an actual examination and collation of the manuscripts, they were at length driven out of this post also, they sought security for themselves by trying to make their adversaries invidious; and held forth to the public the dreadful consequences to religion if it should once be allowed that the Scriptures had not come down to us in their full original purity.'[44]

No doubt Kennicott, Geddes and others of their way of thinking had the Fundamentalists of the Hutchinsonian school in mind. Bishop Patrick Torry, a native of Aberdeenshire and at one time minister in Geddes's home parish, felt strongly on this matter. He flatly denied Geddes's contention that the Massoretic Text was corrupt.[45]

Kennicott explained his procedure thus: 'As to a Various Reading then, my opinion is—*Varia est lectio ubicunque varie legitur.*— wherever in two copies of the same writing the one differs from the other in word or letter or in the position of the same words or letters, every such difference is properly a various reading. And since every Variation from the original of an inspired author is a variation for the worse, every such variation is properly a corruption. Consequently, though every various reading proves a corruption to have happened, every various reading is not itself a corruption, because one of the various readings may be the true reading which obtained at first in the original.[46] Kennicott could not have explained himself more clearly and at the same time demonstrated that he was but a man of his time, confusing, as did his contemporaries, scribal errors with genuine variant readings in the strict sense of the term. Yet it cannot be maintained that no one had perceived the correct distinction to be made. A century earlier, Richard Simon had insisted that copyists' errors must not be confused with genuine variant readings.[47]

Like Kennicott, Geddes too failed to notice Simon's words. All corruptions, he maintained, were the result of either design or oversight. Though a small number of corruptions was due to design, by far the greater number of instances might be due to the ordinary causes that produced them in other writings—the ignorance, the carelessness, the inaccuracy of copyists—and since the number of errors increased with time as the text was copied, no one need be surprised at the number of mistakes. There were in addition special causes in the case of the Hebrew text, namely the change from the old Hebrew characters to the later square or Aramaic letters and the invention of the vowel points. In the latter case not only were vowel letters thrown out as useless but an artificial interpretation was imposed by the new system of vocalization.[48] Geddes does not express himself so clearly as Kennicott on the identification of corruptions with various readings, but a perusal of his treatment of the whole subject sufficiently demonstrates that in this matter he followed Kennicott.

Neither Geddes nor Kennicott appears to have envisaged the possibility of parallel transmission of the text in different localities and traditions. 'When the literary critic of the Old Testament,' writes B. J. Roberts, 'aims at a restoration or reconstruction of the oldest possible textual form of the Old Testament, he must recognise that variations do not necessarily imply scribal errors and deliberate alterations, but may embody variant text forms which had always existed alongside the present text and belong to the traditions of centres and academies other than that whence the accepted text was derived.[49] Paul Kahle too has emphasised that the textual tradition in its early stages was not nearly so uniform as was hitherto supposed and that the Samaritan Pentateuch, the Septuagint and even the Targumim should be regarded as traditions in their own right.[50]

When Kennicott died in 1783 Geddes mourned his loss. Every Bible student, he wrote, ought annually to strew the tributary flower on the grave of Dr Kennicott in recognition of his services to the study of the Bible.[51]

We must now turn our attention to Geddes's literary and historical criticism as expounded mainly in the volumes of his Bible and the volume on Pentateuchal criticism. This will be followed by a chapter devoted to a consideration of the origins of Geddes's critical thought. The chronological account of his writings will be taken up again in chapter five.

CHAPTER THREE

LITERARY AND HISTORICAL CRITICISM:
BIBLICAL INSPIRATION

When Geddes began work on his translation of the Bible, the battle for
the application of critical principles to the Scriptures was far from over.
There was no ambiguity however about his own position. All his life, he
said, he had fought for the unfettered use of his reason. 'A sworn enemy
to implicit faith, as well as to implicit obedience, I have ever been
accustomed to think for myself; I will ever continue to think for myself;
and as often as I shall have occasion, will speak and write as I think.'[1]
In planning his translation of the Bible he stressed that 'the Bible
should be published in such a manner as not to be considered as the
peculium of any denomination of Christians, but given as nearly as
possible as a simple transcription of the original, without pointing out
its conformity or discrepancy to *(sic)* this or that mode of Christianity.'[2]
And some years later he added, 'I have been at great pains to examine
every system of theology, that has come in my way, in order to fix my
religious belief on something like a sure foundation. I have searched the
Scriptures; I have studied tradition; I have read ecclesiastical history;
and the result of my search, my study, and my reading has been, that
reason, reason only, is the ultimate and only sure motive of credibility;
the only solid pillar of faith'. He went on to say that he could not
revere formulas of faith made the test of loyalty, nor penal laws made
the hedge of church establishments. 'In short I cannot revere any system of religion that for divine doctrines, teacheth the dictates of men;
and by the base admixture of "human traditions maketh the commandments of God of none effect".'[3] Replying to his cousin Bishop Geddes
who had expressed the fear that he might flatter the Protestants too
much in his translation, Geddes declared that he would flatter neither
side but apportion praise or blame impartially. 'I will neither betray the
interests of the Church of which I profess myself a member, nor defend
them with reasons which my conscience tells me are bad. To exhibit to
the best of my abilities a genuine transcript of the Sacred Writings in
the most intelligible language, unwarped by controversy or disfigured
by mysticism is my only aim.'[4]

Reason, in the shape of critical principles had to be applied to all the
records, without fear or favour. No exception was to be made for the

Scriptures on the grounds that they were the infallible word of God. As for the Old Testament, 'Shall I grant,' he asked, 'to systematic Judaism what I deny to systematic Christianism? Shall I disbelieve the pretended miracles, the spurious deeds, the forged charters, the lying legends of the one, and give full credit to those of the other? May I, blameless, examine the works of the Christian doctors and historians by the common rules of criticism, explode their sophistry, combat their rash assertions, arraign them of credulity and even sometimes question their veracity; and yet be obliged to consider every fragment of Hebrew Scripture, for a series of a thousand years from Moses to Malachi, every scrap of prophecy, poesy, minstrelsy, history, biography, as the infallible communications of heaven, oracles of divine truth? Truly this is to require too much from credulity itself.'[5]

Setting aside, therefore, any barrier that might be interposed on religious grounds, Geddes approached the Scriptures as he would any other writings of antiquity and gave his opinions on their merits and demerits, beauties or imperfections, as became an impartial examiner. He was well aware that this attitude on his part would be regarded by many as audacious licence but he was prepared to face this opposition. One thing alone he asked. 'I only enter my protest against downright misrepresentation and calumny. I disclaim and spurn the imputation of irreligion and infidelity. I believe as much as I find sufficient motives of credibility for believing: and without sufficient motives of credibility there can be no rational belief.'[6] Viewing the Hebrew Scriptures, therefore, as he would any other literature, Geddes was at first ready to accord them a generous measure of praise. Considering the Pentateuch, he said, as a compendium of history, a digest of laws, a system of theology or a model of good writing, it could be said in some respects to excel or at least to equal the best products of ancient times. Whether one compared the first chapter of Genesis with the cosmogonies of Babylon or Greece, the Mosaic jurisprudence with the Republic of Plato, the songs of Moses with the most sublime Ode of Pindar, the story of Joseph with the best narratives of Herodotus or Livy, one would be induced to give to the former a decided preference or an equal praise.[7] Five years later, however, Geddes had modified his views. The defects of the Hebrew writers were given more prominence. 'But do I, then, really class the Hebrew historians with Herodotus, Thucydides, Livy, Caesar, and Sallust? As mere historians I certainly do; or rather I rank them somewhat lower as mere historians. I am very far from disregarding the Hebrew writers: I have carefully perused them, and know, I think, to appreciate their value (and I value them not the less, because I deem them not divinely inspired); but, I confess, I find not in them that elegance, correctness and lucid order which I find in the Greeks and Romans.

'It would, indeed, be unfair to weigh them in the same scale. The Hebrew historians have a greater resemblance to Homer than to Herodotus, and to Herodotus than to Thucydides. To the first of these writers they in many respects bear a striking similitude. Like him, they are continually blending real facts with fanciful mythology, ascribing natural events to supernatural causes and introducing a divine agency on every extraordinary occurrence. The same simplicity of narration, the same profusion of metaphors, the same garrulous tautology pervade them both; in both we meet with a poetical history.'[8]

The chief obstacle to examining the Scriptures in the way suggested was the prevailing doctrine of inspiration. 'I know well the difficulty of handling so delicate a point as Scripture inspiration, but I know also that nothing has so contributed to throw discredit on the Scriptures and to retard the progress of Biblical criticism as the ridiculous notions that have been maintained both by Catholics and Protestants on that subject.'[9] It was the doctrine of absolute and universal inspiration which chiefly deterred scientists and philosophers from studying the Bible. Inspiration had been made to cover everything; every sentence, word, syllable and apex, of the Bible was regarded as divine, infallible and immutable. Moreover this infallibility not infrequently was made to extend to the translation which was being employed. Again, divine truth was claimed for many a traditional interpretation for no other reason than that it had always been so interpreted. The human author was scarcely considered; little or no account was taken of the circumstances of the writing or the writer's personal qualities and motives. It was even asked if God had a distinctive style or if Hebrew was the language spoken in heaven.[10]

To those who argued that the apostle Paul himself had proclaimed the absolute and universal inspiration of the Scriptures in 2 Tim 3:16 Geddes replied that his words did not necessarily imply what they were made to imply but that even if their contention were established, namely that every part of the Scripture was divinely inspired, 'I would not for that give up my opinion. . . I would say anything rather than believe, even on the authority of St Paul, that everything recorded in the Hebrew Scriptures was dictated by a divine unerring Spirit. After reading the Hebrew writings themselves and finding in them, to my full conviction, so many intrinsic marks of fallibility, error and inconsistency, not to say downright absurdity, I could not, to use the emphatic language of the just-mentioned apostle, believe their absolute inspiration, were an angel from heaven to teach it.'[11] It seems clear from Geddes's further remarks on the subject that he understood the absolute and universal inspiration of the Scriptures to include the supernatural supply of information, and preservation from all error. Thus he argued that it had never yet been proved that Paul or any other always wrote or spoke by inspiration, 'No, they wrote and spoke from more unexceptionable documents; from what they had seen with their own eyes and heard with their own ears; or what they had learned from ear and eye witnesses who had no interest or temptation to deceive; or in fine what was occasionally communicated to them by immediate revelation.[12]

And elsewhere in the same preface Geddes referred to a contradiction which he discerned between Deut 20:16 where Israel was commanded to destroy the Canaanites, and Judg 2:22-23 where God left the Canaanites in the land to test Israel. Geddes refused to accept the usual explanations and roundly declared that it was necessary 'to acknowledge, fairly and openly, that the Jewish historians, both here and in many other places, put in the mouth of the Lord words which he never spoke and assigned to him views and motives which he never had.' To those who protested that this was to abandon a position long held against the opponents of revealed religion, Geddes replied that it was surely wiser to abandon a post which you could not defend, rather than, by obstinately defending it, to risk the citadel. It was better to allow that the Hebrew historians gathered their materials like any other historians, from popular traditions, old songs, public records, were not more judicious or intelligent than they and at least equally credulous, rather than to maintain that their manifest errors and inconsistencies were the immediate dictates of the Spirit of God, for such a suggestion was insulting to reason and prejudicial to the cause of religion.[13]

There was no intrinsic evidence of such absolute inspiration, Geddes argued, and to anyone free from theological prepossessions the marks of human fallibility and error were plain. Nowhere did the writers arrogate to themselves the privilege which posterity had accorded to them. They quoted ancient documents and public records and never claimed to be divinely informed of what they had written. And if they did so claim, he said, 'we should have great reason not only to disbelieve them in this particular, but to conceive in general a worse opinion of them than we can possibly form by considering them as uninspired historians.' The reason, he suggested, was not far to seek. As uninspired historians they could claim the same indulgence as was given to other historical writers. One would estimate their abilities, genius, style and veracity by the same rules of comparative criticism and would make the same allowances for their inaccuracies and oversights. Indeed from their very defects one could draw conclusions in favour of the general authenticity of their narrative, except where one had reason to suspect excessive credulity or designed imposture. But to claim 'a perpetual and unerring sufflation' was to destroy all credibility and was moreover highly injurious to the Supreme Being as it made him author of all that they related, thus bringing both God and religion into contempt and ridicule.[14]

While Geddes was not prepared to concede the inspiration of the Hebrew writers considered as historians, he was nevertheless careful to separate this question from that of the inspiration of Israel's legislators and prophets. 'I may believe that Moses was in some sense inspired as a legislator, without granting that he was, in any sense, inspired as a historian. . . Indeed were there no middle option left me but either literally to believe all that is written in the Pentateuch, by whomsoever written; or to deny the divine legation of Moses; I should not long hesitate in forming my determination; I should deny the divine legation of Moses.'[15] Geddes was careful to insert the qualifying clause 'in some sense' when speaking of the inspiration of Moses as a legislator. Doubtless he would have elaborated this in the General Preface which was never written, but, failing that, we have very little explanation of the inspiration which he allowed. At the end of *Critical Remarks*, Geddes printed a piece of Latin poetry, composed by himself, setting out his views. He saw no essential difference between the gift enjoyed by Moses and that possessed by other secular poets and legislators: the only difference was that Moses had more of it:

> *Motus erat certo coelesti flamine Moses,*
> *Moti quo Teutas, Numa, Lycurgus erant,*
> *Nempe omnes Sophiae sacro de fonte biberunt*
> *Hauserunt large Hi; largius Ille tamen.*

Only one person however enjoyed divine inspiration to the full, namely Jesus Christ—

> *Ille etenim solus, divino Numine plenus*
> *Leges perfectas, jus sine labe tulit.*[16]

While Geddes felt able to concede only this limited form of inspiration to Moses and other legislators and prophets of the Old and New Testaments, he realised that it fell far short of what was demanded by the people and the circumstances of ancient times. It was well-known, he said, that to keep mankind in a state of subordination it was usually thought necessary to keep them in a certain degree of ignorance. This applied both to politics and to religion. Implicit faith and implicit obedience had always been regarded by legislators as the best preservatives from innovations and revolutions in church and state. Thus ancient legislators required a greater or lesser degree of implicit obedience to their respective laws and for that purpose feigned an intercourse with some divinity to make that obedience more palatable to the credulous multitude. Was there any reason to suppose that Moses acted differently from other legislators? This admission, so far from diminishing his character and the wisdom of his laws, greatly enhanced both, he thought. It was perfectly compatible with the only divine inspiration which sense and reason could admit—at least which *his* sense and reason could admit.

Indeed it was hard to see how Moses could have governed a people so rude, stubborn and turbulent and made them accept a code of laws, without feigning an immediate intercourse with the Deity and ascribing to him every injunction laid upon them. And if, in spite of this, the people were constantly in a rebellious mood what would it have been like if Moses had spoken only as if from himself? But Moses was careful, in spite of his frequent communings with the Deity, to keep the people at a distance. No one was allowed to approach the mountain when he was receiving the Decalogue; none might hear God's words but through him nor question their veracity. In a word, the people might have no more religious or political knowledge than Moses was pleased to parcel out to them, either in person or through his brother Aaron whom he made his prophet and priest.[17]

Thus, in place of absolute and universal inspiration, Geddes proposed his own interpretation of the gift which he described as partial and putative: partial, because he allowed it to poets, prophets and lawgivers but denied it to historians: putative, not in the sense that there was no gift at all but in the sense that very commonly the inspired person claimed, whether by force of circumstances or expediency, to possess a direct experience of the Deity which he did not in fact have and he claimed this in order to give greater effectiveness to his words. It was essential that his hearers should be convinced that he was the mouthpiece of God.

Now what advantages would accrue from a theory of this kind? There were many, Geddes suggested. In the first place it would disarm one's adversaries. 'What force would all the erudition of Freret, the sense of Bolingbroke, the wit of Voltaire, the scurrility of Boulanger, the declamations of a Diderot or the sarcasms of Paine have against an Apology for the Bible founded on my principles? Without being presumptuous, I may say that I think I could, on my principles, resist their united attacks; whereas, truly, I cannot see how I could stand before them on the common hypotheses of absolute and plenary inspiration.'[18] In the second place, he continued, we should get rid of a host of useless commentators and an endless tribe of harmonists and conciliators who only serve to puzzle—and biblical criticism could then concentrate on one single aim, namely to ascertain the genuine, grammatical meaning of a genuine text. Thirdly, the Hebrew Scriptures would be more generally read and studied even by fashionable scholars and the many good things they contained more fairly estimated. Were these books presented as human compositions written in a rude age by rude and unpolished writers, in a poor and uncultivated language, many prejudices would be dissipated. Men would discover beauties where they had been led to expect nothing but blemishes and they would become in many cases, instead of scoffers, admirers.[19]

Geddes had one more obstacle to clear away before embarking on his own criticism of the Bible. This was the widely spread method of biblical interpretation by means of allegory. Looking through the writings of the Fathers, he said, it was surprising how little there was that one would select for inclusion in a modern commentary. They could rarely compare their copies of the Scriptures with the originals and furthermore, when they could not find a plausible literal explanation of the text they had recourse to allegory. This disposition to allegorize was also the cause, very often, of imperfect translation inasmuch as they often chose a rendering to fit the allegory rather than one which did not.[20] This recourse to allegory or to a similar mode of interpretation, such as prophetic vision, was prevalent up to the seventeenth century but Cappellus had initiated a new era. There were still authors however who reverted to this method. Reviewing Wrighte's Commentary on Genesis, Geddes noted his remarks on Gen 2:15—to the effect that Adam must have seen all the animals in a vision as it would have been impossible to assemble all of them. On this Geddes remarked 'If whenever a difficulty of this kind presents itself we may have recourse to allegory or prophetic vision to explain it away in opposition to all the common rules of grammar and speech, we shall have no other criterion left to distinguish history from allegory than our own notion of probability. Does no difficulty attend the narration? It is historical; if otherwise, it is an allegory.[21] To a request from his cousin Bishop Geddes to include a selection from the writings of the Fathers, he replied, 'Their writings seem to convey down unbroken the great chain of universal tradition, but the literal intelligence of the Scriptures you seek from them in vain.'[22] Geddes disclaimed any intention to disclose the 'allegories or analogies' of the text. He confined himself to its literal meaning.'[23]

PRIMAEVAL HISTORY

It was usual, remarked Geddes, with the annalists of most nations to begin their histories with some account of the origins of the world. So too with the author of the Pentateuch. It comprised one short chapter, yet it exhibited a grand and singular scene. Without long metaphysical discussions or scientific explanations the author related how an almighty Being made the heavens we beheld and the earth we inhabited. There was no question here of describing the creation of the universe but only of the fashioning of the world we knew from experience. The great solar and starry systems were not here in question except insofar as they were relative to this new creation. 'The world of the Hebrew cosmologist was a recent world, created out of pre-existent matter; and this was the opinion not only of the Jews but also of the early Christian writers. At the same time these writers were quite clear on the point that the primordial matter was itself created by God out of nothing and was in no sense co-eternal with him as some pagan philosophers had imagined.'[24] On the six days of creation Geddes hesitated to pronounce definitely but was inclined to believe it a literary fiction introduced into the narrative to teach the institution of the Sabbath. The narrative taken as a whole he thought was neither literally true nor pure allegory. It 'was a most beautiful mythos, or philosophical fiction, contrived with great wisdom, dressed in the garb of real history, adapted to the shallow intellects of a rude and barbarous nation; and pefectly well calculated for the great and good purposes for which it was contrived, namely to establish the belief of one supreme God and Creator, in opposition to the various and wild systems of idolatry which then prevailed; and to enforce the observance of a periodical day, to be chiefly devoted to the service of that Creator and the solacing repose of his creatures.'[25] A wiser system of cosmogony could not be imagined. The device of making God speak and act in a manner suited to the concepts of the Hebrew nation was calculated to gain their attention and respect. Some of the first scholars of the age, observed Geddes, thought very little differently from this about Genesis chap. 1. Eichhorn for example had treated this subject in his *Repertorium* and with his sentiments Geddes in general agreed, though, he added, 'from him I did not borrow mine.'[26]

In Genesis chap. 2, which Geddes thought to be by the same hand as chap. 1 the author described how man was made in God's image. 'Religious but intelligent reader! Wert thou to read all this in any book but the Bible, what wouldest thou think? Wouldest not thou think and say "It is a pretty poetic tale" and rank it in thy own mind with the *Metamorphoses* of Ovid? – Well, let me ask, what reason hast thou to believe that it may not be a poetic tale, even in the Bible? Are there no such tales there? He will be a hardy man I think who shall dare to affirm it.'[27] The early Jewish writers and Christian Fathers had recourse to allegory when explaining the Hexaemeron in order to avoid the strong objections of their adversaries against the Hebrew cosmogony. And although modern writers had tended rather to follow the contrary opinion of literal interpretation, it was not for that more defensible or more favourable to religion. Better far to allegorize with Origen or Austin than admit an explanation which, if what we were taught to believe about the attributes and nature of God were true, must necessarily be false. This did not mean of course that Geddes was content to accept the allegorical explanation. He spoke of it only to show the difficulties that attended the Hebrew cosmogony considered as real history.

'But let it once be granted that it is a mere poetical mythos, historically adapted to the senses and intellects of a rude unphilosophical people; every obstacle will be removed, every objection obviated, every sarcasm repelled; whether it come from a Celsus, or a Porphyry, a Julian or a Frederic, a Boulanger or a Bolingbroke.' The author of this narrative had two important points in mind: 'to mortify the pride without depressing the dignity of man; and to inculcate the strict and indissoluble union of man and woman in the matrimonial state.'[28] As to the Garden of Eden itself: where else, asked Geddes, could God have placed Adam? Not, surely, in an unproductive desert? He had to be placed in a situation in harmony with his original happy state. Whether such a garden ever existed, said Geddes, was a matter of no importance. An ideal paradise equally well answered the author's purpose which was clearly to portray the original happiness of man. 'The mythologists of all nations have acknowledged a golden age; and this was the golden but short-lasting age of Hebrew mythology.'[29] The creative imagination of the mythologist made it necessary to place the garden somewhere, and he would naturally place it near the source of the two great rivers which were the cause of the fertility in that region and which with two other great capital rivers he made to flow from a common spring. 'If the learned Josephus and the Jews of his day were so ignorant of geography as to make the Nile and the Ganges two of the rivers that flowed from Eden; how easy was it for the Hebrew mythologist to bring rivers together, that never met, to embellish his story; rivers celebrated over all the East for the fertility of soil and the rich productions of their coasts.'[30]

The Fall, thought Geddes, was a wholly mythological event. The present state of mankind was evidently far removed from the happy condition of our first parents when originally made by God. Whence all this misery? Historians informed us that it was due to the violation by our first parents of a divine precept from an ambitious desire of knowing as much as the gods. The gods were jealous of their privileges and were so represented by the mythologists of all nations. For the stealth of a single spark of celestial fire, the box of Pandora, replete with manifold evils, was emptied upon the whole earth. The Hebrew God was described as a jealous God and it was therefore not surprising if the Hebrew author represented him in this way as jealous of man's sharing in knowledge and that the origin of evil should be ascribed to that audacious attempt. It was customary among some commentators to interpret the serpent as the Devil. But apart from the difficulty of introducing a metaphorical expression into a literal narrative there was no trace of the Devil anywhere in the story and nowhere was he mentioned by name. The allegories of Philo and Origen were preferable to literal inconsistencies of this kind.[31] Eichhorn had shown conclusively that the Hebrews knew nothing of the existence of the Devil before the Exile. In his *Urgeschichte,*[32] Eichhorn had suggested that the story of the Fall was of an event that took place in the infancy of the world. It was unlikely to be a myth to explain the origin of evil. Our first parents were innocent of any knowledge of the distinction between good and evil. They had been forbidden to eat the fruit. Eve saw the serpent eating apparently without any harmful result and thought she would do likewise. The dialogue between her and the serpent only represented her train of thought. The serpent could not speak nor did he symbolize the Devil. Adam and Eve learnt from their subsequent misfortunes to distinguish between good and evil. The punishment of the serpent was not really such, but rather a description of the animal's nature. The voice of God in the garden was a clap of thunder and his colloquy with Adam and Eve merely the voice of their conscience; remorse for having disobeyed a divine command. In primitive narratives events were often ascribed directly to God the first cause, when in fact a secondary cause intervened.

Geddes was not in favour of Eichhorn's explanation, though he allowed that it had merit. He did not like mixed solutions—part literal and part allegorical or metaphorical. Though he himself rejected the allegorical that did not mean that he accepted the literal and historical. Why might not the Hebrews have their mythology as well as the Chaldaeans and Greeks? This story would then account for the origin of evil and for man's antipathy for serpents. 'Regarded in this light it will require no straining effort to explain it; it will be perfectly, in all its parts, coherent; it will be attended by no absurd consequence; it will give no handle to the enemies of religion to turn it into ridicule; the serpent will then be a real mythological serpent; will speak like the beasts and birds in Esop or Pilpay; will be a most crafty envious animal that seduces the woman from her allegiance to God; will be punished accordingly with degradation from his original state; and an everlasting enmity established between him and the woman's seed. The respective punishments of the woman and the man will be in the same sense real and the whole chapter an incomparable example of oriental mythology.'[33] In olden times it was thought that animals had the power of speech. The author of Genesis availed himself of this tradition, however fabulous, in his mythological narration of the Fall of Man.[34]

Geddes thought he could detect the same kind of mythological

narrative elsewhere in Genesis. On the subject of Cain's punishment
Eichhorn had tried to show that the colloquy between God and Cain
was not to be taken 'au pied de la lettre' and was in fact only a way of
indicating the effects and consequences of Cain's guilty conscience. 'I
am however inclined to believe,' observed Geddes, 'that the writer meant
to impress on the mind of his reader a real conversation; although that
conversation may never have happened. What I have said of the Creation
and the Fall is equally applicable to the story of Cain.'[35] On the subject
of the Flood, Geddes held that there was a good deal of the fabulous
mixed in with the narrative and this element could be discerned elsewhere. Thus in Genesis 6, on the subject of 'the sons of God and the
daughters of men', Geddes observed that Josephus, Philo and the earlier
Christian writers imagined the 'sons of God' to be angels or 'aerial
beings', who charmed by the 'daughters of men' found means to violate
them'. From this commerce there sprang a race of giants who corrupted
the earth. Geddes thought it very possible that the author of Genesis
had this primitive belief. 'It seems to have been a prevalent opinion
among the antient nations, that the gods had occasionally carnal commerce with the human kind; and that from that commerce the greatest
heroes sprang. Why may not a similar opinion have prevailed among the
Hebrews? That it was common at the commencement of Christianity is
clear from Josephus and Philo and from the earliest Christian writers,
both Greek and Latin.'[36]

To those who objected that it was absurd to imagine that there
could be any commerce between angels and men, Geddes replied that
this was true, but how many absurdities were in fact believed in by
both Jews and Christians? The question was, not, was it absurd, but was
it believed? And of this there could be no doubt. Moreover when one
considered alternative explanations of this passage, e.g. that the sons of
God were the posterity of holy Seth and the daughters of men the posterity of wicked Cain, for which there was not a particle of evidence,
one felt little inclination to adopt such solutions.[37]

Geddes had considerable doubt about the details of the Flood narrative. The story about the making and launching of the Ark he felt was not
necessarily to be taken as historical. Calculations intended to show that
the Ark could hold all the animals he preferred to leave to mathematicians
while he continued his career as a critic. Again, the extent of the Flood
was very difficult to determine. One could not absolutely deny the possibility of a universal deluge but traditions concerning this among different
nations could be explained by local and partial inundations. 'The
daughters of Lot imagined that all mankind were enveloped in the
destruction of Sodom. A traditional tale is easily exaggerated and improved upon by credulous posterity; and the first writer gives it with all the
accumulated circumstances. What reason have we to think that the Hebrew

historian was exempt from the common lot? All we can say is, that he has better told his tale; and this, I presume, will not be denied by the greatest sceptic who has compared it with the similar stories of Chaldee, Phenician, Egyptian, Indian and Greek mythologists.' After all, the story of the Deluge was far too thickly interspersed with great and numerous difficulties if one took it as a literal narration, unless one supposed miracle upon miracle. The inference to be drawn seemed to be that there was a good deal of the fabulous in the history of Noah's Flood.[38]

THE HISTORICAL NARRATIVE

Geddes was of the opinion that Hebrew history properly began with the birth of Abraham. Not that it was thenceforth entirely unmixed with the leaven of the heroic ages: that would be too much to expect of so remote a time. Mythology still tended to creep in. 'Let the father of Hebrew history be tried by the same rules of criticism as the father of Greek history. Let the marvellous in both be distinguished from what is not so, the natural from the unnatural, the highly probable from the barely possible and I believe that we shall find in both, nearly the same marks of veracity, on the whole, though with respect to some particular parts we may be a little inclined to scepticism.'[39] Who could doubt of Abraham's coming into Canaan from Chaldaea, of his sojourning in Egypt and Palestine? Who could doubt that Jacob went down into Egypt and that, after being reduced to a state of servitude, his descendants escaped thence under the leadership of Moses? Nevertheless, not all the narrative was on the same historical footing. On Jacob's struggle with the angel, Geddes recalled that Josephus held the angels to be phantoms–and indeed the whole story had the air of a vision rather than a real occurrence, to be compared with the earlier story of Jacob's Ladder. The same God who had, in a dream at Bethel, encouraged Jacob to proceed without fear on his journey might well have appeared to him again in a dream on his return to Canaan for a similar purpose. Geddes refrained, however, from pronouncing definitely on the nature of the account and contented himself with observing that there was a similar story in Lycophron of Jupiter's wrestling for a whole night with Hercules by whom he was overcome.[40]

The principal events of the Exodus were no doubt substantially historical once they were shorn of their supernatural aura. Who could doubt, Geddes asked, that during the wanderings in the desert the people of Israel received through their leader Moses a body of laws which they believed to be of divine origin? The laws indeed were so interwoven with their subsequent history that no one in their senses would suggest that they were the fabrication of a later forger. The theology and jurisprudence of the Hebrews were so intermingled that one could hardly disentangle the one from the other. Much of the former was framed in a very anthropomorphic manner, full of imagery adapted to a primitive and carnal people, while the legislation was described as issuing from the mouth of God himself in a storm of thunder and lightning, afterwards to be written on tablets of stone by the finger of the Deity. In this way it was adapted to the minds of the people and calculated to command their respect.[41]

But what was one to think of the many wonderful events that were scattered throughout the account of the Exodus? The introductory episode of the rods being changed into serpents ought to warn us, he suggested, not to accept too readily the literal sense of the narrative which followed. Geddes could make no sense of it. What then was he to say? It might be better to say nothing, but that was not his way. 'I am clearly of the opinion that neither the magicians of Pharaoh nor the legislator of the Hebrews, changed their rods into serpents any more than the sorceress Circe turned the companions of Ulysses into swine; but that either the Hebrew historian, whoever he was, invented the whole story; or that if ever any such trial of magical skill took place, the deception was equal on both sides.'[42] The turning of the Nile into blood, once one had eliminated a number of impossible details, was susceptible of a natural explanation. Some critics held that the 'miracle' was not so much in the thing itself as in its having taken place at an unusual season and in having been foreseen and foretold by Moses. This was encouraging, Geddes suggested. This was at least something like rational criticism. Yet the explanation was full of difficulties. What proof was there that Moses foresaw and foretold the phenomenon at a time when it rarely or never happened, other than the bare word of a historian whose testimony bore strong marks of credulity and who told his story with such fantastic detail as to render the whole highly incredible? The mere word of an unknown Hebrew writer might surely be questioned unless we sacrificed our reason to implicit faith and believed stupendous miracles without sufficient motives of credibility. Indeed the intention of the Hebrew historian seemed to be to assemble every sort of calamity by which a nation, situated like Egypt, could possibly be afflicted.[43]

If any unfettered mind could really and literally believe this narrative at its face value, Geddes would only say that he was far, very far removed from scepticism. Did the events then never happen? Doubtless certain phenomena occurred as a result of natural causes. 'But that those events happened exactly according to the Scripture-relation, it requires great faith, or rather great credulity to believe. – It will be said "Is there anything here beyond the power of God?"–What is, or what is not, beyond the power of God I profess not to know; his omnipotence is beyond my very limited comprehension. The power of God, for aught I know, may be able to convert water into blood and dust into flies; but that it did so on any particular occasion and with circumstances similar to those which are said to have accompanied the prodigies operated in Egypt by the rod or hand of Moses, testimonies beyond all exception, and amounting almost to demonstration, would be required to produce a rational belief. Our faith is always in proportion to the motives of credibility: and when these are weak our faith must necessarily be feeble; we cannot believe without conviction, nor disbelieve with conviction. Now I ask what motives of credibility have we to believe that the plagues of Egypt were a continued chain of supernatural causes, operating in the manner related in the book of Exodus? — Why, because the book of Exodus is a part of the Hebrew Scriptures and all that is written in the Hebrew Scriptures is the infallible word of God!" But this suggestion, said Geddes, was a quite inadequate answer. It was based on an assumed hypothesis which had never yet been proved and which, in his opinion, never could be proved. At any rate, until proof were forthcoming with all the force of convincing evidence one was entitled to doubt without being branded as a heretic or traitor to the Church and one should examine their general veracity or probability by the same rules with which one examined the writings of other nations.[44]

In general, the events of the Exodus should be viewed in the light of Oriental ways of thought and expression whereby many of the works of nature or human design were ascribed directly to the intervention of the Deity, and were often exaggerated in the process. Thus pestilence was often regarded as the immediate infliction of the gods and no doubt this attitude had its part to play in forming the outlook of the people on the events of the Exodus. As for the Crossing of the Red Sea, 'For my part, who believe there was nothing miraculous in the event, I am positively for the pass at Suez, or not far from Suez; where at this day there are shallows fordable at low water; and which might at former times have been frequently dry.'[45] Lastly, a sacred fire, was carried about upon a portable altar of which the smoke by day and the fire by night directed the marches of the Israelites. Yet the Hebrew historian, who could not be ignorant of such a custom, made a miraculous cloud of it in which he placed Jehovah or his angel to guide his chosen people.

THE GIVING OF THE LAW

When the moment came to proclaim the law Moses bent his mind to the task of giving it the maximum efficacy. 'Nothing could be better conceived or more dexterously executed than the plan which he adopts to give a sanction to the precepts he was about to promulgate. The highest top of Sinai where he was supposed to have received his first mission, is pitched upon as the secret sanctuary where he is to meet the Deity and receive from him a new code of laws to be ever after observed by the Hebrew nation as coming from their own peculiar God. The people, first purified by ablutions and abstinence from connubial pleasures are forbidden under pain of death to approach the mountain; and the priests themselves who might approach it to offer sacrifice, are inhibited from ascending to its summit. Order is added to order and caution to precaution for the purpose of preventing the smallest infringement of this injunction. While the people wait thus in awe and expectation, a storm of thunder and lightning ensues. This, they are told, is the voice of God, who meanwhile is supposed to give to Moses, in words articulate, the Decalogue or Ten Commandments.'[46]

Geddes was prepared to be called an impious unbeliever for calling the whole thing in question, but he found it impossible to believe that every word of the Decalogue was uttered by the mouth of God. Indeed if there were any articulate voice on that occasion it was more probably the voice of a man rather than that of God, speaking perhaps through a trumpet during the storm of thunder and lightning. But once one accepted the Oriental colouring and phraseology of the narrative so replete with metaphorical personifications, such suppositions were unnecessary. Moses was concerned above all to make his people believe that all his laws were communicated by Jehovah and in this, according to his historian, he certainly used the most effective measures to succeed. 'Yet we find that his divine mission was more than once doubted by the best informed of the Israelites, and it required several new, real or pretended, miracles to remove their doubts. But if persons who had been ear and eye witnesses to all the miracles already performed, doubted of their sufficiency to establish the divine legation of Moses, it may surely be lawful for us, who have neither seen nor heard, to question their veracity, for which we have no other vouchers but an anonymous narrative, composed we know not when nor by whom; for it can never be proved, by any solid, satisfactory arguments, to be the composition of Moses. But were it allowed to be, every word of it, the composition of Moses himself, that alone would not be a sufficient reason for implicitly believing all its contents. Reason bids us appreciate the writings of a Moses as we appreciate the writings of a Livy or of a Herodotus and the same or similar motives of credibility or incredibility ought to be the measure of our belief or disbelief in the former as in the latter; for in this respect I see no difference between a Hebrew historian and a Greek or Roman historian.'[47]

Geddes, like the Deists, appealed frequently to his readers' sense of what was or was not antecedently probable or credible. Thus again, on Numbers 16:31, he asked: was there no reason to suspect the literal truth of the narration? Was it likely that the very next day after the staggering miracle of the destruction of Korah, Dathan and Abiram had been performed, the people would again murmur against Moses and Aaron and a new miracle should have been necessary to establish the authority of Aaron and his priesthood? When one recollected how very fond the Hebrew historians were of the marvellous and how prone to mix history with fable, one should be very careful in accepting as history stories which, if they appeared in the writings of Greece and Rome, would be instantly rejected as fabulous. It had never yet been shown that the Hebrew historians were not to be treated as other historians and it seemed clear that they were just as liable to make mistakes and to misrepresent.[48]

Bold as Geddes frequently was in stating his views without reckoning the opposition which such views were sure to arouse, he was at the same time not slow to quote important authorities in his own favour when the opportunity arose. Among these authorities the German scholars were, not surprisingly, prominent; thus, on Numbers 11:33, the account of the death of the Israelites through eating quails, Geddes quoted Rosenmüller to the effect that the verse merely related the death of a large number of people from an obscure cause which among primitive races would be ascribed to the anger of God. The cause was doubtless natural: the ancients observed that quails often fed on poisonous herbs and plants which gave their own flesh a toxic quality. The Israelites ate the quails and died.[49]

MORAL STANDARDS IN THE OLD TESTAMENT

Like the Deists before him and many of his contemporaries, Geddes was concerned with the problem of the instances in the Old Testament where God apparently commanded something which to the average reader would appear to be immoral. He was particularly opposed to attempts made by well-intentioned commentators to justify these commands while assuming that they came from God. Such scholars kept to the literal meaning of the text but only at the expense of abandoning all hold on moral principles or by putting a meaning on the passage which, to any unbiassed observer, it could not bear. The 'spoiling of the Egyptians' was a case in point (Ex 11). According to the text, the Lord commanded the Israelites to ask of their neighbours 'jewelry of silver and of gold'. Many commentators explained the subsequent departure of the Israelites without returning the jewelry on the grounds that they had been given it by the Egyptians. But, said Geddes: 'It is far more likely that the Egyptians would lend their jewels and their raiments to the Israelites for the purpose of celebrating a national festival than that they would make presents of them. They had no idea that the borrowers were not to return them. But our theologians are afraid that if the word *borrow* were used here, it would make God command the Israelites to do a fraudful, unlawful action: but is this the only instance of an unlawful action being commanded by God. I mean according to the Hebrew historians?'[50] The greatest ingenuity had been used in the past to explain the action in terms consonant with God's having commanded it. Calmet suggested that God dispensed Israel from the law against theft; Melchior Canus held that Israel had the right to compensate themselves for the unjust labour extracted from them in the past. Some of the early Fathers propounded a maxim subversive of all justice and morality, namely that 'whatever is reported by the Hebrew writers to have been ordered and approved of by God must necessarily be right and lawful.'[51]

If this problem were present in the case of the spoiling of the Egyptians, what should be said of the command to slay the Midianites recounted in Numbers 31? There Moses in God's name ordered Israel to slay not only the Canaanite men but also the male children and all the women who had known man. All kinds of improbable reasons had been given to justify this apparently divine command, as that it was punishment for sins committed in the past—or that the Midianites would have constituted a moral danger to Israel if they had been allowed to survive; or that if the male children were allowed to live they would remember the hurt they had sustained and turn against Israel when they had grown up. Fine reasons, suggested Geddes ironically, for justifying such a butchery! Especially when they were commanded to keep for themselves all the females who had not known man, thirty-two thousand of them.[52] The same problem arose in the command to destroy the Canaanites, Deuteronomy 7:2. Up to the end of the seventeenth century this too was judged reasonable and necessary. But in recent times the reasons adduced had been considered frivolous, and modern writers had maintained that the command had never been given by God. Not, however, observed Geddes, the Prelate who recently wrote an *Apology for the Bible* as an answer to Paine's *Age of Reason.*[53] The author of the *Apology* could see no difference between natural disasters like earthquakes on the one hand and the slaughter of the Canaanites on the other. 'Why,' he asked, 'do you not spurn as spurious the book of nature in which this fact is certainly written and from the perusal of which you infer the moral justice of God?' If, argued this writer, the Deist rejected the Bible as an authentic record he should also reject Nature. But Geddes would not allow the validity of this argument. He replied that the principle 'Do as you would be done by' held good, irrespective of any revelation, not only for individuals but also for nations. The Israelites had no more right to dispossess the Canaanites than the latter had to dispossess them. But, could there not be a dispensation for a particular occasion and a special law formulated in its place? Perhaps there could be in the abstract, admitted Geddes, but almost overwhelming proof would be needed in the concrete that God had in fact done such a thing. He professed himself unable to accept any such possibility. His reason and religion revolted against it. To the suggestion that the Canaanites were destroyed for their sins, Geddes asked in whose estimation were they sinners and by whom were they judged? In that of the destroyer? But surely he would not be unbiassed? Moreover God could destroy sinners if he willed without employing men for the purpose. Before believing in the truth of such a command one would require far more convincing evidence than the unsupported word of the interested party.

Indeed, whatever evidence of divine approval or commission the slayer might produce, Geddes declared himself unable to believe that such a command came from the same God who said that the sins of the fathers should not be visited on their children.[54] He was willing rather to believe that the order was the fabrication of some later Jew to justify the cruelties of his nation. Indeed it would be the shortest way to do this by declaring that God had authorized and commanded it, for who would presume to assert that God could be unjust? True, but first we must be sure that he had indeed commanded; and, to Geddes, the very appearance of injustice was a stronger proof that he had not commanded than all the authority of the Jewish historians put together.[55]

THE AUTHORSHIP OF THE PENTATEUCH

Geddes turned his attention to the literary composition of the Pentateuch, when he was engaged on its translation. He intended to deal fully with the matter in the *General Preface* which he was planning. Meanwhile, however, in the preface to the first volume of his Bible, he set out the general lines of his position. Brief though the exposition is, the details given are of considerable interest. He was convinced that the solution of the problem had not been sufficiently thought out. On the one hand there was the great majority of people who held that Moses wrote the whole Pentateuch and that any questioning of this position was at least impertinent if not actually impious. On the other hand there were critics, like Astruc and Eichhorn who claimed to have discovered continuous documents composed of innumerable fragments from which Moses had composed Genesis but that this process had apparently not continued for the other books which were ascribed directly to the authorship of Moses himself, apart from a number of fragments whose origin and date were uncertain.[56]

The Mosaic authorship as traditionally held, Geddes considered to be quite untenable. But he was almost equally critical of the alternatives commonly proposed. He saw that the evidence which led to the dissection of Genesis did not stop there but continued through the Pentateuch, so that if one recognized the existence of such documents one could not stop at Genesis, but should continue through Exodus to Numbers, or that alternatively the evidence should be reassessed. He chose the latter alternative and concluded that the fragments said to form continuous documents did not in fact belong one to another but were largely independent. In the second place he had no hesitation in abandoning the traditional belief in the Mosaic authorship altogether and ascribing the composition of the work to a date several centuries later. Indeed Geddes went even further. He saw in Joshua signs of composite authorship such as he had discerned in the books of the Pentateuch and decided that that book must join the preceding five so far as the circumstances of its composition were concerned.[57] Thus was the Hexateuch considered as a unit forty years before Bleek.

Undaunted by the weight of tradition in favour of Mosaic authorship Geddes noted that external evidence was of no great assistance in this matter; one had to assess the internal evidence of the work itself.

Summarizing the position, three things seemed to him clear: (1) the Pentateuch in its present form was not written by Moses; (2) it was written in Canaan and probably in Jerusalem; (3) it could not have been written before the reign of David nor later than that of Hezekiah. Solomon's reign seemed most likely, but there were signs of later date or at least of later interpolation.[58]

Geddes recognized that much of the material incorporated in the Pentateuch was older than the probable date of composition or compilation. There were 'ancient documents' as he termed them used in its compilation some of which were coeval with Moses and some even anterior to him. But by using this term 'ancient documents' Geddes did not apparently commit himself to the view that there were *written* records before Moses. Whether all these ancient documents were written or many of them only oral, it would be rash, he said, to determine. He permitted himself however the expression of the opinion that the Hebrews had no written documents before Moses. All their history before that date was derived from 'monumental indexes and traditional tales'. 'Some remarkable tree under which a patriarch had resided; some pillar which he had erected; some heap which he had raised; some ford which he had crossed; some spot where he had encamped; some field which he had purchased; the tomb in which he had been laid; — all these served as so many links to hand down his story to posterity and corroborated the oral testimony transmitted from generation to generation in simple narratives or rustic songs. That the marvellous would sometimes creep into these we may easily conceive but still the essence or at least the skeleton of history was preserved.'[59]

From the time of Moses however Geddes felt certain that there were written records. Indeed Moses himself was very probably the first Hebrew writer, or at least the first who applied writing to historical composition. From his journals a great part of the Pentateuch was composed. Whether Moses actually composed the narrative of events prior to his own day Geddes would not positively assert. He may have collected much of the material which was afterwards worked up into their present form by the compiler of the Pentateuch. On the whole however Geddes thought that the later compiler also collected his material, both from his own people and among the neighbouring nations.

The theory of Astruc and Eichhorn that Genesis was composed of two main documents distinguished by their use of the divine names, was looked upon by Geddes as a work of fancy, though he realized that he might be wrong in this assessment. He proposed 'elsewhere' to try to prove the correctness of his own position. Evidently this was a reference to the *General Preface*; but he did at least, in his later work, *Critical Remarks*, state briefly: 'I hasten to the second chapter which is at present pretty generally supposed to be another cosmogonical fragment written by a different person and inserted by Moses in his commentaries as a curious piece of antiquity. I confess I have never been able to view it in that light; after all the pains that Astruc, Eichhorn and others have taken to prove the diversity, I can find nothing in it but a natural resumption of the subject by the same pen which wrote the first chapter and with the same wise, political and religious views.'[60]

Thus Geddes saw no need, in the composition of the Pentateuch as a whole to suppose the existence of strands or strata of traditional written narrative such as later Pentateuchal study elaborated. Among the individual fragments he would at times identify particular items but without attempting to link them together. The isolation of the fragments was the first consideration. Their individual differences seemed to him more readily discernible than their points of likeness. Moreover the signs of posterior date were unmistakable. Thus, for example, on Genesis 49 Geddes wrote: 'I do not believe it to be the real composition of Jacob, but of some Hebrew bard who lived posterior to Joshua, perhaps posterior to David. That Jacob may have blessed his children and accommodated his respective benedictions to the known bent and disposition of each is highly probable; but that he should accord his benedictions

to the future situation of the tribes will not readily be believed by those
who have critically examined the subject.' And on Numbers 21:27-30
Geddes observed: 'The piece of poetry here quoted is by some thought
to be that of an Amorite bard who related the conquests of Sihon over
the Moabites. I cannot be of that opinion; I believe it to be the work of
a Hebrew poet, who after the defeat of Sihon, and the overthrow of his
capital city, excites his countrymen to rebuild it and repair it as the
strongest city of that territory which had formerly defeated the Moabites and might still be a formidable rival to Ar. Considered in this light
it is a beautiful fragment of an old ballad quoted by the writer of the
Pentateuch; but such a quotation could not be made by Moses, although
Moses may have composed the ballad.[61]

When commenting on the Balaam stories, Numbers chaps 22-24,
Geddes clearly declared that they were written 'not by Moses, but by
the compiler of the Pentateuch from such traditional stories or scraps
of written documents as he could find.'[62] He felt he was in a stronger
position to study the evidence objectively than were those of his contemporaries who still kept to the Mosaic authorship and were thereby
forced to resort to what seemed to him subterfuges. Since the Balaam
stories were so clearly legendary, even the staunchest supporters of the
Mosaic authorship shrank from ascribing them to Moses and allowed
for the development of a parallel legend incorporated at a later date in
the Pentateuch.

Again the statement in Numbers 12:3 that Moses was the mildest of
men suggested to Geddes that the writer of that narrative was later than
Moses; although he was aware of the alternative explanation offered,
namely that the sentence was a later interpolation in a narrative written
by Moses. He noted that Eichhorn proposed the latter in his *Einleitung. . .*[63]

On Deuteronomy 2:12 'like as did the Israelites in the land which
the Lord gave to them for a possession', Geddes observed that this
could not have been written by Moses because it recorded what took
place after his time when Israel were in possession of Canaan. 'There are
critics however,' he added, 'who fancy that this difficulty is fully obviated by giving to *ntn* 'he gave', the meaning of 'he meant to give'. It
gives one pain to find Rosenmüller adopting this conceit.'[64]

The whole of the passage of Deuteronomy 2:10-12 Geddes considered to be an interpolation, though present in all the copies and versions
(except that the Samaritan Pentateuch lacked verse 11). He thought it
was probably made 'by him who redacted the *Memoirs of Moses* into
their present form. I have placed it here [in a footnote] separate from
the text, not to interrupt the Legislator's narration.' On Deuteronomy
2:10-12, 20-23, von Rad comments: 'a later hand has now amplified

this original form of Moses narrative by means of the insertion of various antiquarian notes about the earliest inhabitants of these regions.'[65] Geddes does not seem to be clear in his own mind what he is trying to reconstruct: the Pentateuch as it left the hand of the final redactor or as it stood at some earlier stage of its evolution. He is over-concerned with consistency in the narrative as were all the earlier critics, before its composite character was properly understood. At any rate this is one of the very few passages where he speaks, at the same time, of the interpolator and later redactor. Occasionally he identifies the source of some 'interpolation' as in Deuteronomy 10:6-7 which he describes as either an interpolation and so to be left out (Geddes puts it in a footnote) or else out of place and to be repositioned after verse 11. He considers it to be a fragment of the record of the stages traversed by Israel on their journey from Mt Horeb—a recapitulation of Numbers 33, though (in view of the discrepancies between the two) an account which has suffered some corruption. On this passage von Rad comments: 'There is hardly any doubt that these verses are a secondary interpolation. . . inserted into the text rather clumsily.'[66]

Apart from these few passages, Geddes contents himself with pointing out what he considers to be interpolations without further indentifying them; these he usually removes from the text and puts in a footnote; occasionally he leaves the passage in the text with brackets round it. His reasons for thinking them interpolations are usually their omission from the Samaritan Pentateuch or one or more versions or fairly clear indications in the text that they are not of the same literary origin as the sections in which they are inserted. One particularly disjointed chapter, Deuteronomy 31, undergoes considerable rearrangement at the hands of Geddes and he adds this comment: 'If the arrangement I have ventured to make displeases any reader he may easily restore it to its former state of confusion.' Apart from this, Geddes has very little to say on the editorial work present in these final chapters of Deuteronomy.

The inclusion of Joshua in the first volume of his Bible raised hopes which were unfortunately not fulfilled. In the Preface Geddes wrote, 'To the Pentateuch I have joined the Book of Joshua both because I conceive it to have been written by the same author and because it is a necessary appendix to the history contained in the former books.'[67] But apart from a few references to interpolations and a comment on the 'Book of Jasher' nothing whatever is said in the appended notes about the composition of the book.

CHAPTER FOUR

ORIGINS OF GEDDES'S LITERARY
AND HISTORICAL CRITICISM

PHILOSOPHICAL PRESUPPOSITIONS

It may be assumed that when Geddes arrived in Paris in 1758 fresh from the remote Highland seminary of Scalan he was unfamiliar with the work of philosophers such as Hobbes and Locke and had certainly never read any of the writings of the Deists. Thus his first introduction to the world of the Enlightenment was through the French, and his works bear unmistakable signs of the influence of that environment. Though his general training in Paris would have been within the scholastic framework and mould of thought for which he later expressed so great a distaste, Geddes would have had plenty of opportunity during his years of attendance at the Sorbonne of absorbing elements of the dominant intellectual attitudes of his time.[1]

The Gallicanism which he displayed in his later years was largely acquired during his stay in Paris, where he had seen it all around him. Likewise the foundations of his biblical criticism must be traced back to those years in the French capital, though free expression of such ideas and principles during his student days would not have been tolerated. Even the *philosophes* had to tread carefully.

Geddes's principle of free inquiry[2] implied the obligation to follow the argument wherever it led, unimpeded by considerations of authority or tradition and to test one's beliefs at the Bar of Reason. But this was not a principle exclusive to the French. It was basic to the reaction against the authoritarianism of the Reformation controversies and was inherent in the work of the principal philosophers of the preceding century. 'The doctrine of implicit faith has lost its vogue. Every man will judge for himself in matters that concern him so nearly as these do. And nothing is now admitted for truth that is not built upon the foundation of solid reason.'[3] The movement of thought then in progress in England was widespread on the mainland of Europe and was to have far-reaching effects.

This was the century of Descartes, Spinoza, Leibnitz and Locke, all of whom, in their different ways had so powerful an influence on the

movement of thought we know as the Enlightenment, but in considering the antecedents of Geddes's general intellectual moulding in the
land of the *philosophes*, few of this period are of greater significance
than Pierre Bayle, the French Calvinist philosopher.[4] Though a genuine
forerunner of the *philosophes*, Bayle was strangely different from them
in at least one important respect, namely in his scepticism. Where the
French thinkers of the eighteenth century were, for the most part,
supremely confident in the power of reason to attain all truth, Bayle's
overriding concern was to question every assumption. For him, facts
were everything and in his zeal to reach them he mercilessly attacked
whatever stood in his way—superstition, intolerance and ecclesiastical
authority. But having got the facts Bayle considered his task done. He
felt under no obligation to draw conclusions or to collate his material
and produce any pattern of knowledge. Above all he attacked the attitude of mind which considered any argument justified so long as it
reached the 'right' conclusion. Ultimate truth, Bayle considered to be
unattainable and he was strongly opposed to any coercion of belief. A
man's conscience was the supreme arbiter. Indeed Bayle caused a sensa-
tion by maintaining that a man who sincerely professed error or even
atheism might be a better man than a believer. Sceptic though he was,
Bayle was deeply attached to the principle of ethical criticism so dear
to the Deists and the *philosophes*. Applying it to the Scriptures Bayle
held that any interpretation of the Bible which offended our moral
consciousness should be rejected. He refused to accept the common
view of the 'infallible' Bible and made havoc of many customary interpretations of familiar episodes and personalities. Indeed he seemed to
go out of his way to assimilate the Bible to other ancient literatures and
to disperse the sacred aura which enveloped the text. It was in the
article on David written for his *Dictionnaire* that he reached the peak
of destructive criticism. Without actually denying miracles he constantly discredited them and hinted that belief in such events was tantamount to superstition. Bayle was particularly opposed to *odium theolo-
gicum* which had been so evident during the Reformation. Not that it
was confined to that period. Indeed Bayle held the view that Christianity, for all its seventeen centuries of existence, had had remarkably
small influence on mankind for good and seemed to have little to do
with morals.

Perhaps nowhere was he better known than in Germany. Frederick
the Great, who was probably the greatest single influence in introducing
into Germany the thought, literature, and culture of the French, once
described Bayle's *Dictionnaire* as the 'precious monument of our
century' and he sponsored a special Berlin edition of Bayle's works.
Lessing, who spent some years in Berlin, was much influenced by Bayle,

particularly in his rooted opposition to dogmatism and intolerance, but differed from him in his general judgment on Christianity. Just as Bayle's disparaging and generally irreverent attitude to religion had influenced the Deists so now it was not without its effect on German thought.

Geddes shared Bayle's reaction against ecclesiastical authority, which figured so largely in the Enlightenment, but in his case it was something less than complete rejection. While criticising severely his own superiors he looked forward to an ideal period in which Church authority would be exercised in a manner consonant with the Age of Reason.[5] The investigation of the mysteries of faith by human reason he felt, like the philosophers and thinkers of a century earlier, to be a duty on the individual conscience. This might well lead, and in his case did lead, to a reduction of the basic content of his creed. But as a Roman Catholic he found it difficult to follow men like Semler into the field of religious experience and to separate religion from theology.[6] The blurring of the distinction between natural and supernatural revelation characteristic of this period was also mirrored in Geddes's writings but he never lost hold altogether of a belief in a personal and supernatural revelation given to man through Jesus Christ.[7] To some extent he shared the anthropo-centric outlook of the Deists and the *philosophes*, especially in the judging of actions and words ascribed in the Bible to God. Here he was content to doubt the historical accuracy, rather than ridicule the narra-tive in the manner of a Tom Paine. Indeed he maintained that the explanation he gave for this type of account was the best answer that could be given to accusations levelled against the Bible by writers such as Paine.[8]

In his philosophical attitude to miracles, Geddes was prepared to agree with Hume that the evidence required to verify an event had a strict relation to the marvellous character of that event.[9] On the other hand, he did not exclude, (as Hume, in effect, did), that adequate evi-dence for its having taken place as described, was at least theoretically possible. What Geddes ruled out was any suggestion that he ought to accept the event as literally true because it was recorded in a divinely inspired and infallible Scripture.

Geddes's attack on the still prevalent notion of absolute and univer-sal inspiration of the Scriptures likewise found an earlier link in the writings of Conyers Middleton, librarian of the University of Cambridge for a number of years, a liberal thinker who propagated his views vigor-ously and in consequence forfeited all hope of advancement in the Church of England. As Geddes also was later to suggest, Middleton argued that God might use the prophets as his instruments, enlighten their understanding and preserve them from error on certain occasions yet at other times leave them destitute of supernatural assistance. 'It is as extravagant therefore and contradictory to the testimony of Scripture to believe the prophets and apostles to have been at all times incapable of error because they were sometimes guided by an unerring Spirit; as to imagine that they were always exempted from fatigue or hunger, because the effect of those sensations was sometimes miraculously suspended in them.'[10] Middleton went on to criticise those who said that to abandon absolute inspiration was in effect to have no inspiration at all. On the contrary, he argued, absolute inspiration 'is so far from being of service to Christianity, that it has always been, and ever will be, a clog and incumbrance to it with all rational and thinking men; and to impose it as necessary to the Creed of a Christian, and on the authority of those Sacred Books in which everyone may see the apparent marks of human frailty, not only in the style and language, but sometimes also in the matter of them, can have no other effect but of reducing us to the dilemma of distrusting either those books or our senses.'[11]

The difficulty lay in finding a theory of inspiration which would adequately allow for the part played by the human writer. Many critics fluctuated between limiting the incidence of the divine influx in the writers and reducing the influx to an inspiration of a natural kind, such as that enjoyed by poets, lawgivers and other historical figures. Either way, it seemed not far short of abolishing inspiration altogether, because, it might be argued, in the first alternative, the critic could extend or narrow the field of its influence as he willed; and in the second alternative he could afford to ignore it when assessing the standards of morality, the probability of error or the human characteristics of the writer. The old conception was manifestly wrong, in the view of many scholars, but it was by no means agreed what should take its place.

THE GERMAN CRITICAL SCHOOL

In Germany, about the middle of the century, Christian Wolff's philosophy was setting its mark on the progress of thought.[12] H. J. Kraus notes that the German biblical *Aufklärung* drew heavily on the English Deists. Ideas on nature and revelation were taken up in their Deistic sense. The effect was specially noticeable in the matter of revelation. Deism and *Aufklärung* marked the end of supernaturalism in its older sense.[13] Another thirty years however were to pass before Geddes was in a position to embody any of these ideas in his own critical work and in consequence much of this way of thinking was mediated to him through the German critical School.

The Germans succeeded where English Deism failed because their approach was both more scientific and, on the whole, more moderate. It was established on a basis infinitely more sound than anything the Deists could show and, on the other hand, with few exceptions, they made no attempt to get rid of revealed religion in favour of natural religion or no religion at all. Lastly, the German critics did not make fun of traditional beliefs and practices after the manner of the English Deists. Reimarus was a rare exception in this respect. Thus it was that besides the conservatives, who constituted the majority in Germany, as in England, and the 'Naturalists' who were relatively few in Germany, there arose a third group who, though they refused to ridicule religion, were nevertheless unable to accept it on the terms hitherto regarded as normal; and they rationalized it according to their critical principles. As Georg Pfleiderer has said: 'German Rationalism bears the marks of its origins in the idealistic optimism of the philosophy of Leibnitz and Wolff and remains in sympathy with the ethical spirit of biblical religion, while the but faintly religious naturalism of the English Deists leads them, with their rejection of the biblical miracles, to attack the religion of the Bible and drag down into the mire its representatives and heroes. With this, the German Rationalists have no sympathy. They were unable to treat the Bible narration of miracles as historical occurrences, but they were not prepared on that account to regard them as deceit and delusion on the part of the Bible heroes or as the invention of the Biblical narrators. Their reverence for the Bible kept them from both of these inferences.'[14] The spirit and tradition of German pietism remained very much alive throughout the whole period of the *Aufklärung* and had a notable influence on it.

At this time Germany was embarking with traditional thoroughness on biblical research; investigation of ancient manuscripts and their history, study of oriental languages, research into ancient literatures and the history and customs of the ancient inhabitants of Bible lands. More and more the critics were coming to treat the books of the Bible as they would any other ancient literature and apply the same critical principles. Sigismund Jacob Baumgarten had succeeded Wolff at Halle and he too, notwithstanding the Pietistic tradition of the University, made a special study of the English Deists, drawing what he considered valuable material from their writings which he reviewed in his periodical *Nachrichten von einer Hallischen Bibliothek* (1748-51). At the same time he disapproved their hostile attitude to religion.

But it was Baumgarten's gifted pupil and successor at Halle, Johann Salomo Semler, who made the greatest single contribution to biblical criticism in his time and had considerable influence on Geddes. Semler was the critic rather than the theologian or philosopher. While insisting on the free exercise of reason in biblical and theological matters, he aimed at a harmony between faith and reason by separating religion from theology. For him, religion was personal experience of Jesus Christ his saviour and this was a reality which no criticism however destructive could touch. Theology, on the other hand was an affair of the intellect and was liable to change, under the influence of criticism, from age to age. Having thus placed, as it were, his faith out of harm's way, Semler proceeded, in a manner not unlike that of John Locke, to apply the strictest principles of reason to this theology and bible study. Geddes too, while applying the strict rules of criticism, never failed to profess his undying allegiance to Jesus Christ, his saviour.

Semler was concerned to bring about nothing less than a total change in approach to the Bible, and in particular to the Old Testament, but the old ways died hard. 'Carpzovii introductionem illam scimus quasi regnare per Germaniam—nec invidebimus amatoribus!' he wrote in 1773.[15] Carpzov, though a great Orientalist in his day, had also been a firm believer in the infallible Hebrew text. Let those who thought like Carpzov follow him, said Semler. But if others wished to follow the path indicated by himself let them not be persecuted in the name of sacred orthodoxy. Nearly all the commentaries were useless, he observed, for knowing more about the text; they only conveyed theology. Books of sermons also kept repeating doctrines which though well known were not to be found in the text. It was not preachers that one needed now, he suggested, but grammarians, philologists, and above all critics. He would spare his readers all those allegorized interpretations of Hebrew history and the discernment of types of the New Testament in the Old where there was no trace of them and no authority for discerning them.[16] Semler indeed seemed almost obsessed by the need to get rid of the old ways of biblical interpretation and above all the allegorical method, by which, he said, one could make a text mean almost anything. It was critical principles that were needed and especially the principles of historical criticism.

One might be pardoned for thinking that it was Geddes speaking rather than Semler. Almost everything stated above was echoed in Geddes's writings for he found in England a similar situation and attacked it with equal vigour. Geddes however did not achieve a like success. There were many reasons for this. His learning did not equal that of Semler; his manner of expression at times acquired an intemperate note and his views an extremist character that Semler would not have imitated. Lastly he was almost alone among the British in sustaining the views he put forward, whereas Semler, twenty years before Geddes wrote a line of his Bible, had a large following of his own. Semler aimed to dissipate the aura of sanctity which surrounded the Old

Testament and effectively prevented any real examination of its contents. The human origins and contents of the books had to be considered. They originated in a period of culture and morality much
inferior to that of the New Testament. Moreover they differed widely
in their spiritual value. In some books it was hard to find, as he put it,
any Word of God, by which he meant some spiritually elevating
passage.[17] Semler tended to make this quality or spiritual value the criterion by which he judged the inspiration of a book and in consequence
found it difficult to regard the Old Testament as inspired in any extensive or effective sense. Moreover, insofar as it had this quality, it could
be said to share it with the best in pagan literature. It was difficult to
separate the wheat from the chaff. Where did one draw the line? One
was in danger of losing inspiration altogether in the process. This was
precisely the problem facing Geddes. Some writers solved it by keeping
the name and discarding the substance. 'The phantom of inspiration
continued after the reality had vanished, like a morbid impression on
the retina after the disappearance of the object.'[18]

All the evidence of the so-called Jewish and Christian Churches was,
for a searcher after truth about the purpose and message of Scripture,
quite insufficient to produce personal conviction. The relativism of
history did not lead to truth but only to confusion. To unravel this
there was only one way. Only man's present-day needs could serve to
lead him through the garden of errors. The worth of a thing could not
be established by its age or ancestry, and especially not historically, but
practically, through use. The real worth for the present day was
decisive.[19] These ideas, surprisingly modern in their appearance, found
little echo in Geddes with his Roman Catholic and Gallican background. Not that Geddes had an adequate substitute for religious
experience. While asserting the overriding claims of reason to be able to
discover the truth, he was as ready as any Semler to cast doubt on the
cogency of historical evidence. How exactly Geddes reached his religious
conviction is not apparent. But certainly he absorbed many of Semler's
critical views and profited by his achievement. This was mainly: (1) to
ascertain the literal sense of a passage, rather than any spiritual or allegorical meaning; (2) to insist on grammatical correctness; (3) to introduce historical interpretation. This led to a radical transformation of
the previously held dogma-bound interpretation.[20]

Johann David Michaelis of Göttingen, though by nature more conservative than Semler, nevertheless vigorously applied the principles just
enunciated. Thus in his notes to the German translation of Lowth's *De
Sacra Poesi Hebraeorum* he expressed his dislike of the allegorical
method of interpretation adopted in certain places by Lowth. Then
again, armed with his wide knowledge of oriental languages, he was un-

rivalled in his philological approach to the Bible text. In the matter of his attitude to the miraculous in the Bible, Michaelis tended to adopt the Naturalist interpretation, e.g. as regarded the miracles of the Exodus. The destruction of Korah, Dathan and Abiram was caused, he thought, by an earthquake (Num 16:31-32) which perhaps Moses had foreseen.[21] But such an explanation did not make clear how the narrative originated. Believing as he did that Moses wrote the Pentateuch, Michaelis would have had to admit that either Moses or a collaborator had somehow devised this miracle story out of something which was in fact a purely natural event. Michaelis however refrained from going into details. His main concern was to avoid any explanation of a Deistic nature involving a charge of deceit or imposture. He also wished to show that he believed there was a historical event underlying the narrative.

Geddes put forward as many naturalist explanations as Michaelis, but on the whole more plausible ones. This was due, in the first place, to the fact that he was not hampered, as was Michaelis, by considerations of Mosaic authorship, and, secondly to his adopting Eichhorn's principles of literary criticism discussed below.[22] Michaelis's position was in fact clearly a compromise. He lived at the time of transition from the Carpzov period (for which he had so great a distaste) to the new criticism of which Eichhorn was the real pioneer. Eichhorn gave Michaelis full credit for his great contribution to biblical science but considered him too dogma-bound in his exposition.[23]

The abuse of the biblical writers so characteristic of the English Deists and which Geddes so studiously avoided, was bound sooner or later to raise its head in Germany. It did so in unexpected circumstances in the shape of the Wolfenbüttel Fragments of Reimarus, selected and published by Lessing. Reimarus, unlike the English Deists, had not risked his reputation by publishing his revolutionary work[24] during his lifetime. His daughter agreed to the publication of the extracts on condition that they were anonymous. Six pieces entitled *Fragmente eines Ungennanten* were published between 1774 and 1777 and a seventh in 1778. The result was electrifying. The trend of the extracts was unmistakable. Rationalism was the only true basis of religion. Supernatural revelation in which all men could believe was an impossibility because all but the first recipients of that revelation would have to rely on human testimony which could not be a sufficient guarantee — and as time passed there was the added defect of historical transmission. Moreover, since many men had never heard of Christianity it could not be for all men. Besides, it had a great deal of fraud mixed up with it. The resurrection, for example, was an invention of the disciples. As for the Old Testament this was even more clearly not a divine revelation. Many of those who proclaimed it were unworthy men; the content of the 'revelation' was both defective and of a low standard of morality; finally, the miracles and prophecies proposed as proof of its authenticity were both incredible and absurd. The Fragment which had the greatest impact was also the last, *The Aims of Jesus and of his Disciples,* in which Reimarus accused the disciples of removing the body of Jesus and spreading the rumour that he had risen from the dead, in order to build him up into the leader that he had never claimed to be. In the *Israel's Crossing of the Red Sea,* Reimarus made great play with the impossibilities and inconsistencies of the story, to show it must be fictitious. He had of course no notion of the composite nature of the narrative. Thus, in different ways, Reimarus, by discrediting the account, aimed to show that there was no real evidence for a special revelation either to the Jews or to the Christians. Traditional apologetic had tied Christianity to the historicity of the Bible as literally understood. The Deists thought that they only had to dispose of the literal historical sense to do away with Christianity altogether.

In his notes accompanying the Fragments, Lessing explained that he did not necessarily agree with their contents but felt that they expressed a point of view which should be made known. Truth should be gathered from every quarter. Lessing, like Geddes, had been strongly influenced by the French Enlightenment and also by Hume's scepticism. Lessing agreed that history could not prove the truth of Christianity. Historical evidence could not produce conviction. Thus miracles and prophecy which had been traditionally produced as proofs did not in fact prove what they claimed to prove except perhaps to the first witnesses. If we had personally seen Christ's miracles they might have been a guide and inspiration to us, but we were separated from them by a wide gulf in time. These miracles now had to be judged historically, but no historical truth could have the certainty of demonstrated truth. Mediated as they were through history, miracles necessarily partook of the character of history and shared its weakness. The most you could be (historically) sure of was that Christ's disciples were sure they had seen a miracle. But even if you could prove historically the fact of a miracle you would not be justified in drawing a conclusion outside the domain of history. You might accept the resurrection but that would not justify you in believing that Jesus Christ was the Son of God. History could not prove this. It was a conclusion outside reason. It was useless to appeal to the inspired writers. How did one know they were inspired? By historical evidence. There was the famous ditch across which Lessing professed himself unable to jump.[25]

Lessing, however, felt under no obligation at this point to draw with Reimarus the conclusion that Christianity—indeed all revealed religion— was a fraud. We had no right, he maintained, to expect that religious truths could be proved in this way. Eternal truths could never depend for their validity on contingent facts. Lessing argued against those who wanted proofs for the Christian mysteries and excluded them if proof was not forthcoming. What was revelation if it did not reveal? Christianity was accepted by the believer through an intuitive realization of these tenets in his life. Christianity was true because it was experienced to be true. The rational acceptance could be said to be provisional and the truth realised in practice. Thus reason had a part to play in the initial act of faith but it did not itself account for the whole proof. Even if criticism did discredit the Bible record it would not follow that we must discard Christianity. Both Lessing and Semler were conscious of the inroads made by historical criticism on the credibility of the Bible. But while Semler tended to bring the facts of Bible history into the present, Lessing dug an ever wider chasm between the 'discredited narrative of a past age' and the 'eternal truth' newly perceived in the present. Indeed, in insisting that events cannot prove truths of religion Lessing was in effect separating the two to the point where the historical basis for Christianity could be said to be irrelevant. Furthermore, the knowledge of God which comes to us through Nature could be seen to be in a different category altogether from that of historical Christianity. What then was this eternal truth which Lessing claimed to hold? It may be questioned whether he held anything beyond certain moral and philosophical truths and a recognition of Jesus Christ as a teacher of an elevated moral doctrine. Transcendental revelation seemed to vanish into thin air. Religion in his view was evolving all the time as truths were realised in our lives. Indeed there was no 'fixed' positive revelation and the search for truth was more important than the attainment. Starting from the basis of a religion of nature, Lessing saw positive religions not as corruptions but as necessary stages in the evolution of religion from infancy to a state of maturity. In his *Education of the Human Race* he superimposed the idea of human progress on to a religion of nature.

Semler's disagreement with Lessing centred mainly on the question of the distinctive character of the Christian revelation and the reconciliation of man to God through Jesus Christ. Right up to his death Semler kept this conscious and firm attachment to his Saviour even at the price of being thought by Lessing illogical and inconsistent. What Semler found most shocking in the Fragments was that Reimarus ascribed the defects and corruptions of Christianity not to Christians of later ages but to the conscious and deliberate deceptions of its first founders.[26] Lessing's treatment of historical Christianity was far more subtle than that of Reimarus but it may be argued that his destruction of it was scarcely less thorough. Geddes would have seemed to Lessing as incon-

sistent as Semler in his attachment to basic truths of Christianity, given
his position in the matter of historical truth and the principle of free
inquiry. Perhaps in his last years Geddes had not worked out a consistent theological position. We can only be sure that he retained to the
end, as did Semler, a genuine allegiance to his saviour Jesus Christ, to
which the inscription on his tombstone is eloquent witness. Geddes
appears never to have doubted the possibility of producing basic evidence for Christianity and to the end of his life accepted the essential
connection between religion and historical evidence, even if, in the
process he found himself severely restricted as to the area of reliable
evidence and of revealed truth. Thus he would have by-passed Semler's
insistence on the significance of religious experience and rejected
Lessing's idea of a relative Christianity continuously evolving. Though
he often expressed his hopes and desires for a purified and more liberal
Christianity in terms which perhaps did not differ so much from
Lessing, nevertheless, at the final count, Geddes must be judged by his
professed allegiance to the person of his Saviour. This was the main
issue. If the only absolute truths of religion were those which made up
the religion of nature, then not only did the distinctive character of the
Christian creed fade into the background but even the person of Jesus
Christ lost the significance given to him by traditional Christianity and
one was left with a code of morals but little else. Pastor Goeze who
attacked Lessing so strongly was himself criticized as intolerant and even
slow-witted. But perhaps the Pastor saw farther than his critics thought.
He realised very quickly, as others did not, the direction of Lessing's
thought and that, however he might camouflage it, his ultimate aim was
as much the destruction of traditional Christianity as was that of the
head-on attack of Reimarus. Lessing's arguments were not new but the
literary quality and vigour of his writing gave them a special force.
Doubtless too, the subtlety of his thinking disarmed many of his
opponents; but it did not disarm Semler, who made it clear in 1779
that he could not follow in the direction Lessing was taking.

JOHANN GOTTFRIED EICHHORN AND PRIMITIVE HISTORY

With the publication of the Fragments and their accusation of fraud the
time had come for a new development in biblical criticism. Many
scholars agreed that the supernatural as portrayed in the Bible was unacceptable but they were not prepared to accuse the biblical writers of
fraud or deceit. What alternative was possible? The 'Naturalist' view,
favoured by earlier writers, such as Michaelis, was unsatisfactory because
it offered no sound reason for the explanation given. The only evidence
available was in the Bible text. How then could the interpreter be sure

his explanation corresponded to what happened? But worse than this was the implication of dishonesty on the part of the writer of the narrative. This point requires some consideration. We mentioned above Georg Pfleiderer's contention that the German reverence for the Bible kept critics on the whole from making such accusations. Doubtless this is the true reason in many cases, but it is not true of Eichhorn, at least from 1788, whose whole critical outlook lay in applying to the books of the Bible the same principles which were applied to other ancient literatures. Eichhorn refrained on other grounds. His contention was that those who accused the biblical writers of deceit or imposture were ignoring a fundamental truth, namely the gradual development of human reason and experience. These Naturalists were supposing that human reason had always been the same and that the writers of the biblical literature were moved by the same considerations and enjoyed much the same background of knowledge and experience as do we today. This misunderstanding had been powerfully helped by the widespread belief in a primitive Golden Age at the beginning of human history in which our first parents enjoyed a developed intelligence which later deteriorated. Michaelis, great scholar though he was, accepted this interpretation of the early history of man without apparently questioning it. Eichhorn would have none of this and strongly maintained that, on the contrary, mankind had developed from a primitive state of intelligence in which his standards of judgment and facilities for acquiring information were widely different from those enjoyed in later times. It was thus possible to admit the good faith and sincerity of those early writers even though their own interpretation of events differed so greatly from our own. In developing his concept of the evolution of human intelligence Eichhorn was but following up certain ideas of Semler who had insisted so strongly on studying the biblical authors and their writings in their historical context. Eichhorn's views on primitive man had a further consequence, namely in the matter of revelation. The childhood of the human race seemed to him at variance with the idea of a special revelation to the Jews such as normally envisaged in the Bible. Either one should suppose a general revelation to all nations proportioned to their state of development at the time of their 'childhood' or one should make an exception for the Hebrews and allow them a more advanced state in keeping with such a developed revelation. But Eichhorn had already rejected the latter alternative and was moving towards the former conclusion. In this he approached Lessing much more nearly than Semler. These considerations must now be treated in some detail.

It so happened that in the very year of Semler's attack on Lessing (1779), Eichhorn, then a young professor of oriental languages at Jena,

published a long article entitled *Urgeschichte–ein Versuch,*[27] in which
he attempted an interpretation of the early chapters of Genesis. Accepting the distinction between Gen 1:1–2:3 and Gen 2:4–3:24, he regarded Gen 1 as a word picture painted to describe the divine origin of the
world. Gen 2–3 he regarded as a tradition coming down from the origins
of the human race. Basically it was history, but written in a simple and
anthropomorphic manner, characteristic of primitive peoples. Thus the
narrative constantly ascribed to the direct action of God many things
which we know to have been produced by secondary causes. But Eichhorn was insistent that it was history.[28] If Moses had inserted a mythological fragment in his first book would he have supplied a solution to
this important question of the origin of evil which had no guarantee of
correctness? Could God make a place in his revelation for something
mixed with error and falsehood? And even if he could, was it really
possible or fitting that one of the most important objects of revelation,
namely the origin of evil, should be wrapped up in it? How could one
discover with certainty the divine meaning in a myth? Moreover, there
was little of the miraculous in this story and a usual sign of myth was
the presence of the wonderful or miraculous.[29]

At this stage then, Eichhorn held (a) that there was a chain of history coming down to us from the beginnings of the human race, and
(b) that the concept of myth involved error and in other ways too was
unsuitable as a means of interpreting Scripture. But in view of the
inadequacy of the current 'natural' explanation of the Bible account,
Eichhorn introduced his theory of the *infantia generis humani* which
was to lead in a direction he hardly expected. Whereas hitherto exegetes
had supposed that man at his first appearance had lived in a Golden Age
of high intelligence and prosperity unencumbered by many of his later
disabilities, Eichhorn now suggested that, on the contrary, the first man
lived in a very primitive state of culture and undeveloped intelligence. It
was an illiterate and unscientific age in which man knew little of the
forces and powers of nature around him, and he tended to ascribe the
phenomena he experienced to God, the first Cause, being ignorant of
secondary causes. There was no evidence of a Golden Age in the sense
so beloved of theologians as an interpretation of Genesis.[30] Eichhorn
considered the possibility of an allegorical interpretation of Gen 2–3. It
was difficult, he said, to suppose such a method of describing a spiritual
reality and moreover a reality in a narrative which was otherwise
entirely historical. The topography of Eden and much else in Gen 2
gave so definite an impression of history that it seemed laughable to
suggest allegory. If an allegorical fragment had been inserted, it must
have been done long before the composition of the book as we now had
it–perhaps near the origins of the human race. But then was allegorical

expression really to be expected at the origins of mankind? Was not allegory rather the fruit of a developed human understanding? Would it not be to falsify the continuity of history and the development of human reason to suggest that men of both the childhood and adulthood of mankind played with toys of the same kind? Eichhorn admitted that Gen 3 was not proof against every argument for myth or allegory and he was only concerned, for the moment, he said, to show that Gen 3 — light and artless as it was — *could* be explained as actual history.[31]

Eichhorn's special contribution to criticism at this stage therefore was his introduction of the principle of the *infantia generis humani* into the interpretation of the early chapters of Genesis, though he had not as yet envisaged all the consequences of that application. At the time of the publication of the *Urgeschichte* Eichhorn still found it possible to believe in a thread of history that had come down to us from the beginnings of the human race. Without that of course he would have had no grounds for supposing the Genesis account to be in any way historical. Moreover he had to suppose that the accounts were originally composed by or depended on evidence of eye witnesses because otherwise he would have had difficulty in separating fact from opinion. If the account were dated long after the event there would be no grounds for making any separation at all between the ordinary and the wonderful events there narrated. The adoption of this view on the historical character of the narrative led to many inconsistencies in his interpretation, and this demanded further clarification which he undertook later. But he was conscious of having reached a significant stage in the history of biblical criticism. 'Here I bring to an end my investigation and now quietly await the judgment of worthy critics on the new viewpoint which I have opened up for commentators of the Old Testament and especially for biblical historians.'[32]

Eichhorn was not of course the originator of the *infantia generis humani* idea, but he was the first to apply it to the Bible records. The idea itself had long been known to classical critics and in particular to Christian Gottlob Heyne, professor at Göttingen since 1768, who specialized in classical mythology. Its full development however could not yet take place, for Eichhorn still held principles which restricted him in that direction, e.g. on primitive history and on the Mosaic authorship of the Pentateuch.[33] He was well aware that Heyne's researches into the nature and composition of classical literature had revealed that myth was the earliest form of the traditions of ancient nations. Moreover Eichhorn was one of the foremost opponents of the prevalent view that certain critical principles might be valid enough when applied to classical literature, but were inapplicable to the Bible because of its inspired and sacred character. The Bible, he argued, was literature like any other ancient literature and the same principles applied. But Eichhorn's approach to the full application of the mythical principle was gradual. Already he had established the unreasonableness of judging these writings by contemporary standards and thereby had eliminated any suggestion of dishonesty. 'The supernatural colouring of ancient story,' said Eichhorn, 'is not fraudulent invention, but the genuine reflection of antiquity; we must decipher the records by discarding the bewildering haze of the miraculous, and seeking out the natural occurrences which were so obscured by simple imaginations.' This 'natural' theory of Eichhorn is what, from the ancient Epicurean expounder of mythology, has been termed 'Euhemerism'; it means the view of *mythi* making them unintentional misrepresentations of an historical tradition. On this principle Eichhorn explains 'naturally' the stories of the Fall, of Noah, Abraham, Moses, etc; the forbidden fruit, he tells us, was poisonous; the divine voice is to be understood as a clap of thunder; the serpent's temptation was not a speech, but the example given in eating; the cherished project of the patriot Moses to emancipate his people presented itself to his own mind as a divine commission; the flame and smoke of Sinai arose from a fire purposely kindled on the mountain to produce a theatrical effect, increased accidentally by a thunderstorm; the luminous column was a torch carried in advance of the caravan and the shining of the countenance of Moses the natural effect of his being hurried and overheated, etc.'[34]

This 'natural' interpretation, so greatly employed by Eichhorn at the beginning, was gradually to be decreased as the understanding of myth increased.

THE MYTHOLOGICAL INTERPRETATION

In 1788 Eichhorn wrote a book review taking his ideas a stage further. He now applied his principles more thoroughly to the Bible. In Stendal's book *Die Ältesten Urkunden. . .*[35] the author saw many affinities of Genesis 2 with the traditions of other ancient peoples. Thus the story of the creation of Eve reminded him of the Indian myth concerning the creation of Vishnu from the side of Brahmah. Eichhorn observed that his own thinking had been developing along similar lines. The narrative of Genesis 2 now seemed to him to be a *Philosophem* or philosophical myth about an original Golden Age and this had developed into a Saga. Eichhorn next considered this tradition of a Golden Age. He personally did not believe in it as it was commonly understood. But the tradition was there. How should one explain its existence? There appeared to be a true idea underlying it. The highest happiness of mankind could be realised in two situations: (1) at the lowest stage of development, in a state of utter simplicity, segregation, ignorance and lack of familiarity with other situations. A people could be, and often were, happy in such conditions. It was when man, with his developing intellect, and advancing experience, realized that other situations and conditions of life were possible that contentment and happiness vanished. (2) In the second situation, that of the highest enlightenment, principles of the greatest wisdom would be the source of peace and happiness. An ancient philosopher observed that envy of another's condition of life was the ultimate cause of man's unhappiness. It was hardly necessary to observe that the happy state described here had not yet arrived. It was an ideal for the future. The original happy state of man, said Eichhorn, was just such a condition of primitive simplicity as was described above. This happiness was lost because through developing experience man became conscious of another desirable objective which he did not yet possess. He wanted the food of the gods. All this had to be expressed metaphorically and poetically because only thus could spiritual concepts be expounded. Later, such a poetical account would take the form of a Saga and from this there originated a Mythus as in similar circumstances in Greek times. Certainly the first attempts of the ancient nations at philosophizing were clothed in metaphor and their description of the transition from the *Aetas aurea* to the *Aetas argentea* was set down immediately after the cosmogonies. Need one be surprised if the Semitic nations had something like it? The history of literature showed that similar situations of man led to similar ideas and presentations of those ideas, allowing of course for possible modifications due to differences of circumstance, climate, food, customs, etc.[36]

Here, for the first time, the principles of mythological interpretation, as developed by Heyne, were directly applied to the Bible.[37] And this confirmed what J. P. Gabler[38] said of the first edition of Eichhorn's *Urgeschichte*. 'Eichhorn blazed the trail. He pointed out an entirely new way, not yet trodden by man, whereby one could rationally defend these ancient documents against the ridicule of their enemies and correctly explain the nature and way of thinking of the ancient world.'[39] As in the case of most pioneers Eichhorn met with considerable opposition from the more conservative scholars.[40]

In applying myth to the Bible records, Eichhorn was logically facing up to the shortcomings of the Rationalist or Naturalist explanations which he himself had employed for so long. Not only did such explanations frequently make the narrative stilted and artificial but, as already noted above, [41] there was no evidence at all on which to base it. The story which lay before the critic was the only source of information on the episode in question that claimed to be supernatural. The Rationalist therefore was simply drawing on his own preconceived ideas as to what he considered appropriate in the case. Such procedure could be compared to the conjectural emendation of the Hebrew text which was practised to an alarming extent in the eighteenth century and was condemned by more moderate scholars.

While Eichhorn was now prepared to interpret much of the early record as myth, certain well-defined limits were set, because of his views on the authorship of the Pentateuch. One essential requirement in applying myth is length of time for it to develop. But Eichhorn held that Moses himself composed the Pentateuch, though he incorporated earlier traditions in Genesis. In consequence Genesis was the only part of the Pentateuch in which Eichhorn could admit myth for there alone was there sufficient time to allow for its development. Geddes with his different views on the authorship was in a better position for introducing myth into his interpretation of those books. But the main point was that the mythical principle was now being applied to the Bible without any preconceived notions that it was somehow unworthy of the inspired text.

No doubt this reluctance to admit myth was largely due to historical circumstances. Spinoza's denial of miracle could be seen as leading to the admission of myth in the Bible. If miracles were impossible since Nature *was* God's will, they could be said to exist only in a subjective sense. Primitive man beheld a wonderful event which appeared to him to be contrary to the laws of nature; but this was only because he was ignorant of natural causes and ascribed many phenomena to the direct action of God. Thus his explanation of what he experienced was passed on as tradition and miracles became a myth expressing man's ignorance of natural causes.

A second reason for the delay in admitting myth was no doubt its superficial likeness to allegory, against which the tide of opinion was running strongly in the eighteenth century. In earlier times the allegorical interpretation had been made the vehicle for all kinds of exaggerated interpretations. Much of the Christian creed had by this means been read into the Bible text. As a method of interpretation it was now regarded as totally opposed to the later historical and literary criticism.[42]

A third obstacle to admitting myth was the prevalent idea that myth was synonymous with fable. Since fable had no historical basis—being a fictitious story to point a 'moral'—it was assumed that myth was equally unhistorical; and therefore to admit myth was equivalent to denying the historical character besides bringing Scripture down to the level of many not specially edifying stories.[43]

Mark Pattison has written that Heyne was the first to work out a clear analysis and classification of myth by means of an application of the rules of historical criticism, whereas before his time the mythology of Greece and Rome had been 'a farrago of nursery tales.'[44] Heyne was not content like Lowth[45] merely to examine the structure and development of ancient poetry. He went back behind the poetry and investigated the earliest forms of the traditions themselves. He was concerned to separate the contents of the record from their literary dress. The introduction of myth followed from the unacceptability of the literal interpretation of the story as fact. Before Heyne, poetry and myth were interwoven and confused. It was his special achievement to isolate myth as the material of the traditions of ancient nations on which later poets worked. Myth was the stuff of ancient oral tradition before written records began. *'A mythis omnis priscorum hominum cum historia tum philosophia procedit.'* From this unformed material the later poets shaped their artistic products. Homer and Hesiod did not make up their stories; they gave them poetic shape.[46]

Heyne went on to analyse the imperfect modes of expression at the disposal of primitive man. In this *infantia generis humani* there was a threefold lack. (1) Lack of knowledge–knowing nothing about the causes of things he ascribed all to the direct action of God. Ignorance was at the base of every myth. (2) Lack of ability to express oneself–primitive man was unused to abstract thought and grasped only what came within the range of his senses; hence the concrete and individual. This *sermonis egestas* was basic in Heyne's theory of myth and he made use of Lowth's explanation of primitive forms of expression, metaphorical usage and personification. (3) The third lack was that of ability to detach oneself from one's own experience. Primitive man became more involved than would a more cultured and educated person. Being thus more impressed, often to the exclusion of other experiences, primitive man saw the particular thing or event under consideration as larger than life. Thus many events, unusual though natural, might become exaggerated into something greater. The *sermo mythicus* whereby these early ideas were expressed was distinguished by Heyne from the *oratio poetica* of a later age. The former belonged to the age of formation of myth; the latter to the time when myths were shaped into poetic form.

By making this distinction, Heyne provided an answer to the Rationalist who made no such distinction and judged the whole to be the conscious product of the artistic intention of the poet who composed the Saga. For the Rationalist it was only a short step thence to charges of imposture and deceit on the part of the poet. Consider, for example, the wonderful events of the Exodus many of which could not have taken place literally as described. Heyne ascribed the more wonderful features of the narrative to the *sermo mythicus*, i.e. to the primitive people who first formulated it, and not to the more sophisticated writers of a later age who were responsible for the actual formation of the book. The former would have been in good faith; if the latter made use of such language to describe what was impossible by the law of nature such use would have been conscious and intentional and there-fore involved deception.

We come then lastly to Heyne's classification of myth. There were two main groups, with a third of less importance. (1) *The historical myth.* About a real occurrence or person but with attendant mythical circumstances, e.g. an account of the foundation of a city, the story of an eponymous hero. (2) *The philosophical myth* or Philosophem. This contained speculation by primitive man about ethical problems of human experience, or the phenomena of nature, e.g. theogonies, cos-mogonies, origin of evil. (3) *The poetical myth.* This was used by the poet to express his aesthetic intentions but in mythical style.[47]

The full application of the mythical principle to the Bible in the light of Heyne's analysis was eventually made not by Eichhorn, as one might have expected, but by his brilliant pupil Johann Philipp Gabler. In a new edition of Eichhorn's *Urgeschichte*, undertaken with his full permission[48] and published in three volumes, 1790-93, Gabler applied myth to the Bible record, taking account of all developments since the first appearance of the work in 1779. The revision was so thorough and the notes so copious that it almost amounted to a new work. Whereas in the first edition Eichhorn had but tentatively outlined his views, in this new edition Gabler openly adopted the mythical interpretation and as openly attacked opposing views. The work is one of the outstanding critical achievements of the period and it is therefore all the more curious that Geddes appears to have been unaware of its existence.[49] He quotes the first edition of *Urgeschichte* in the first volume of his Bible (1792) but nowhere is there a reference to this important second edition though it had been published two years previously.[50] In his edition of the work Gabler made it clear what his intention was: 'to provide an exact and complete historical-critical review of the different methods of interpretation.[51]

The appearance of the work was made the occasion of a new attack by the supporters of the traditional interpretation. Even now they fail-ed to see any inconsistency in their parallel denial that the Greek myths should be taken literally. Eichhorn and Gabler however were attacking principally the Naturalist, Deist or Rationalist interpretation. Both sides agreed in rejecting the literal interpretation as impossible but parted company in their explanation. The Naturalists said the biblical authors deceived us: Gabler said no—the unacceptable features of the narrative must be ascribed to an earlier stage of the tradition and were composed by honest but primitive folk. The Naturalists or Rationalists ignored historical development. 'The dispute was not about the literal truth of the biblical history, but about the method of interpretation which laid the biblical authors under the general suspicion of intending to deceive their readers,'[52] Gabler's debt to Heyne is very clear, and he emphasized the need to transfer oneself back into the spirit of the age in which the books were written, the *Kinderalter* of the human race.

In applying Heyne's principles, Gabler considered primitive man's tendency to 'blow up' events to more than life size.[53] This could lead to a belief in the miraculous if it were coupled with the other tendency to ascribe unusual happenings to the direct action of God. But besides physical phenomena, there were also internal, e.g. dreams. All these figured largely in primitive records and traditions. The changing character of oral tradition, emphasised by Heyne was taken up by Gabler. Referring to the Mosaic records in Genesis, he stressed the distance in time separating the original events from the setting down of the record in writing and noted how great an accumulation of detail might have taken place in the intervening time. In the case of great men, the recollection of what actually happened became more and more vague as time passed. The great names were clothed with new details; they became stereotyped personages, and stories in keeping with this new role were added to the collection. Thus on two counts, myth had a character all its own: (1) it was expressed in the sense-modes of thought and expression of those days; (2) the tradition could have undergone an indefinite amount of modification in the course of transmission down the ages.[54]

Heyne's important distinction between myth and fable was taken up by Gabler. Heyne defined fable as a poetic fiction. Myths were not fables or tales without foundation but old Sagas. Mythology was not fable-lore but the oldest history and philosophy, couched in the rude and sense speech of those early times.[55] Gabler's most personal contribution to this analysis of myth was his distinction between the content of a myth and the intention or purpose of it. It was not enough, he said, for a myth to contain historical matter for it to be classed as a historical myth. One had to discover the purpose for which it was composed. A myth containing historical material might be used to illustrate an idea—and this would be a philosophical myth. The distinction was not between historical myth, which dealt with a real event, on the one hand, and the philosophical myth, treating a pure speculation, on the other. There could be an event in the latter without it being a dominant element.[56]

Gabler did not look on himself as the author of an original work. He considered it his task to apply the principles he had learnt from Heyne and Eichhorn and gladly rendered to his masters the credit for anything he wrote. He was always ready to consider, he said, any new contribution on this subject, especially if it came from a scholar of the school of Heyne with its appreciation of the spirit of ancient times; and in this consideration he would have Eichhorn as his guide. '*Er war mein*

Lehrer, und ich lernte so viel zu seinen Füssen—Er sey es noch! Er sey es in der Ferne. Er sey es vor der Welt!'[57]

THE COMPOSITION OF THE PENTATEUCH

Geddes's remarks on this subject, though tantalizingly few, are important and suggestive. Like many other matters, it was to be discussed more fully in his General Preface. In asserting that the Pentateuch in its present form was not written by Moses, Geddes was echoing Richard Simon of the previous century.[58] Simon had suggested multiple and indeed collective authorship spread over a number of centuries. The bulk of the work was carried out by official or public secretaries under the general direction of the 'Hebrew Commonwealth'. Only a selection of the original records survived. There are in the Pentateuch many references to lost works. Simon of course distinguished Moses from these secretaries and he was author of a part. It was perhaps Ezra, he thought, who was responsible for the completion of the work, as Spinoza had already suggested. Simon's work was in fact an answer to Spinoza on the one hand, who sought to discredit the authority of the Bible by noting its inconsistencies, and Protestants on the other, who took, in his view, insufficient notice of tradition. Simon insisted that though the inconsistencies, especially the chronological ones, might militate against Mosaic authorship, this did not destroy the authority of the Bible.[59] It was collective or community authorship which was all important—an idea which is today coming back into prominence. Geddes agreed with this position, though he put the completion of the work much earlier. Simon was mainly concerned with the broad historical situation. He hardly entered into the literary dissection. Thus he distinguished two accounts of the Creation, and two of the Flood and suggested they were by different authors whose work Moses had put together. Geddes agreed the accounts were different, but not that they were by different authors. Simon, at any rate, had established two important points—that the Pentateuch was, in substance, later than Moses and secondly that the actual author was of less importance than the fact that the work had been produced under the general direction of the community. His conclusions however, as noted already, were rejected by his Church, indeed by all Christian denominations at that time, and not taken up again until nearly a century later.

The gibe of Spinoza that nothing in Genesis was in its right place[60] still needed to be answered and it was in effect to supply this answer that Astruc wrote his *Conjectures. . .* He is remembered for his isolation of documents on the basis of different divine names. What is often forgotten is that, holding the full Mosaic authorship of the Pentateuch, he sought to absolve Moses from responsibility for the dislocations of Genesis. He did this by suggesting that Moses had several documents at his disposal which he arranged in parallel columns, like synoptic Gospels; but later scribes put them together in a defective way. Astruc's treatise was to be a vindication of Moses. He pursued his work as far as Exodus 2 but no farther, since at that point contemporary history was reached, and he did not question Moses' authorship.[61] Well meaning though Astruc was, his detailed dissection of Genesis inspired other scholars to try their hand at dissection too and a rash of differing analyses resulted. This alarmed the conservatives and, ignoring the solid achievement of Astruc in his distinguishing of sources, they pointed to the differing results (as many conservatives have done since) as proof that they cancelled one another out. There was some truth in this insofar as many analyses were perhaps put forward without enough evidence in their support. But in general the conservative argument was made to prove too much.

Johann August Dathe, in condemning this wholesale dissection was at the same time careful to point out that he was not against it in principle. All he asked for was proof; and this, he maintained, was just what he could not get. At the same time, he went on to provide a most elaborate defence of the Mosaic authorship of the whole Pentateuch.[62] Doubtless bearing Dathe's advice in mind, Eichhorn embarked on the task initiated by Astruc. The difference now was that whereas Astruc, the king's physician, had studied Genesis as a hobby, Eichhorn brought to his task all the formidable mental equipment and training of one of the foremost scholars of Europe. Eichhorn always maintained that he did not use Astruc's work, though he had of course heard of it, but analysed Genesis in accord with his own principles. This means that his results must be given that much more weight. He confirmed Astruc's distinction of two sources on the basis of the different use of the divine names and went on to analyse them with a great weight of learning, which put the basic distinction beyond the possibility of doubt, up to the end of Exodus 2.[63] Eichhorn was therefore all the more surprised when Geddes rejected the different use of divine names as a criterion for distinguishing between documents and concluded that Geddes could not have studied recent German work on the subject.[64] Doubtless Eichhorn put the emphasis on the word 'recent'. He could not have been unaware that Herder, with whom he had so much in common, was extremely sceptical about the validity of such analysis and was of the opinion that Eichhorn had done the job too thoroughly. Pieces which should have been left intact, being clearly of the same period and probably by the same author, had been divided. The criterion of the use of divine names he thought very unreliable. It was not difficult to con-

ceive other reasons for the difference in usage. The oldest pieces had
Elohim—as also those parts which followed the oldest passages, or
perhaps related something which was not entirely fitting the honour of
Jehovah.[65]

That Eichhorn should have continued, unlike Geddes, to believe in
the Mosaic authorship of the Pentateuch, was even more surprising and
his explanation of the evidence in Exodus and Leviticus, to the effect
that these books had partly grown out of separate documents during
the Mosaic age, hardly carried conviction. Eichhorn's analysis of documents stopped short, just when it should have continued. But his
scientific dissection of Genesis provided the groundwork on which
future Pentateuchal analysis could be based. Unlike Astruc, he made
some attempt to characterize the documents isolated—as for example
that the Elohist (actually P) followed a chronological method, whereas
J had an interest in cosmography.[66]

Eichhorn was of the opinion that Exodus 1–2 had originally belonged to the book of Genesis. An editor cut off this portion and attached
it to the book of Exodus so that the two books might constitute two
works, each independent of the other: the former, Genesis, contained
the history of Israel's ancestors; the latter, Exodus and the other books,
comprised the history of the nation; the former concluded with Jacob;
the latter now began with his descendants. These first two chapters of
Exodus belonged, thought Eichhorn, to the E source. Today, of course,
we would observe that the two chapters contain considerable portions
from J. Furthermore, if one accused Geddes of arbitrary action in
dividing the narrative in Genesis 2 after verse 6, one might equally criticise Eichhorn for his decision to draw a line after Exodus 2. True, the
distinction between the divine names no longer helps much after
Exodus 3 but Eichhorn in any case did not confine himself to that
criterion.

CHAPTER FIVE

CONTEMPORARY COMMENT
ON GEDDES'S BIBLICAL CRITICISM

The appearance of the *Prospectus of a New Translation of the Bible* in 1786 brought about a distinct improvement in Geddes's situation. Hitherto he had been the obscure protégé of Lord Petre, welcome in his patron's circle of society for his lively conversation and ready wit, or as a friend of the Bishop of London in whom he had found a staunch supporter of his project for a new translation of the Bible. But now Geddes was a biblical scholar in his own right; the *Prospectus* was recognised everywhere as an able work. Geddes made sure it reached everywhere by sending out a large number of complimentary copies, not only to leading scholars and dignitaries of the Church in Britain and eminent professors abroad, especially in Germany, but also to members of royal families.

As time passed, however, this favourable reputation declined in Britain for a variety of reasons. When the French Revolution first broke out it attracted a large measure of sympathy and open support in Britain among all classes of the population. But as the Revolution developed and became more violently opposed to existing institutions, whether political or religious, British opinion became alienated and the Government began to take repressive action against sympathisers. Though Geddes had never taken any active part in subversive movements nor carried his sympathy to extremes, he had written more than once in its favour, as indeed had many others in Britain; and he had contacts with men who were far more compromised than he. In the dark days of 1794 indeed there was some reason to think that his own freedom might be in danger.[1] As for his biblical criticism, the *Proposals and Specimens* (1788) gave the first signs of his advanced views on the subject. Moreover, they were expressed in too blunt and too brief terms, as Eichhorn observed. Lastly, during the 1790's Geddes began to gather round him a circle of friends of the Unitarian persuasion — a movement then making progress in Britain. Geddes counted among his friends men such as Dr John Disney, Dr John Mason Good, the Rev. Theophilus Lindsey, George Dyer and Gilbert Wakefield. Some of these were members of the Chapter Coffee House Club in Paternoster Row, and it was there that Dyer, and possibly Geddes, first met the young Samuel

Taylor Coleridge in 1794 who had Unitarian leanings at that time.[2]
During the early 1790's Geddes also became acquainted with Dr Joseph
Priestley when he came to London from Birmingham for a few years
before his departure for America.

The welcome given to the *Prospectus* (1786) by the educated public
both of Britain and Germany must have been a source of great satis-
faction, not to say solace, for Geddes.[3] Even among his co-religionists it
went far to reversing the judgment which many of them had already
formed of him as a priest of unorthodox tendencies. The British
periodicals of the time gave the work considerable notice, concentrating
naturally on his plans for a new translation of the Bible rather than on
the textual or literary criticism. It is noteworthy that the reviewers
agreed among themselves that the Common Version was, and should
stay, in possession, and that if textual criticism showed that changes
had to be made, such changes should be few and disturb the translation
as little as possible. Those who ventured on Bible translation at that
time were acutely conscious of the climate of opinion. The scholars saw
the need of a revision based on a more critical text but the public
grudged every change introduced into the familiar Version. There were
many in those days who translated the New Testament and individual
books of the Old Testament but few who attempted the whole Bible.
This may have been one of the reasons why Geddes's project attracted
such attention when it was announced. Among those who had produced
a translation of several books of the Old Testament was Dr Benjamin
Blayney, Regius Professor of Hebrew at Oxford University, and he
made no secret of his desire to see a new translation of the Scriptures
for the public service. After speaking of a project for a new translation
in Sweden, he went on, 'And, which may more excite our wonder, we
are credibly informed that a similar work is set on foot in our own
language, at the sole expense of a single Nobleman of princely spirit for
the use of the English Roman Catholics. And shall the British Nation
ever accustomed to rank with the foremost in learning and piety be the
last to hold forth to her members those sacred writings in their utmost
perfection and purity the free use of which she has ever taught them to
consider as the most invaluable of their privileges?'[4]

When the *Prospectus* was published the *Critical Review* enlarged on
the need for emending the faulty text of the Bible, as had been done
for the classics of Greece and Rome. The reviewer was happy to see this
being undertaken at last, with care and attention, and that, after Dr
Kennicott and de Rossi, other labourers were executing the task with
industry, so that one might look forward with confidence to the Word
of God cleared from the errors of ignorance and superstition. In this
very able and intelligent *Prospectus*, the reviewer continued, the author

gave us an account of the state of the text, pointing out its defects which he attributed to a superstitious veneration of the Masora. The effects had been covered up because the text was regarded as sacred and to reform it would seem to many little less than changing the national religion itself. Few people, he observed, could distinguish verbal and essential errors, between the mistakes of a translator and the dictates of heaven.[5]

In Germany the *Prospectus* was equally well received. The venerable Johann David Michaelis, professor at Göttingen, was evidently attracted by the idea of a new English translation and commented at length on the project. What was especially novel about this venture, he observed, was that it had originated among the Roman Catholics and that they wanted to produce their translation from the original languages according to the scientific principles acknowledged by the best Protestant scholars. This was real progress and true Aufklärung. This did not mean that the Catholic Church would now be untrue to its principles. At a time when the Protestants held firmly to the infallible Hebrew text, the Catholic Church had proposed emendation. Moreover, she never exalted the Vulgate above the originals. If now, a new translation were to be produced, making use of the work of Kennicott and de Rossi, by a scholar well versed in Oriental languages, it would be an immense advance over preceding translations. It might even come to be used by Protestants. Michaelis then speculated on whether this might open the door to proselytising, given the Roman Catholic practice of adding notes to the Bible text. Reaching no conclusion on this point, he returned to his criticism of the *Prospectus*. He disagreed with Geddes's view that the Massoretes were responsible for eliminating the vowel letters and he maintained that this view was contrary to the general opinion. On the other hand he was critical of the spurious uniformity of the Massoretic Text and agreed with Geddes who likewise put little trust in the vocalisation and regarded the points as of late date.[6] On the subject of the Vulgate, Michaelis observed that Geddes appeared to rate it lower than he himself did; 'indeed a reader, not knowing to which religion we belonged, might take me for the Catholic and him for the Protestant!'[7]

Geddes, said Michaelis, was loud in praise of Lowth's translation of Isaiah and with this judgment he was inclined to agree. He felt that if Geddes took Lowth for his guide, especially in his philology (England had had no one equal to Lowth in that field during the present century), the prospects for his translation were good.[8]

On the whole, Catholics had been inclined to prefer the versions, especially the Vulgate and Geddes was trying to steer a middle course. Michaelis approved his critical principles but thought he exaggerated the corruption of the Massoretic Text. Geddes gave an excellent account of the versions, in particular the English versions. What especially pleased Michaelis was Geddes's familiarity with German scholars and their work: an unusual accomplishment in Britain and if Geddes did not know them all, who, among foreign scholars did? The German language was not well known abroad.[9]

The *Prospectus* was favourably noticed in other German periodicals: in particular the *Annales Literarii* of Helmstädt and the *Diarium* of Würzburg which last also recommended its translation for German readers. The suggestion was speedily put into effect by a monk of the Benedictine Abbey of Banz, in Bavaria, named Ildephonsus Schwarz, who translated the work into Latin, adding copious notes.[10] Dom Ildephonsus Schwarz translated the *Prospectus* (he wrote in the fore-word), not because he thought it the best work on the subject, but because it contained material which could be useful for German readers and because it had been recommended by many different scholars, both Catholic and Protestant, for its elegance of language, its order and its erudition. But there were parts of it which would displease some readers: e.g. its excessive admiration of Houbigant and certain remarks on the Samaritan Pentateuch and the Hebrew language. Moreover it was not a complete introduction – thus it was too exclusively concerned with the Old Testament.

The notes to this Latin edition for the use of students add much useful information, correct a number of points and, where necessary, put an alternative point of view. In general Dom Ildephonsus is concerned to moderate Geddes's 'liberal' views where they seem to him to depart from the path of accuracy, to supply for his German readers a much more detailed account of German literature on the subject under consideration, and to substitute German titles and examples where Geddes quoted English ones. Dom Schwarz was particularly anxious to counteract Geddes's immoderate enthusiasm for Houbigant. Thus (note 84) he comments: 'De Houbigantio non ita amice Critici nostri iudicarunt.' When Geddes remarks that the first vernacular version made in Europe from the originals is the German of Luther (*Prospectus*, p. 82), Schwarz comments (note 86): 'Lutherus pro suae versionis fundamento non archetypum sed Vulgatam habuit. V. Ernesti *Bibl. Th.* 7, s. 777. Et ex ipsa versione ostendi id potest.' When Geddes enlarges on the history of Bible reading over the centuries, Ildephonsus Schwarz comments at great length, modifying and correcting his statements or amplifying them to give a more balanced impression. Thus when Geddes affirms that the Fathers of the Church are full of exhortations to read the Scriptures Schwarz observes that one must distinguish Scripture reading from Scripture knowledge and there were often many good reasons why a poorly educated people in later times should not be urged to read the vernacular Scripture for themselves. In the early centuries people were instructed in the doctrine and history of the Scripture; and then could read it with profit. When Geddes declares that apart from a small handful of Fathers one will look in vain for anything of value in their writings, Schwarz points out that we have no right to look for what we know could not be there, for example a philological exposition. In those days no one had the knowledge. Lastly, he disagrees with one of Geddes's principles for translation, namely that 'not a single ambiguity should be left which can be removed'. On this Dom Schwarz quotes Ernesti who warns that the translation should be as accurate as possible and that all interpretations be put in the notes or commentary rather than in the text. 'Bene Castalio ad 1 Pet. 4:6 –"Haec non intelligo – itaque ad verbum verti".' On the other hand Schwarz is in entire agreement with Geddes when he declares that the translator or interpreter should under no circumstances put into his translations his own dogmatic presuppositions. Lastly, Schwarz clearly divides up the work into sections and subsections with appropriate titles, thus greatly enhancing the appearance and utility of the book. It is a strange thing that Geddes provided not so much as a single title or chapter division throughout the entire book.

When Geddes's *Proposals and Specimens* appeared in 1788, Michaelis wrote a review in the *Neue Orientalische. . .* In this he expressed his disappointment at the selection of variants put forward by Geddes. Moreover, there were no examples from the New Testament and that was more difficult to translate than the Old Testament. In Gen 1:26, in place of 'and in all the earth', Geddes put 'and all other terrestial animals', on the strength of the Syriac reading. But could one follow this alone if all the others were opposed? And was it so certain that the Syriac read this? It could be an interpretation or an implication rather than an explicit reading. Geddes devoted valuable space to the recording of minutiae of the Hebrew text which were of no real value for the ordinary reader for whom he professed to be writing. Geddes should make up his mind whether he was addressing the expert or the average reader.[11]

In Exodus 16 Geddes transposed verses 11-12 and placed them between verses 3 and 4 without any evidence at all from the manuscripts. On this Michaelis commented: 'This is sheer Houbigantian criticism to which he is very much inclined.'[12]

Soon after the appearance of Geddes's *Proposals* (1788), the first signs of trouble began to appear. There were those who criticized him for departing from the Common Version; but more serious were the objections of those who criticized him for making rash and unfounded emendations of the text and for commenting on it in so novel and

daring a manner. In the *Proposals*, Geddes gave for the first time his
own literary criticism and interpretation of the Bible text. It was this
especially which provoked opposition. For this reason and because of a
certain deterioration in health, brought on, in part, by the difficulties
he encountered, the publication of his Bible was delayed. Writing to his
cousin Bishop John Geddes in April 1788, he said: 'The first volume of
my great work shall certainly, Deo volente, be put to the Press next
year and published the spring after.'[13] The following month he received
at his home a visitor from Germany, the young scholar H. E. G. Paulus,
who described Geddes as 'an enlightened critic of the present state of
the Hebrew text and experienced in the use of the various Hilfsmittel
for the study and translation of the Bible'.[14] During his prolonged visit
to England Paulus visited Geddes many times, mostly during May and
October of 1788 and met a number of scholars at his residence. In the
October he met Raspe there, who, he said, was preparing his catalogue
of a Collection of Gems.[15] Geddes was very busy sending copies of his
Proposals to everyone of importance. 'Copies (of the *Proposals*) have
been submitted to all the royal personages and well received. Del Pinto
has carried one to the Queen of Portugal and I believe I shall find means
to transmit one to every crowned head in Europe.'[16]

Over a year later, there was still no sign of the promised volume. He
wrote to his cousin the Bishop: 'You have been a long time indeed
before you would tell me that you were not pleased with my *Specimens*.
Your objections would have come with a much better grace on your
first receiving them than after a second edition was published. However
the admonitions of a friend are never out of season and I will always
avail myself of these as much as I can.'[17]

Meanwhile Geddes was becoming more and more deeply involved in
the efforts of the Catholic Committee[18] to pilot the second Catholic
Relief Bill through Parliament. The Bill was eventually passed in June
1791 after a bitter struggle between the Catholic Committee and the
Vicars Apostolic over the nature and wording of the proposed Oath of
Allegiance to the Crown. Meanwhile, Sir John Throckmorton, a prominent member of the Committee, was busy writing a book on the
right of the people to elect their own bishops. Geddes was convalescing
at Thorndon in Essex, one of Lord Petre's residences, when the passage
of the Bill was announced. 'I believe,' he wrote to his cousin, 'I shall
remain here a week longer and then return to my tremendous labours.
I had gotten to the end of Numbers at the period of stopping, and part
of Deuteronomy is in the Press.'[19] The first volume of his Bible eventually appeared in the following year, 1792,[20] about the same time as
Geddes moved into his new house in Allsop's Buildings, New Road,
Marylebone. Sir John Throckmorton's book on the election of bishops

issued from the Press in the same year. Though Geddes must have been only too well aware of the serious nature of the dispute between the Vicars Apostolic and the Catholic Committee, he appears to have greatly underestimated the permanent effects of this and to have thought that the worst was over. He was soon to be disillusioned.

On 10 July 1792 Geddes sent a copy of his Bible volume to Bishop Douglass, the new Vicar Apostolic of the London District, asking him to accept it as a mark of his Catholicity, whatever his critics might say, and regretting that the bishop could not see his way to subscribe to it or otherwise give it his official approval.[21] To this letter no reply was sent. Geddes was too deeply implicated with the Catholic Committee and the breach had not been healed. On the contrary, the appearance of Sir John's booklet on the election of bishops (evidently aimed at Bishop Douglass) made matters worse.

Among Geddes's numerous critics at this time, one of the most outspoken was the Rev. John Milner, an able and learned priest of extreme conservative views, then resident at Winchester. A man of rigid orthodoxy, he spared no pains in criticizing those whom he considered to be deviating from the truth, and did not shrink from abuse where he thought it suited his purpose. Accusations of the gravest kind poured from his pen. These were often not only exaggerated but even inconsistent with one another. Writing about Geddes's Bible some months after the appearance of the first volume, Milner observed: 'A man who thinks the Creation a myth and who treats the Scriptures as any other author, breeds in my mind a jealousy which will not permit me to trust the translator any farther than I can see him.'[22] He urged Bishop Douglass to excommunicate Geddes. The bishop however was unimpressed by this show of zeal, probably because he suspected that it concealed an ambition for preferment in the Church.

Not long afterwards the Vicars Apostolic issued a joint Pastoral condemning a number of propositions drawn from Sir John's work but not otherwise censuring him. In the same Pastoral they warned the faithful against Geddes's Bible which, they said, had been published without episcopal approval.[23] Geddes naturally protested to Bishop Douglass, who swiftly replied: 'Sir. Since it is evident from your letter to me that you adhere to and maintain the doctrines which were censured by the Pastoral Letter to which you allude, unless you signify to me in writing, on or before Friday, the fifth day of July next, your subscription to observe the injunction contained in the 21st page of the said Pastoral Letter, viz. "We prohibit our clergy in particular from preaching, teaching, maintaining or supporting any of the aforesaid condemned opinions", I hereby declare you suspended from the exercise of your Orders in the London District'. (signed) John Douglass,

Vicar Apostolic, 27 June 1793.[24]

While this momentous decision was being taken by Bishop Douglass, Geddes was spending the summer months at Oxford, collating texts for his Bible. Writing to Miss Howard on 15 May from Oxford, Geddes confessed that he was not overworking, as he had not been well lately. 'I never sit down to write after dinner; that is, after three, which here is the canonical hour... I have some thoughts of being in London next week; but it will be only toward the end of it and that too will depend on the progress I shall make this week through 57 volumes of Various Readings.' There can be little doubt that the volumes in question were the collations of Septuagint manuscripts, gathered from all over Europe by Dr Robert Holmes.[25] Geddes also found time to take some part in the academic life of the University and from time to time was invited to dine in college. As for Bishop Douglass's letter of 27 June, Geddes found himself unable to comply with the Bishop's request and the censure took effect therefore from the date specified. The issue of what amounted to a condemnation of his Bible as well as a censure of himself affected Geddes deeply. To condemn his Bible was to touch him where it hurt most.[26]

Fortunately for him, there were many favourable opinions of his work to which he could turn for encouragement. The *Monthly Review* was consistently, though not uncritically, favourable. The reviewer of volume I announced with pleasure the appearance of 'this great and important work on which Dr Geddes has been long and assiduously employed and for the appearance of which his *Prospectus* and other preliminary writings have prepared the public mind and have excited in lovers of sacred criticism great expectations.

'It will be unnecessary for us in this place to pay any compliments to Dr Geddes's learning and abilities or to offer any remarks, after what he himself has advanced in the *Prospectus*, to shew that he is sensible of the qualifications which are necessary to constitute a good translator. That he has undertaken the task with a mind richly stored will be acknowledged, whatever opinions may be formed of the merits of the version.'[27]

The reviewer went on to speak of the defects of commentators in the past and the present need of a judicious and up-to-date exposition. Past commentators had too often tried to defend many interpretations which did not properly belong to the province of religion and this had turned many philosophers with disgust from the sacred text. 'From such men as Dr Geddes, who is uninfluenced by the vulgar prejudices and childish fears of ordinary theologians, biblical criticism may acquire some valuable accessions. He enters on his understanding with an openness and manliness which evince that he has no party views to serve;

and whatever may be his mistakes or omissions, his labours are evidently intended to support that religion which is founded on truth and which shrinks not from the severest scrutiny.' Dr Geddes wished, continued the reviewer, to study and interpret the sacred books as he would any other ancient literature and so revive the declining taste for biblical learning by means of motives similar to those which incite us to study the classics of Greece and Rome. Something of this kind was necessary, not for the vulgar, but for the educated reader. The current notion of biblical inspiration had hitherto prevented many readers from assessing the merits of the Scriptures as literary compositions. By inviting the critic and man of taste to estimate their value by the rules of taste Dr Geddes would advance rather than diminish their reputation. Referring to Geddes's explanation of the Hebrew cosmogony the reviewer observed that by this means he had rescued Moses from the attack of modern philosophers − and however he might be at variance with the common herd of modern commentators, he proved that he had many of the Fathers on his side. His examination of the narrative induced him also to note that the ancient Hebrews were real anthropomorphites and to this circumstance we should ascribe those expressions about the Deity which seemed to degrade it.[28]

The *Critical Review* was equally effusive in its praise (1794) of Geddes's first volume and contented itself with what amounted largely to a transcription of parts of its contents. The reviewer was understandably interested in the translation more than the literary criticism and ended with these words: 'The importance of the undertaking is great, the learning, sagacity and liberality of Dr Geddes we cannot sufficiently admire; and we sincerely wish him health, with every requisite to the full completion of his hopes.'[29] Others however were less complimentary. The *British Critic* noted Geddes's denial of inspiration as commonly understood and his interpretation of the early history of the Bible as a mythologue. This, said the reviewer, was how Dr Priestley spoke; and it was alarming to think that the teaching on the origin of evil or the Sabbath observance might rest on a myth or fabulous history. He concluded that he must warn Christians 'to beware of an interpreter, who appears to us, under the disguise of that character, to conceal at least Latitudinarian principles of the most dangerous tendency. We know not well how to distinguish between an insidious friend, who gives up almost every essential point, and a real enemy.'[30]

Another critic declared: 'The literary world has long acknowledged that no man is so well qualified for translating the Scriptures as Dr Geddes, not only from his superior attainments in languages but also from his enlarged understanding and singular liberality of mind.' But many were tired of his constant promises and continual delays, especially as he more than once had written a eulogy on his work, before it was half-finished. The doctor was angry at the opposition he had met with but had not for all that modified any of his positions. There was nothing new in all his preface except the comparison of the Pentateuch with Esop and Pilpay.[31]

Meanwhile, in Germany, Michaelis had died and been succeeded in his professorship by Johann Gottfried Eichhorn—a man who inclined more to Geddes's way of thinking and with whom he formed a friendship which lasted until Geddes's death in 1802. This did not mean that Eichhorn was blind to his shortcomings. But Eichhorn, unlike Michaelis who was first and foremost a philologist, was far more interested in literary and historical criticism. Reviewing the first volume of Geddes's Bible, Eichhorn contented himself largely with generalities. First he discussed the chances of a new translation being produced by the English Church and judged them not good. Next he went on to speak of the plan produced by Geddes and made known to the public in 1786 through his *Prospectus*. It was that book which convinced Europe that he was competent to undertake so considerable a task.[32]

The approval which Geddes earned thereby was second only to that accorded to Lowth on the publication of his *Isaiah*. The *Prospectus* was followed by the *Proposals* and now by the first volume of his Bible. It was the result, Eichhorn noted, of long preparation, with the help of a fully critical library furnished by the munificence of his patron Lord Petre. The appearance of this first volume was an event not only for the Roman Catholics of Britain but also for Bible scholars everywhere. Eichhorn regretted that the first volume of *Critical Remarks* had not appeared with the Bible translation. One could see only the finished product and not the reasons which led up to the translation. When the full apparatus was published this volume would be reviewed again in greater detail. Meanwhile, Eichhorn allowed himself some observations on Geddes's criticism. His views on the Semitic cosmogonies approached closely to the progressive outlook of the German critics and were shot through with bright and enlightened ideas. Eichhorn singled out a question asked by Geddes on Genesis 3. 'Why should not the Hebrews have their mythology like every nation...?' Eichhorn went on to make some fairly critical comments on the translation. He thought Geddes was too much inclined towards the Samaritan Pentateuch and too free in his criticism. One must await the *Critical Remarks* to learn the full reasons for his choice. Lastly, the notes; these were short, full of useful information and explanations. The full evidence would be in the future *Critical Remarks* but already one could see evidence of a free, objective spirit, no ordinary knowledge and an acquaintance with all the best literature on exegetical, antiquarian and critical matters. Geddes had kept to his promise to give the grammatical sense and not a sense conditioned by theological systems. Hence some of his conclusions were novel. Eichhorn waited for the future explanations with eagerness.[33]

The second volume, like the first, was delayed by ill-health brought on by disagreement with his ecclesiastical superiors and the attacks of his enemies. The work, completing the historical books, appeared at last in 1797.[34] On its publication the volume attracted a good deal of attention. The *Monthly Review*, undeterred by the adverse criticism, continued to be favourably inclined to Geddes's work and critical position. 'Among the literary acquisitions of the present age,' the reviewer wrote, 'we cannot but rank the work before us. In this second volume as in the first, a free and manly judgment, associated with real learning and rational criticism, will be found in uniform exertion, regardless of the censures of those whom the author deems ignorant, bigoted and superstitious.' After referring again to Geddes's method of regarding the Scriptures as he would the classics, he observed, 'The appearance of such a translator and commentator will, no doubt, be hailed by every liberal advocate for Revealed Religion; for the age of enlightened criticism is at hand, if not already arrived; and whatever cannot bear the touch of Ithuriel's spear will be considered as belonging to the region of error and darkness.' Too many Christian commentators had thought that, like Mount Sinai, the sacred books were not to be approached and that learning and criticism were to regard them at a reverential distance. But 'Dr Geddes leads, the way in a new march of Hebrew criticism. He neither appreciates the writings of the Jews too highly, nor does he interpret, as has generally been done, the bold and highly figurative expressions of the east, according to the frozen conceptions of the inhabitants of the north. Scripture language he weighs in the scale of Oriental philology, and thus endeavours to ascertain its true meaning and value. It is wonderful that this should not have been oftener attempted, as many stumbling blocks to the faith might by these means be completely removed.' Referring again to the traditional doctrine on inspiration as an obstacle to the correct understanding of the sacred books, according to 'many judicious divines', the reviewer suggested that it was a matter of importance to discover how far such a view was supported by the evidence and by reason. Dr Geddes, he noted, was decidedly against the inspiration of the books and however one might differ from him on many points, one was bound to admire the plain and unequivocal manner in which he expressed his views on the subject.[35]

Geddes's explanation of the discrepancies in the commands to Israel concerning the Canaanites, namely that 'the Jewish historians put in the mouth of the Lord words which he never spoke and assigned to him views and motives which he never had', forcibly struck the reviewer. 'This vast concession, by which, in the opinion of some, the cause of revealed religion is completely surrendered, naturally leads to the question about the absolute and universal inspiration of the Hebrew writers. The observations advanced on this subject deserve much consideration. They may at first startle weak minds; but Dr Geddes will affirm to such readers, that the more these arguments are examined and considered, the more will they make their way to the conviction of the judicious part of mankind, and will establish the only true basis on which the explanation of the Hebrew Scriptures can be erected.'[36]

The *Critical Review* was noticeably cooler towards volume two than it had been regarding volume one. Referring to Geddes's discovery of a supposed contradiction between the commands to destroy the Canaanites and the statement that the Lord left them in the land to test Israel,[37] the reviewer continued: 'Attached as we are to freedom of inquiry, from its obvious subservience to the attainment of truth, we cannot forbear to express our surprise at such a discussion in this part of the work. Surely an attack on the veracity of the Bible is not likely to increase the list of the doctor's subscribers; and, if the starting of such difficulties evinces his candour, would not this piece-meal objection have been better postponed till the appearance at least of the General Preface to which for other topics we are often referred?' The reviewer rejected Geddes's solution as foolish, especially his statement that there were similar contradictions in many other places. Surely, he remonstrated, this was travelling towards conclusions with seven-league boots? Because Dr Geddes saw no solution therefore no solution existed. The reviewer preferred the traditional solution. As for Geddes's view that the narrative often recorded words of God which he in fact never uttered and views which he did not hold, this was to destroy all confidence in the account as a record of events. It did not help to say that the narrative contained inspired prophecy, for why should one give that any more credence than the rest of the history? Finally, when the reviewer reached the actual translation he was able to impart some words of approval: 'On the whole,' he said, 'the performance reflects great honour on the doctor, and, notwithstanding the peculiarities that attend it, deserves to be considered of inestimable value. The notes though brief, abound with information; and the various readings will be found of essential importance.'[38]

The *British Critic*, which had warned its readers against the dangerous tendencies of volume one of Geddes's Bible, had evidently been encouraged and strengthened in its opinion by the opposition which had grown since then. 'We cannot wonder,' the reviewer of volume two wrote, 'at the general indignation of the Christian world against an attempt to shake to its basis the admirable and revered fabric, whose foundation-stone was laid by the Hebrew legislator, inspired, as we believe, by the sacred Spirit.' After discussing his treatment of the Mosaic cosmogony, the reviewer observed, 'To Dr Geddes, as a Christian, if he be one (a thing which he seems very angry to have for a moment doubted) we will put an important question, to be evaded by no sophistry, to be shaken by none of that raillery in which he so much delights: Will he reject the attestation borne to the Jewish Scriptures by Christ himself, and by the Apostles, whose inspiration we conceive he must, as a Christian, admit?' The reviewer went on to 'prove' by quotations that Moses must have written the Pentateuch. Furthermore, he argued, inspiration could not have been partial and putative in the historical books, as Geddes suggested; it must have been plenary and entire or non-existent. Geddes maintained that on his principles one understood the Scriptures much better, inasmuch as one was freed from the necessity of taking literally the many prodigies and wonderful interventions of God. So the sacred books, commented the reviewer, were merely a poetical kind of historic rhapsody? The reason why Geddes was against inspiration was because he was reluctant to admit the historicity of God's command to destroy the Canaanites. 'For ourselves,' he concluded, 'convinced that on such a basis as that which this translator has laid, no solid or lasting fabric can be erected; disgusted with the barbarous phraseology that prevails throughout the work; with the manifest perversions of the text, and the audacious scepticism of the comment; we shall not continue the toil of further examination, but leave the work to its fate; a fate not the most envied or honourable, and to which it appears to be rapidly hastening.'[39]

Geddes was warned more than once that the open and blunt expression of views which were completely unfamiliar and unacceptable to most Englishmen was bound to excite opposition. Thus the *Monthly Magazine* while recognising 'the same liberal independent spirit which adorned the first (volume)' nevertheless pointed out that his version was so different from the accepted version and his critical views so much at variance with those commonly regarded as established that 'he must expect very copious torrents of calumny and abuse, from many a stupid and malignant bigot; and the Doctor's opinions on the subject of inspiration, will expose him to peculiar insult.'[40]

But there were others, besides bigots, who opposed him. The Rev. John Earle, chaplain to the Spanish Embassy Chapel in London, wrote a series of four letters in reply to the prefaces to volumes one and two of Geddes's Bible. Earle noticed that in the second preface Geddes had a rather worse opinion of the Bible as literature than he expressed in the first and this was borne out by his classification of the Creation story and other parts of the Pentateuch as mythological or fabulous. Who, Earle asked, had yet dreamed of Pilpay and Esop being divinely inspired? Was this not to do away with all inspiration? Earle was not clear as to what exactly Geddes meant by partial and putative inspiration. It seemed largely unintelligible to him, 'unless you mean the partial and putative inspiration of Homer or of Hesiod, of Horace or of Lucretius; and in that sense it would be mere tautology. But the main question should be the honesty of your hero, Moses'. This was Earle's main point − Geddes's views made Moses an impostor.[41]

Earle denied the validity of Geddes's distinction between the historical and legislative parts of the Bible relative to their inspired character. One could not regard the legislative material as authoritative and exclude the historical. Geddes admitted that the two were interwoven. If therefore he suspected the one he should also suspect the other. If Geddes suspected the historian he should also suspect the legislator, but that made them all impostors, including Moses himself. This showed that Geddes was worse than Tom Paine. 'When Paine thought proper to call Moses "an arrogant coxcomb, a stupid pretender to authorship", and his works "a book of fables, contradictions and lies" he was at least consistent with his own principles. But you affect to honour and revere an illustrious personage whom you perpetually insult.'[42]

Earle argued 'ad hominem' that there was every reason for Geddes to accept the historical parts as reliable if he was prepared to apply to them the same tests that he used for secular history. There was as much reason, argued Earle, to believe 'Moses' as to believe the secular historians. There was a continuous chain of tradition from Abraham to Moses —and, as for the history of the times before Abraham, it was important to recollect that Abraham lived 150 years with Seth so that he could have learned many interesting facts which Geddes chose to regard as fables. 'The same principles which lead us to believe the veracity of their (secular) writings must at least equally lead an unprejudiced person to believe the veracity of his.'[43]

Earle returned to the subject of inspiration. Referring to Geddes's 'middle option' between the extremes of admitting absolute inspiration on the one hand and denying Moses' divine legation on the other, Earle remarked that the middle option did not seem to him very different from the latter alternative. First Geddes said Moses was *in some sense* inspired as a historian and then added in a footnote that he was far from thinking he was so in the strict and theological meaning that was now generally annexed to the word 'inspiration'. So, declared Earle, if not a theological meaning it must be a mythological meaning. Hence the middle option which Geddes applied to Moses as legislator must be referred to the putative inspiration which he allowed to the

sacred writers in general. 'And what is that? Why, an inspiration which
is supposed to arise from art and genius—you believe them to be
inspired like Pilpay or Aesop, (that is to say) you believe a sort of
middle inspiration which, viewed in a theological or religious light, you
must allow to be no inspiration at all—and your middle option vanishes
with it.'[44]

Earle suspected that Geddes's views on the subject were strongly
influenced by ideas prevalent across the Channel. 'The public may judge
whether your sentiments or mine have the greater appearance of truth
and whether your *pupillage* has been much improved upon by the
sudden blaze of philosophic light—and the sublime effort of gallic
liberty-with which you have been so much enamoured.'[45]

Bishop John Douglass, feeling a justifiable pride that one of his
priests had written so telling a reply to this wayward critic, wrote in his
Diary of 9 May 1799, 'took 50 copies of Rev[d]. Mr Earle's *Remarks
upon Geddes's Prefaces to his Translation of the Bible*, wh[ch] I mean to
give to the priests at 2 shillings each copy, total 5£.'[46]

Though the long awaited volume of *Critical Remarks* on the Pentateuch had still not appeared, enough comment on the text, both in the
prefaces and in the notes, had been published to allow a more extended
appreciation of Geddes's views. It was in Germany, however, rather
than in England that anything like an unbiassed and at the same time
penetrating analysis appeared. 'I have had a most polite and elegant
Latin letter from Eichhorn of Göttingen,' wrote Geddes, 'together with
his review of my second volume, in his Oriental Library. He says he has
no scruple in subscribing to every word of my preface and assures me
that all Germany applauds my work. My *Critical Remarks* have been
unutterably retarded, but are now in a fair way of appearing. One
hundred and twenty pages are printed off. I expect a new torrent of
injuries on their publication but I am prepared for it.'[47]

In his review, Eichhorn treated at some length Geddes's arguments
on Inspiration and his examination of the evidence with which he substantially agreed. His aim was to give a rather more detailed exposition
of the matter and add weight to Geddes's conclusions. Aristeas was a
spurious author who in any case was concerned to affirm the inspiration of the Mosaic law without any express consideration of the
history in the Pentateuch. Philo too regarded Moses as an inspired
prophet and lawgiver and the authors of the books as prophets but
hardly as inspired writers. Moreover he allowed Balaam and the Septuagint translators to share in inspiration which showed he was not thinking of it in the same sense as we. As for Josephus, he expressed himself
very guardedly on the origins of the sacred books and based their trust-
worthiness only on this that they were composed with the greatest

accuracy and embodied no contradictions. A special providence of God guided and directed them, he said. Not everybody could write history in this way—only the prophets could do so.

A curious explanation, thought Eichhorn, and one would like further details. If one could only get to know in what consisted the writing of history according to God's will. But Josephus did not explain. In any case the canonical status of the books was settled, as far as Christians were concerned, by their own authorities, which made the opinions of the Jews irrelevant. Meanwhile he had no hesitation in endorsing the conclusions reached by the author. He permitted himself however some observations concerning the production of evidence. In order to allow one's opponent no escape from the force of the conclusion, one should at the outset clearly define the various meanings which could be attached to the word 'inspiration'. Even the theologians did not always take it in the same sense. One would then go on to show that in none of these senses could the word 'inspiration' be applied to the historical books; neither in the sense of a dictation by God, nor as an equivalent of revelation, nor as a miraculous and divine preservation from error, nor as a raising of the spiritual powers of the writer. A copious use of illustrative material from the historical books should make clear the inadmissibility of any of the above senses. For further elaboration of Dr Geddes's views one would have to wait for the full treatment in the forthcoming *General Preface*.[48]

On the appearance of *Critical Remarks* in 1800 Eichhorn was at last able to deal in some detail with Geddes's views on literary and historical criticism; and this evaluation was all the more necessary, he considered, in view of the unfavourable climate of opinion in England for work of this kind. The difficulties with which Geddes had to contend were surely an illustration of this. In these *Critical Remarks* one saw clearly the evidence of the author's wide reading, critical acumen and what was more rare, especially abroad, a true feeling for the explanation of the Old Testament.

On Genesis 1—3, Geddes's views, said Eichhorn, were similar to those currently held in Germany but expressed in his own personal manner. Thus the Creation story was for Geddes not an allegory or a literally true account but a beautiful mythos or philosophical poem clothed in the garb of real history to inculcate belief in a High God and Creator of the Universe. The Garden of Eden was a creation of Semitic mythology and the Fall a mythological drama. Informed readers would be able to judge from these examples what direction the author's exposition was taking. The difficulty was that the v ews were set down with such brevity and force that their acceptance by the English might be thereby impeded, for there was less receptivity there for such ideas than elsewhere. There were fewer in that country who had made the attempt to investigate fields and discover positions for themselves where our author himself had not yet penetrated. If only his *General Preface* had been printed and published before these *Critical Remarks* one would then have had his full explanations and a ready answer to many of the objections and criticisms now being launched against his expositions in his own country. Geddes had gone far towards destroying traditional belief in the Bible but the brevity of his treatment meant that he had not succeeded in establishing a satisfactory substitute in its place.[49] When Eichhorn said that Geddes's views were like the German but expressed in his own personal way, he did not single out the features in these views which were personal to Geddes but contented himself with giving an outline of his exposition.

Like Michaelis before him, Eichhorn thought some of Geddes's philological derivations surprising in the extreme. Thus on Gen 49:10 Geddes suggested that *Shiloh* was the same as the Latin *salus*, which was probably derived from it.

On the other hand, as against derivations such as the above, Geddes produced the best work of the basic philologists abroad, particularly Michaelis's *Supplements* to the Hebrew Dictionaries and Rosenmüller's *Scholia*. In his literary criticism, continued Eichhorn, Geddes seemed only occasionally familiar with the results of the Higher Criticism as commonly accepted in Germany. Thus he did not consider that Gen 2 was from a different author from that of Gen 1. Unfortunately the discussion of the recently accepted theory of the formation of Genesis was held over by the author to be dealt with in his *General Preface* which would also furnish the reader with the reasons why he, throughout Genesis, even in the account of the Flood, rejected the hypothesis of the incorporation of different documents or Memoirs.[50]

Johann Philipp Gabler, the man who developed Eichhorn's mythical interpretation of the *Urgeschichte*, was naturally excited by Geddes's interpretation which was so similar to his own. 'A very important work,' he wrote, 'which will certainly be attacked by the orthodox English theologians, because the author has made his own the principles and ideas of the latest German exegetes and their free interpretation of the Bible.'[51] The liberal interpretation displayed in the notes was no longer new in Germany because the path had been cleared by Michaelis, Semler, Eichhorn and others, before it was taken up by the expositors. But in England it could frighten the Bible interpreter for he had had no opportunity to reflect on the method. But perhaps, thought Gabler, Geddes was more interested in the text and philological derivation to which he devoted so much space. His mythical theory of Genesis 1 Geddes evidently got from Eichhorn, said Gabler, as indeed he himself admitted, so it was really surprising that he refused to recognise in Gen 2:4ff the hand of a different author. After criticising some of Geddes's derivations Gabler felt obliged to conclude that in spite of his great learning and wide reading Geddes did not have a solid grounding in oriental languages, not even in Hebrew.[52] But what he lacked in this he made up for by his clearsightedness and diligence in setting forth and comparing various views old and new in which activity there was no one in England like him. The work of a man like Geddes belonged to a category quite different from the usual theological products of England which for the most part one could do without and not suffer the slightest disadvantage.[53] Eichhorn and Gabler were right in thinking that Geddes had not worked out a fully developed alternative to the traditional belief.[54] It may however be doubted if he had made any serious inroad into that established position, let alone destroyed it, as Eichhorn suggested. On the whole, opinion in England was hardening against him, irrespective of religious differences. The *Critical Review*, commenting on Geddes's views on Genesis observed, 'Dr Geddes asks rhetorically "Do I believe that Genesis is not literally true?" . . . In our poor judgment it is but of little moment to the world what the Doctor does or does not believe − the question being, what is the sense of the narrative?' Geddes called it a mythos and said it was a fiction adapted to the shallow minds of its readers. 'That the Mosaic history is wisely adapted to these two ends [belief in one supreme God and the Sabbath observance], we do not think anyone will have the folly to deny; but that the history is not literally nor allegorically true, and therefore wisely contrived to effect them, appears to us stark nonsense.'[55]

The *British Critic* was even more emphatic. If the Mosaic history was an allegory, it said, it was an allegory without a key and the inspired writer might as well have left the tale untold. If Paradise was not a garden but a condition of the first man, what *was* the reality? Again, Geddes had said that the narrative must be either all literal or all allegory. But then if the woman's formation was allegorical, the woman herself was allegorical too and the whole narrative was allegorical, which was absurd. The real question was whether what was given as history could be considered as fiction without discrediting the Bible. A writer who meant to impress on his readers a belief of what never happened meant to lie and this was Geddes's opinion of Moses. Such views were but 'the idle dreams of a hare-brained critic'. The Doctor appeared to think, observed the reviewer, that the majority of Christians 'have no ground for the faith which they profess; and Alexander Geddes is raised up, after the lapse of 18 centuries, during which the faithful have been wandering in mists and darkness, to set these matters right, to reform the principles of belief, and to fix our faith on an immoveable basis. The method taken by this Catholic Christian (for by that name he desires to be called) of strengthening foundations, seems very extraordinary. For it consists in tearing up all the foundations which the learning and piety of the divines of former ages had been employed to lay.' Continuing the review in a later issue, he said he had heard that since the previous issue Geddes had died; but, he added significantly, the poison remained and the antidote had to be provided.[56]

The circumstances of Geddes's last years thus become fairly clear. The publication of his *Prospectus* in 1786 had established him as a man of learning with an international reputation. The appearance of his subsequent volumes had been the occasion of a sharp difference of opinion between those who considered him as a man of bold and original, if at times erratic, thought, and those who on the other hand regarded him as a dangerous innovator, who, by introducing the latest German critical views, was undermining the very foundations of Christianity. Not surprisingly Geddes found most of his explicit support in Germany, and during the last decade of his life he kept up a regular correspondence with several professors, notably Eichhorn, Paulus and Timaeus. He was untiring in sending them detailed news of everything that happened in the learned world in Britain and sought equally full information from his German friends. He sent copies of his books to them and solicited their opinions of his work. Indeed he felt, with reason, that he was more likely to get a discerning and unbiassed view from them than he would from his fellow countrymen.

It was not that he had no friends in Britain. A man of his intellectual stature and reputation would not lack friends and acquaintances. But there can be no doubt that with the growing conservatism both of Church and State during the 1790s, Geddes must have stood out as a man to be treated with caution. It was clear by now that not only had the State set its face firmly against the expression of revolutionary sentiments such as Geddes had earlier indulged in but also that the Church had made up its mind to regard the new trends of thought coming in from Germany as subversive of religion and to be excluded from serious consideration.

So far as these trends of thought were concerned, the attitude of the Church of England did not differ materially from that of the Roman Catholics. Both Churches totally rejected them. As in former days with the Deists, so now with German criticism; anyone openly professing or promoting such ideas could relinquish any hopes of advancement in the Church or even in University life—and indeed in some cases could count himself lucky to avoid a worse fate. Geddes still had his friends in academic circles and he continued to correspond with a large number of professors at Oxford and Cambridge but it was recognised that such contacts could not amount to open support of his ideas, where they deviated from the accepted viewpoint. This recognition was reinforced in the late 1790s by Geddes's friendship with a number of prominent Unitarians—once more, an association not calculated to lead to ecclesiastical promotion. In the political sphere too there were heavy blows. The imprisonment of his friends Gilbert Wakefield and Joseph Johnson for writing and selling a pamphlet regarded as subversive, coming so soon after the death of his patron, Lord Petre, added sadness to his advancing years. All this had a disastrous effect on his health. Though he was busy right up to the end with the preparation of further volumes of his Bible there can be no doubt that these sorrows with the consequent ill-health seriously impeded their appearance. Indeed the illness which was to prove fatal began to show itself about the time of his patron's death in the summer of 1801. Not least among his burdens was the Church censure imposed in 1792 and the consequent isolation from his fellow clergy. This was a continuing source of sadness to Geddes, as Charles Butler testified.

On his death, some journals at least were prepared to say a good word for him—for example, the *Monthly Review*: 'Vain is the hope of man. From this able and intrepid theologian, we expected a body of notes and dissertations on the Hebrew Scriptures, distinguished by a new and superior character; which, however it might have displeased the ignorant and the bigoted, would be admired by all rational scholars and have exonerated future defenders of revealed religion from much embarrassment. Alas, Death has stopped him, we cannot say in the midst, but at the very commencement of his career; leaving us only a solitary volume of *Remarks* to meet our sanguine anticipations.'

The reviewer however was not uncritical. He went on to admit that Geddes had many defects. His judgment was often at fault; he frequently took great liberties with the text. But Geddes's faults were very largely the result of exaggerated attitudes towards the Bible then current, especially the superstitious reverence for the Hebrew text.[57]

The following year there appeared a book by Dr Robert Findlay, professor of theology at the University of Glasgow, in which he attacked Geddes for denying the absolute and universal inspiration of the Hebrew Scriptures. Had he meant, argued Dr Findlay, that not everything therein was the immediate dictate of the Spirit of God he would have given less offence, for many admitted that the sacred writers set down many things from their personal knowledge or from records and tradition. But Dr Geddes had gone on to assert that there were falsehoods in the narrative and proceeded to argue that there were no convincing proofs from the Scriptures establishing their inspiration. Dr Findlay then expounded 2 Timothy 3:16 in an attempt to refute the arguments of Dr Geddes.[58]

CHAPTER SIX

THE DEATH OF DR GEDDES.
LATER DEVELOPMENT OF HIS CRITICAL THEORIES

HIS DEATH

Towards the end of the year 1800 in a letter sent to Miss Howard, Geddes wrote: 'My friend and patron, Lord Petre, is again very poorly; and I greatly fear that his end is approaching. He was in town for a few days in order to consult the physicians; but has returned to Buckingham in Norfolk.[1] Should anything happen to him great indeed would be my loss. He has been for these twenty years my uniformly constant friend.'[2] When Lord Petre died in the month of May, 1801, Geddes himself was ill at the time and the shock was great. Though Lord Petre's son and successor generously continued Dr Geddes's pension, thus relieving him at least of financial worry, Geddes never regained his health and found it impossible to give himself seriously to biblical work. He wrote an elegant Latin Elegy on the death of his friend and patron which was translated into English verse by a friend.[3]

Lord Petre's death seems to have coincided with the appearance of the first symptoms of the disease which was to prove fatal to Dr Geddes. At first he took little notice but it rapidly increased in gravity and very soon he was obliged to transfer his bed to the ground floor of his house in order to avoid the stairs.[4] When the end seemed to be approaching one or two priests of the London district made attempts to visit him but were refused admittance. Evidently Geddes regarded them as mere emissaries of Bishop Douglass and he easily calculated the terms on which their ministrations would be available. The day before his death, however, a French émigré priest, the abbé de St Martin, who had been a frequent visitor since his arrival in England some years previously, was admitted to see Dr Geddes. Though the abbé could hardly speak English, communication was not a problem on those grounds, since Geddes spoke fluent French. But unfortunately by this time the disease had advanced so far that Geddes could hardly speak and indeed was in a comatose state. Anything like a searching interrogation was clearly out of the question, and the abbé confined himself to the essentials. He explained clearly why he had come and Geddes understood. On Geddes's signifying his sorrow for sin and desire for absolution, the abbé gave him conditional absolution, considering that he should be given the benefit of the doubt. He remained with him throughout the day in the hope that his state might improve. As however no improvement showed itself the abbé suggested staying the night. On Geddes intimating that he would see him more willingly next day the abbé took his leave. When he came back next morning, the housekeeper informed him that Geddes had died during the night. 'Elle me dit qu'il avoit été en pleine connoissance avant de mourir; qu'elle avoit laissé approcher une femme catholique, avec laquelle il avoit récité l'oraison dominicale et le symbole des Apôtres. . .; qu'ensuite il avoit donné sa bénédiction a cette bonne femme, et que peu après il avoit expiré.'[5] The notice in the *Times* gave the information that Geddes died at about four o'clock in the morning. It was Friday, 26th February, 1802.[6]

The question now arose as to what form the funeral should take. Dr Belasyse, a priest of the London District, urged Bishop Douglass to allow a Requiem in view of the conditional absolution received by Geddes. The bishop however was adamant and refused to accede to this request.[7] The funeral took place in St Mary's, Paddington, and was attended by a large number of people. It is not recorded however what kind of service was held. Geddes was buried in the cemetery there, and, in 1804, Lord Petre placed a tombstone over the grave to his memory. [8]

Shortly after Dr Geddes's death, Lord Petre asked Charles Butler, a lawyer and historian, who had also been secretary of the Catholic Committee, to go and examine Geddes's papers.[9] It was well known at the time, and can easily be deduced from his frequent references to such writings in his published works, that he had a considerable quantity of manuscript material awaiting publication shortly before his death. Butler therefore, together with Dr John Disney, an old friend of Geddes, went to carry out this task. 'This was the more proper, as a report had been widely circulated that the Catholics had caused his papers to be destroyed. Dr Disney and the present writer made as complete a search among them as their avocations permitted. To their great surprise, although they found several literary manuscripts, they did not, with the single exception of a rough version of the last Psalm, find a single scrap of paper that related to his biblical pursuits. This was signified to Lord Petre with a recommendation that further searches and inquiries should be made by some person possessed of greater leisure. These were made but they were equally unsuccessful. All this was the more surprising as from the doctor's declarations to his friends and from other circumstances there was great reason to suppose that he had made considerable progress in the continuation of his work, or at least that he had collected ample materials for it. Probably, in view of his approaching dissolution he had committed them to the flames.'[10]

The slender connection between the last sentence just quoted and the one that precedes it did not escape the attention of Henry Cotton, in his meticulous account of Roman Catholic Bible work. He writes: 'How is it possible that the last sentence of that preface could have satisfied the mind of such a man as Charles Butler, especially as the same volume informs us that Dr Geddes continued to send copy to the printers till within a few days of his death?'[11] No answer however to that question was forthcoming. Certainly Butler's attempted explanation did nothing to allay doubts. On the other hand it is difficult to see how any emissary of Bishop Douglass could have gained admission to the house, much less have destroyed any papers. It is clear from St Martin's account of Geddes's death that his housekeeper[12] who was a member of the Church of England, regularly declined, on orders from her master, to admit priests sent by Bishop Douglass. Is it likely that she would have admitted them after his death and without the knowledge of Lord Petre? And is it even conceivable that she would have allowed them to burn her master's papers? In an admittedly obscure situation, Butler's solution seems less unlikely. One is reminded of a parallel situation in the case of Richard Simon, whose biblical works likewise incurred ecclesiastical censure. Before his death he committed all his unpublished papers to the flames, in order to avert a possibly more humiliating fate after his death.

LATER DEVELOPMENT OF HIS CRITICAL THEORIES

Of all the praise bestowed on Geddes's work, none perhaps was so generous and candid as that of Johann Severin Vater, the young professor of Theology and Oriental Languages at the University of Halle, to which chair he had been appointed in 1800, at the age of twenty-nine. On the appearance of *Critical Remarks* Vater paid it the compliment of incorporating a great deal of its material in a work of his own on the Pentateuch.[13] His object was to produce a work which would be of use to the serious Bible student and enable him to understand the text without the aid of lectures. Vater wanted to put before the reader all the available evidence in manageable form to enable him to reach a rational judgment on the matter under consideration rather than dictate his conclusions to him.

For this purpose he found Geddes's work highly useful. The sheer abundance of various readings drawn from a great number of manuscripts in many different languages, the variety of rabbinical interpretations and the many shrewd, sometimes brilliant, insights into the meaning of the text could be, he thought, of great value to students. Vater put Geddes's notes, taken from the *Critical Remarks* and his Bible, vol. 2, in square brackets, but recorded in summary and not verbatim. The use made of his notes was very extensive and it is clear that Vater's primary aim was to make use of the textual criticism. But he then moved on to questions of literary and historical criticism. In the third volume of the *Commentar,* Vater published a long *Abhandlung über Moses und die Verfasser des Pentateuchs* which took up the main ideas outlined in Geddes's brief notes on the authorship,[14] and now noticed at length for the first time, apparently, in any language.

In his *Vorrede,* Vater spoke of Geddes's translation as an enduring monument to his learning — indeed all the more remarkable since there were so few scholars abroad who, like him, unhampered by prejudice, sought unswervingly to reach the truth guided only by sound principles of criticism and interpretation. Geddes's wide reading was remarkable, observed Vater, covering as it did nearly all the new German publications, and he would now pay him the compliment of taking the fruit of his study.

Like Geddes, Vater too considered unsound the distinction of documents in the Pentateuch on the basis of the use of different divine names.[15] There were passages beginning with titles such as *'elleh toledoth* which appeared to have no connection with the context; there were also 'End' formulae, such as Lev 7:37, 38; 27:34, similarly independent. These passages showed the need for separating them from their surroundings. Then a comparison of such passages with the nature of the preceding or style of the following passage could provide grounds for excluding the possibility of one author.

Thus, Vater went on to analyse the whole of the Pentateuch beyond Genesis, as Eichhorn had not done, and found a great number of separate and, for the most part, independent fragments of varying length. Vater was more impressed by the inconsistencies of the fragments and other signs of discontinuity than by the evidence for their connection, one with another, and he concluded that the Pentateuch was put together from a great variety of fragmentary records by an unspecified number of redactors. Whereas Geddes would not put the final redaction later than Hezekiah, Vater was prepared to postpone it towards the time of the Exile.[16] Both Geddes and Vater were convinced that the five books could not possibly have been put together during the forty years in the desert, in view of the abundant evidence of later composition. Vater thought the Pentateuch was built round the book of Deuteronomy as the original law book, parts of which evidently dated back to Moses, though its literary composition and final redaction were completed only by the time of Solomon.

This view of the Pentateuch, later described as 'le désordre dans la multiplicité',[17] was strengthened in Vater's eyes by the publication of K. D. Ilgen's work in 1798.[18] In this study, Ilgen minutely divided Eichhorn's Elohist into two which he called, First and Second Elohist; ascribed much of Eichhorn's Jehovist material to one or other of his Elohists and occasionally assigned passages of Eichhorn's Elohist to his own Jehovist. Vater argued that an analysis which could produce such different results could hardly be a correct estimate of the evidence; and he printed the analysis of Genesis by Astruc, Eichhorn and Ilgen in parallel columns to reinforce his argument. [19]

For the purposes of our discussion the term 'document' is understood as a continuous source traceable in the Bible, made up of detached sections of the text with common characteristics of style and contents suggesting that these sections once constituted a single record, before incorporation in the Bible. The term 'Fragment', explains Vater, is used to indicate sections which in his view appear to be independent of one another.[20] He distinguished six in Genesis 1:1–9:27 and regarded Genesis 10:1–11:9 as two (ch. 10 and 11:1-9) ethnographical fragments. In the following section, Gen 11:10–50:26, Vater said that several of the Fragments were clearly not from one author, while others had no positive evidence that there was any connection intended by the authors or that they were the work of a single author. The connection between these Fragments amounted to hardly more than their common subject, the history of Abraham, Isaac and Jacob, except in a number of the larger ones in which there was a continuous thread of narrative which doubtless indicated a whole, e.g. Gen 12 and 13; 18 with 19; 27 to 33; 37 to 47. Altogether in Genesis, Vater found about forty fragments, though in a number of cases he professed himself undecided. Unfortunately, a strict comparison with Geddes's views is not practicable as he did not work out his division of fragments in any detail.[21]

While recognizing the value of the criterion of the divine names, Vater said it was more important to decide the character of the passages from their connection and mutual relation to one another. This would lead to an answer to the question how the thread of a narrative ran through, and *where* a new one began. Sometimes an event was ascribed to different persons — and this an author could not do, but a collector or editor could do. The interwoven duplicates could not be by the same author. What then of the use of different names for God (Yahweh and Elohim) and for the mountain of God (Sinai and Horeb)? This could not be pure accident but equally it did not appear to indicate, in itself, difference of authorship. That a writer should consistently use one particular name for God seemed to Vater an artificiality which had to be explained, not just in one or two but in a great number of passages. Suppose one had German songs, some of which used the name 'Jesus' and others 'Christus'. Must one conclude that this necessarily indicated difference of authorship? There were many other criteria to consider. The difference must be explained. If it did not indicate different authors, then it might be due to differences of place and time in the circumstances of their composition.

Indeed the usage was much more reasonably explained on the basis of different circumstances than different authors. There might well be a case for similar editorial background rather than for identity of authorship. Of course one might suppose that an editor or collector would have made a better job of the editing, but we should always recall that not every editor is in full command of his materials.

Vater allowed that Deuteronomy contained Moses's *Reisejournal*. It was difficult to believe that anyone else could have written that, but the final editing of the book was much later. Vater could not follow Eichhorn in his placing Deuteronomy wholly within the Mosaic age. Again, the Egyptian spirit in the Pentateuch Vater held to indicate that its contents substantially dated back to the Mosaic age, though composed and edited at a later date. Even Genesis, Vater thought, was probably not put together by Moses from earlier traditions.

While Vater dealt at great length with questions of text, authorship and literary analysis, he was sparing with his remarks on the historical character and the relationship of the narrative to myth. Yet much had happened since the appearance of Gabler's edition of Eichhorn's *Urgeschichte,* in the field of the mythological interpretation of the Old Testament. Georg Lorenz Bauer, professor of Oriental Languages at Altdorf, published his *Hermeneutica Sacra* in 1797; and in 1802 his *Hebräische Mythologie des A. und N.T. mit Parallelen aus der Mythologie anderer Völker, vornehmlich der Griechen und Römer,* 2 vols, Leipzig. Hartlich and Sachs are of the opinion that the development of the mythological school could be said to have reached its peak with the publication of the last mentioned work; and it satisfied Gabler's desire for a *Mythologia Sacra.* Bauer strongly promoted the historical approach to the Scriptures which he insisted must be studied like any other Oriental literature. He stressed that the grammatical approach advocated by Ernesti was not enough. In another of his works written at this time he wrote: 'One must first explain each Book according to the language in which it is written and this is called the grammatical interpretation; it gives the understanding of the words. The ideas contained therein are, from the customs and ways of thought of the writer himself and of his time, nation, sect, religion, etc. and this is called the historical interpretation; it gives the explanation of the thing itself.'[22]

Different as was Bauer's interpretation from the Naturalist interpretation of Paulus,[23] there was nevertheless a distinct Rationalist strain running through his work. Nothing might be admitted as historical which could not be conceived as happening and hence such statements were to be relegated to the realm of myth.[24] Furthermore, one had to ask, not only could it have happened but, how could it be known?[25] Since much of the early narrative was of its nature unverifiable in addition to containing a substantial element of the marvellous, Bauer was able to consider large parts of the Pentateuch and the following historical books, Joshua and

Judges, as myth. One should apply to the Old Testament, he argued, the same principles which were applicable to the early traditions and literature of other nations and peoples. Angel stories were a relic of polytheism — 'Wo bei den Hebräern ein Engel erscheint, da erscheint bei Homer ein Gott' (*Hebräische Mythologie*, p. 129).

The important works of Bauer referred to above appeared too late for Geddes to make any considerable use of them. It must be recalled that *Critical Remarks* had been completed in manuscript some time before it was finally published. The delay was largely due to the author's ill health and for the same reason he was not able to take account of the most recent German literature before the publication of his book. Nor on the other hand is there any evidence that Bauer made use of the early volumes of Geddes's Bible.

It is in the work of Wilhelm Martin Leberecht de Wette that we pick up again the thread of Geddes's work and are able to study its later development. Here too, and to a much greater extent, the influence of Johann Gottfried Herder is manifest. This was the man who seemed to de Wette 'on the barren steppes of Criticism and Rationalism, to be an inspired seer who pointed out the way to the eternal pastures fed by the Water of Life'.[26] De Wette absorbed Herder's ideas concerning the human origins of the biblical literature, of its character as a product of the *infantia generis humani*, of its natural and loosely defined poetic character. Popular songs often changed the historical elements into the miraculous and ideal, cf. Jos 10:14 where the miracle was attributable to the lyrical hyperbole of the previous verses. Two factors had their influence on the formation of the traditions — theocratical pragmatism (or the plan of the divine government of the world), and theocratical mythology (whereby the divine influence was shown by means of miracles and revelations). 'If an historical narrative,' he argued, 'written without critical investigation of facts, but treated so as to suit religious and poetical ideas, is an epic composition, then the Pentateuch may be called the theocratical epic poem of the Israelites, without denying that there is an historical basis at the bottom.'[27]

The Pentateuch was built up from poems and traditions into wonderful and supernatural events and anyone wishing to take it as historical would meet with serious difficulties. The story had a mythical character which contradicted the law of nature, experience and historical probability. A magician could not pollute all the waters of Egypt; Moses could not have produced so developed a Law; the shepherd Abraham could not have had so developed a religion.[28]

But above all there was the myth by which God came forward as a person to be treated with. It was impossible to say how much and what historical fact underlay the myth. Indeed there were no sure criteria for reaching a conclusion. Even apparently historical detail had mythical

roots. De Wette was opposed to the attempt made by earlier representatives of the mythical school (Eichhorn to Bauer) to isolate the historical
fact in the myth. There was no criterion for doing this and hence, in the absence of any evidence, one must regard the whole narrative as myth. This
was de Wette's special contribution to the investigation. He regarded the
Pentateuch as a mythical whole; and in this he clearly followed Herder
rather than Eichhorn.[29] Without denying any historical substratum he held
it was not recoverable. It is possible that in his suspension of judgment he
was influenced by Herder's and his own antipathy for Paulus and his
Naturalist interpretations.[30] De Wette opposed the attempt to interpret
some parts of the Pentateuch in the naturalist-historical way — as Paulus
did — and other parts as myth. The work had to be treated as a whole. He
allowed himself to draw one conclusion at any rate from the non-recovera-
bility of the historical basis, namely, that, in consequence, the 'historical'
books had no historical value.[31] In saying this, de Wette certainly went
further than Herder would have gone.[32] But then, in spite of his admiration for Herder, de Wette was more Rationalist than he, and furthermore
stated his critical views more clearly, as will appear below.

Geddes was inclined at times to 'naturalize' Old Testament events as
Eichhorn tended to do in his earlier work and as Gabler and Bauer were
anxious to avoid. But, as already mentioned, Geddes does not seem to
have been familiar with the work of these last two scholars. It is worth re-
calling, however, Geddes's disapproval of Eichhorn's use of a 'mixed' solution of Genesis 3, where he took parts of the narrative as literal and part
as allegorical.[33] Geddes was emphatic in his dislike of mixed solutions of
that kind and proposed a mythical interpretation throughout that chapter.
But he was not consistent. If a mixed interpretation of the kind he mentioned was unacceptable, why was it not equally so where it was a case of
myth in place of allegory, e.g. in the case of Balaam's ass? Part of the
explanation perhaps is that Geddes had not yet reached firm conclusions
regarding the mythical character of much of the narrative. It is relevant
here to recall Geddes's attitude to the historical reliability of the record,
and his conviction that certainty was not obtainable.[34] All this seems to
point to the general conclusion that had Geddes continued his research he
would in all likelihood have reached very much the same position as de
Wette, who, it may be noted, does appear to manifest the influence of Gabler and Bauer.

On the authorship of the Pentateuch, de Wette expressed his view very
clearly in his first considerable work, published when he was twenty-five
years old. 'Pentateuchum non esse a Mose conscriptum, sed seriore aetate
ortum.' The Mosaic authorship, he said, would be maintained only by
those people who are more interested in defending a cause than in searching for the truth.[35] Eichhorn would not have been pleased to hear that,

written, as it was, in 1805, and thirteen years after Geddes's equally definite statement.[36] De Wette's chief aim was to show that not only Genesis but also the subsequent books of the Pentateuch were of multiple authorship; and stimulated by Vater's exhaustive analysis, he began his own dissection in his *Beiträge,* and later in the various editions of his *Lehrbuch.*[37]

The theory of Witter, Astruc and Eichhorn of two parallel and continuous sources or documents in Genesis, one distinguished by the use of the name Elohim and the other by Jehovah, de Wette considered to be doubtful. 'At most, in the E sections there is evidence of a unified plan and coherence whereas the J sections are more loosely-knit and are probably from diverse sources.'[38] What is specially interesting here is that, though he considers with Vater and Geddes the distinction on the basis of the names to have been exaggerated, he does admit, unlike Vater and Geddes, that the 'E' fragments have a certain coherence; and are drawn from an *Urschrift Elohim,* into which the less coherent 'J' fragments have been interpolated. De Wette goes on to say that the two groups of fragments are distinguished one from the other, not so much by the names of God as by their style and contents: 'The "E" fragments by their inner unity; the "J" passages through their mythological character'.[39]

As regards the rest of the Pentateuch, de Wette notes that the evidence for the *Urschrift Elohim* is less clear after Exodus chapter 6 since the distinction of names no longer obtains in the same way as hitherto. De Wette made his first distinctive contribution to the debate by suggesting, in his *Dissertatio. . .* (1805), that Deuteronomy was the Book of the Law discovered in the time of King Josiah and that it was written shortly before that time, i.e. in the seventh century B.C.[40]

As to dates, de Wette suggested that the *Urschrift Elohim* seemed to be the oldest source and was probably to be dated in the time of David or Solomon. Geddes too thought that Solomon's reign was the earliest date for the composition of the Pentateuch, but his latest date, the reign of Hezekiah, eighth century, was a good deal earlier than de Wette's.

CHAPTER SEVEN

GEDDES'S PLACE IN THE HISTORY
OF BIBLICAL CRITICISM

Geddes died at a moment of transition in the history of religious thought. The older Rationalism had nearly run its course. It had been, at least to outward appearance, more successful in pulling down the existing structure than in building up an adequate alternative. The Deists had long since been silenced by greater scholars than they, but not perhaps altogether answered. A sign of the continued vitality of their ideas might be seen in the sudden irruption of Tom Paine's *Age of Reason* at the end of the century and the disturbance which it caused. Geddes was no Deist but he was not uninfluenced by their thought. In the last decade of the century, the Unitarians, who inherited deistic teachings, could claim Geddes as a friend, if not as a follower. Coleridge on the other hand, had accepted their doctrine so far as to become, if only for a short time, a Unitarian minister. When Coleridge later rejected their tenets, Geddes manifested no corresponding attitude. Coleridge found that the Unitarian tendency to reduce Christianity to a few easily grasped truths of natural religion satisfied him not at all. He denied that this was an adequate description of Christianity and was equally sure that it could never satisfy the mind and heart of man.[1] This form of Rationalism left out of account vital areas of human nature and experience, past as well as present, which had their part to play in the search after ultimate reality.

Coleridge was influenced by the Romantic Movement which had already begun in Germany. This reaction against the older rationalism passed Geddes by; but on the other hand the development of the historical study of the Scriptures, initiated by Semler, Herder and Eichhorn, commanded his full attention. He was not slow to appreciate the significance of a method which steered a course between dogmatic authoritarian interpretation on the one hand and extreme rationalistic criticism on the other. Though Geddes never showed much inclination to follow closely in the path of Paulus, he never lost his confidence in the power of unaided reason to seek out all truth. But in pursuing this line of study Geddes remained almost alone; and in publishing the results of his investigations he had few imitators.

In the early stages of preparation, however, for his translation of the Bible, Geddes was necessarily occupied in research that gave less scope for unorthodox views or hostile accusations. Thus, his conviction of the corrupt state of the Hebrew text, exaggerated as it may appear today, was but an echo of the widely shared opinion of the time. Even in this, he made efforts to steer a middle course, in spite of his earlier studies under the shadow of Houbigant. In reviving his knowledge of textual criticism Geddes came more and more to rely on the work and authority of his friends, Kennicott and Lowth, while making occasional contact with professors at Oxford and Cambridge, such as Blayney, Dimock, Hodgson and, láter, Holmes and Lloyd. In the early years in London, he was less familiar with the German scholars, evidently because he had not yet learnt German and because, at that time, as already noted, contact with those scholars was not common in Britain. Though Geddes in his *Prospectus* had professed great admiration for Johann David Michaelis, the veteran biblical scholar of Göttingen, it cannot be said that in the first volume of his Bible there is a corresponding evidence of his influence, which might partly explain that scholar's rather severe strictures on Geddes's work. Michaelis rightly accused him of being too much under the influence of Houbigant and if Geddes had not been conscious of the need not to antagonise his readers he might well have followed the French critic even further.[2]

Geddes's tendency to attach greater weight to readings of the Samaritan Pentateuch and the Septuagint than was approved by the more conservative scholars of his time, and his insertions, omissions and transpositions on the basis of those authorities, attracted a certain amount of criticism. So too with his conjectural emendation. It is clear that, without going as far as Houbigant, he shared the tendency to break away decisively from the slavish following, as he regarded it, of the Massoretic text; and this led him into making emendations without textual authority, that even in his own time elicited rather sharp reaction from the more conservative scholars. If his textual criticism leaned rather heavily on the French and British critics this was because he had been trained in Paris and resumed his studies in London. In general, Geddes's work in this field showed him to be but a man of his time, with his contemporaries' familiar shortcomings. He had little new to contribute beyond a number of ingenious emendations of the text. Indeed it is hard to see how he could have contributed much more, in view of what Gabler called his lack of a really thorough knowledge of oriental languages.[3]

It was otherwise, however, with his literary criticism. When Geddes first resumed his biblical studies in 1782, biblical criticism meant for him, as for most of his fellow-countrymen, textual criticism.[4] Unlike them, however, Geddes went on to give his attention to the requirements of what Eichhorn had named Higher Criticism; and, when composing the explanatory notes for his Bible translation, he did not flinch from accept-

ing the consequences of so decisive a departure from usage. Geddes occupies a modest niche in the history of biblical criticism as author,
together with Johann Severin Vater, of the Fragment Hypothesis[5] and
even here he is somewhat overshadowed by Vater, who did the lion's
share of the work. Nevertheless, two things should be borne in mind: first,
that the idea of the Pentateuch as a concatenation of largely independent
fragments of different dates, put together centuries later, was substantially Geddes's own conception at least in the form known to us as the
Fragment Hypothesis; second, this hypothesis not only held the field for a
time but had a permanent influence on the development of Pentateuchal
criticism. Though further investigation showed that the evidence brought
to light by Witter, Astruc and Eichhorn could not be adequately explained
in terms of Vater's hypothesis, it is nevertheless true to say that the
Documentary Hypothesis which eventually emerged owed a good deal to
the investigations of Geddes, Vater and de Wette. The Fragment
Hypothesis proved to be a useful corrective to the tendency to discover
continuous documents on too slender evidence. But its influence has extended even further, as may be seen in attempts made this century to question the basis of the current Documentary Hypothesis.[6]

Carpenter-Harford have noted that Eichhorn's view of Exodus-
Leviticus as a collection of separate documents, many incomplete and
fragmentary but all dating from the Mosaic age, and his omission to link
them together or with the documents analysed in Genesis, meant that
later a decision would have to be made: either Exodus-Numbers must be
regarded as continuous with Genesis, or Genesis must be reduced to a
similar collection of fragments.[7] Geddes and Vater chose the second alternative; but, though it succeeded for a time and underlined important data,
it could not maintain its position indefinitely in that form. Even those who
held it basically, introduced significant modifications; so that while Eichhorn appeared to have combined elements of the Fragment Hypothesis
with his Documentary, de Wette now seemed to be introducing the
documentary principle into his Fragment Hypothesis.[8] But on the questions of date and authorship, these scholars were far apart. Indeed Eichhorn in the fourth edition of his *Einleitung in das Alte Testament* (1823),
produced twenty years after the third edition (during which time so much
had been written), felt able to make no considerable modifications in his
own view of the Mosaic authorship. Though he made a long and exhaustive examination of Vater's *Abhandlung* he still maintained substantially
his original analysis of the documents and fragments and, as to the date of
these, allowed only that materials contemporary with Moses might have
been put together in the time of Joshua or at any rate before the time of
Samuel.[9] The success of the Fragment Hypothesis, however, he appeared
to recognise.[10]

But it is in the field of mythological interpretation of the Scripture that Geddes made his most extensive, if not his best known contribution. He was quick to recognize that it was illogical to interpret the traditions of other nations as myth and to exclude the early traditions of Israel from the application of similar principles on the grounds that the Scripture was the inspired and infallible word of God. Eichhorn put his finger on the significant question of Geddes: 'Why might not the Hebrews have their mythology as well as other nations?'[11] This was the crux; and Geddes was working along the same lines as Eichhorn at about the same time. Indeed, in view of his apparent lack of acquaintance with the second edition of the *Urgeschichte,* it seems probable that he developed his ideas in independence of Eichhorn. Furthermore, as has been already noted, he was able to go further than Eichhorn in the application of the myth principle because he did not hold the Mosaic authorship of the Pentateuch. It is certain that Eichhorn read his views with pleasure and this provided Geddes with the encouragement to continue his researches in the same field. Most of the further development of the mythical interpretation however was to be undertaken by others, notably Gabler, G. L. Bauer, and later, W. M. L. de Wette, and D. F. Strauss. The mythical school then went into eclipse, partly because Strauss had travelled too far in the non-historical interpretation of the New Testament, partly because, while the mythical interpretation did take account of historical development, it did not do it completely. It was a case of working from the outside into the Hebrew traditions and arguing that the kind of literature found elsewhere must also be verified in the Scriptures. This was true but it was not the whole truth. The detailed examination of the actual records and the tracing of their development both literary and theological, had yet to come and was undertaken by the Tübingen School.

At the same time, the achievements of the mythical school, though obscured for a time, were of permanent value. Geddes's outspoken advocacy of the myth interpretation earned him many hostile attacks in his time, yet perhaps his very outspokenness, which even Eichhorn appeared to deprecate,[12] had more effect in the long run than milder statements would have had, even if the immediate result was disastrous. It is true that many conclusions reached were inaccurate. This was inevitable at a time when knowledge of ancient literature was so overwhelmingly a matter of study of Greek and Latin classics. It followed therefore that when the principles of C. G. Heyne were first applied to the Bible, insufficient allowance was made for the special character of the Hebrew literature. Indeed it could be argued that only in the present century as a result of the numerous and remarkable discoveries of ancient literatures in the East, have we been able to acquire a knowledge of the Old Testament literature which takes adequate account of its own peculiar characteristics, and fully complies with the appeal of Lowth and Herder to think and feel as a Hebrew.

Geddes was often accused of reducing the whole of the historical narrative to a mere myth. But though he allotted a larger place for myth than did Eichhorn he was far from dispensing with history altogether. Who could doubt, he asked, of Abraham's coming into Canaan from Chaldaea. . . ?[13] Generally speaking Geddes was prepared to accept the narrative as in substance historical though with his customary reservation. But when he came to those events which transcended human experience and understanding he seems to have divided his explanations fairly evenly between the mythical and the natural.[14] De Wette, however, looked upon the Old Testament record with different eyes. He felt under no obligation to save the historical character and could indeed see no criteria whereby it might be recognized.[15] In effect then, de Wette discarded the historical myth and looked on the whole narrative in terms of philosophical myth. In so doing he went much further than Eichhorn, as well as Geddes, whose views approached those of Eichhorn.[16]

A decisive step in the reassessment of the historical basis of the records was taken by de Wette in his work on Chronicles and the Pentateuch. The existing belief in the Mosaic authorship had led everyone to accept the levitical law as belonging to the Mosaic age; and the discrepancies between Samuel and Kings on the one hand and Chronicles on the other had been explained largely in terms of a difference of outlook; the latter books concentrating more on religion than the former: a conclusion which however was not supported by the evidence. Now that the barrier of the Mosaic authorship had been removed, it could be seen that there was an evolution in religion and that the situation described in Chronicles belonged to a later age. In other words, the author was projecting back into earlier centuries religious ideas and institutions which in fact only came into existence at a later period. Once this was understood, many of the difficulties disappeared.[17]

This point was further elaborated by Wilhelm Vatke, with the addition of a philosophical basis.[18] It is interesting to recall that Vatke's book appeared in the same year as D. F. Strauss's *Leben Jesu,* which represented the culmination of the work of the mythical school, and could be seen as an answer to the Naturalism of H. E. G. Paulus. It is true that, in quantitative terms, there is more of the Naturalist than of the Mythical interpretation in Geddes's work. Nevertheless, a careful reading of his views suggests that his thought was tending in the direction of de Wette's later interpretation and perhaps ultimately that of Strauss rather than the position adopted by Professor Paulus. Geddes had been too well schooled in Eichhorn's principles not to appreciate the artificiality of Paulus's interpretation.

Though Geddes was not entirely alone in voicing unpopular theological views in Britain,[19] or in acquiring a familiarity with the work of German biblical scholars[20] he appears to have achieved a certain singularity in combining both of these accomplishments. Among the German scholars, J. G. Eichhorn was closest to him and the correspondence between them continued till Geddes's death. J. M. Good, Geddes's biographer, publishes a letter from Eichhorn to Geddes in which Eichhorn took occasion to say how much he would appreciate Geddes's opinion on a biblical work he was sending to him. He valued Geddes's judgment the more highly, he said, inasmuch as he was well versed in biblical literature and thoroughly acquainted with its difficulties and problems.[21] Geddes's friendship with the young professor Paulus, twenty-five years his junior, was no less warm, as is testified to by the letter printed in Good and by the entries in Paulus's *Reisejournal*.[22] Both Eichhorn and Paulus were regarded by British scholars as representing all that was most pernicious in German Rationalist criticism.[23] Few made the attempt to distinguish between the solid attainments of biblical criticism and its contemporary exaggerations. Indeed one of the rungs on the ladder of advancement in the Church was the condemnation of German criticism. Writing in 1825 Bishop Connop Thirlwall observed: 'It cannot be concealed that German theology in general, and German biblical criticism in particular, labours at present under an ill name among our divines; so that no one is more sure of an attentive and believing audience than he who undertakes to point out its mischiefs and dangers, and no one of course has need of greater caution than he who thinks of importing any novelties from that suspected quarter.'[24]

English theological output at this period was correspondingly meagre. 'Since the fifteenth century, Theology has emigrated,' wrote Mark Pattison. 'Extinct in Italy, and all but so in France, it is now in Germany alone that the vital questions of Religion are discussed with the full and free application of all the resources of learning and criticism which our age has at its command.'[25] And writing some years later, F. W. Farrar asked, 'Is there a single English commentary, before the last generation, except the *Isaiah* of Bishop Lowth, of which anyone could say without extravagance that it struck out a new line or marked a new epoch? Can there be a better proof of the stagnation of fifty years ago than that the popular commentary was the 'variorum' mediocrity of D'Oyly and Mant?' The infallibility of the Bible, he continued, had been weighed and found wanting, 'And yet for a considerable period the main body of the English Church, ignoring the philosophy and the history of the Continent, clung with tenacity to obsolete conceptions, and failed not only to further the progress of Scriptural study, but even to avail themselves of the sources of knowledge which other Churches so largely used. Fifty years ago the shibboleth of popular orthodoxy was the indiscriminate anathema of German theology.

If in later days the Church of England has made an immense advance the progress is perhaps more due to Samuel Taylor Coleridge than to any ordained or professional theologian.'[26]

What was the issue? It was this. Was a biblical critic to be allowed to apply to the Bible the same principles which were applicable to any other ancient literature or was he to be forbidden on the grounds that the Bible was a book every syllable of which had been committed to man by God, as divine and unerring? The view of absolute and universal inspiration current in the seventeenth and eighteenth centuries was incompatible with the application of critical principles to the text of the Bible. But as knowledge of oriental literatures and the physical sciences grew, so the position of the Traditionalists became more and more untenable; and, insofar as they kept rigidly to their view of inspiration, this laid them open to the charge of insincerity.

The theory of inspiration which emerged in the seventeenth century (noted E. B. Pusey), envisaged the divine influx as extending not only to religious truths, as hitherto, but to every word and matter contained in Scripture. The purpose of this development was to exalt the Bible above the Church, a need experienced in the acute religious controversies of that time.[27] It its earlier phases this was taken to involve the divine provision of information and even the mode of expression as well as a divine guarantee of its infallibility, not only with regard to religious truths but all other matters related in the Scripture. To this must be added the contemporary ignorance not only of ancient oriental literary forms and modes of speech but likewise of any conception of a developing morality in a primitive people. This was the impenetrable wall that faced those who first attempted to apply to the Scriptures the principles which they were accustomed to make use of in reading and understanding the classical literature of the ancient past. Apart from the writings of the Deists the effect of which was seriously blunted by their exaggerations, no real breach was made in this barrier until the middle of the eighteenth century. It was Ernesti who first insisted that the verbal sense of Scripture must be determined in the same way in which we ascertain that of other books; and Semler who followed this up with his untiring advocacy of the historical method of interpretation, stressing the circumstances and conditions by which the writers were surrounded.[28]

In the early part of the nineteenth century there were not lacking men in Britain who showed signs of breaking through the British reluctance to modify the current view of inspiration or give attention to German critical research.[29] Samuel Taylor Coleridge, already referred to, was responsible for sowing seeds which later resulted in fruitful developments. His visit to Germany in 1798 appears to have been in a real sense a watershed in his life and he came back to England with a renewed sense of purpose. On the one hand he learnt a great deal from the study of Kant which had a profound effect on his later religious development; on the other he was much impressed by the principles of methodical and critical study which he was taught during his months at Göttingen.[30] Coleridge was irrevocably opposed to the current view of scriptural inspiration which was responsible for lack of progress in biblical knowledge, for downright evasion and even dishonesty. 'The Doctrine', as he called this rigid view of inspiration, was to be deprecated because it 'evacuates of all sense and efficacy the sure and constant tradition, that all the several books, bound up together in our precious family Bibles, were composed in different and widely distant ages, under the greatest diversity of circumstances, and degrees of light and information, and yet that the composers, whether as uttering or as recording what was uttered and what was done, were all actuated by a pure and Holy Spirit.'[31] The Bible, he maintained, should be considered not so much to be the Word of God as to contain the Word of God. In saying this Coleridge was echoing what Semler himself had formulated many years previously. Those who went to great lengths to reconcile conflicting texts were those who took 'The Doctrine' literally. But they were inconsistent. They censured John Wesley for objecting to the Copernican system as being against Scripture, but how did *they* reconcile Scripture with the views of Copernicus in the light of 'The Doctrine' of inspiration which they held?[32] Coleridge deprecated the collection of texts detached from their context and brought forward as infallible dicta to prove some new credendum. Not only Roman Catholics but also Protestants had done this.[33] But it was wearisome, he said, to discuss a tenet 'which the generality of divines and the leaders of the Religious Public have ceased to defend and yet continue to assert or imply.'[34]

Here Coleridge put his finger on the significant point of the problem as it existed in his day. Scholars and indeed educated people in general could no longer consistently apply the outdated doctrine of inspiration to the Bible, in view of the great advances of science and other branches of knowledge. Yet they continued to accept that doctrine unchanged. Herein lay perhaps timidity in not facing up to the discrepancy and, at the least, a danger of dishonesty. Coleridge was susceptible to the former but he was not guilty of the latter. These *Letters on Inspiration* he did not dare publish during his lifetime and they eventually saw the light in 1840 six years after his death.[35]

The explosive reaction to the appearance of the volume *Essays and Reviews* in 1860 showed that there was still a long way to go before anything like a general acceptance of critical principles of interpretation was reached.[36] Indeed the avalanche of replies seemed to suggest that nothing had changed since the previous century. The writers were denounced as 'Septem Contra Christum' and the book censured by both Houses of the

Convocation of Canterbury. Dean Burgon took this occasion to restate the traditional doctrine of inspiration in its most extreme form.[37] But there was worse to come. It was Bishop Colenso's frank facing of the critical problem which produced the crisis of the century. The inconsistencies, anachronisms and other signs of multiple authorship convinced him that the Pentateuch must have been composed long after Moses. Further, he was concerned with the clearly imaginative figures given for the Exodus and the obvious immorality of certain acts apparently commanded by God. In short, like Geddes, Colenso jettisoned the traditional doctrine of inspiration, and the historical character of the Pentateuch at least in the sense hitherto accepted. Colenso's main objective was the same as that of Geddes — the scientific examination of the Bible text without prohibition by authority.[38] The reaction however was even more violent than that against *Essays and Reviews*. His superior, Bishop Gray of Capetown, 'deposed' and 'excommunicated' him and only two of the British Bench of Bishops spoke in his favour, namely Tait of London and Thirlwall of St David's.[39]

Meanwhile the adverse reception of his work induced Colenso to publish in the second part of his study, a defence of his position. He began by prefixing to it a long quotation from Geddes's work *Critical Remarks* in which he proclaimed his inalienable right to examine the Scriptures as he would any other writings of antiquity and to pass judgment on them as a free and impartial examiner without being denounced as a heretic or an infidel.[40] Colenso argued that to go on handling the obsolete view of inspiration when it was patently irreconcilable with the facts was simply to foster insincerity and even infidelity. Yet no scholar raised his voice against that Doctrine even though none could possibly hold it in practice. Colenso claimed that the only surprising thing about his own work on the Pentateuch was not that a bishop of the Church of England should thus criticise the Scriptures, but that he was, so far as he knew, the first bishop to do so. It was his duty to speak out and thus bear witness to the truth.

There were those who questioned whether in fact such a declaration of critical principles was necessary. To this Colenso could only point to the stream of publications issuing from the press which evidenced a considerable need for his own book.[41] Thus in 1863 D. Moore published *The Divine Authority of the Pentateuch Vindicated,* in the preface to which, he referred to the Bishop of Natal as 'a Prelate who has taken advantage of his high position in the Church and of his previous reputation in another line of study to aim the more deadly blow against the ancient Scriptures. . . The verdict of the public has been declared both upon the author and his book. It pronounces a sentence upon the one of an unhonoured and speedy oblivion. It convicts the other of the sin of religious unfaithfulness and the signal folly of having made a great mistake.'[42] Moore's words on Colenso are reminiscent of a similar pronouncement on Geddes.[43] The barrier seemed outwardly as firm as ever; Colenso's efforts just one more failure. But it was not so. Change was taking place.

Professor Andrew White compares the last stages of biblical criticism's struggle for acceptance against the traditional doctrine of inspiration to the break-up of the ice on the River Neva at St Petersburg. 'This barrier is already weakened; it is widely decayed, in many places thin, and everywhere treacherous; but it is, as a whole, so broad, so crystallised about old boulders, so imbedded in shallows, so wedged into crannies on either shore, that it is in great danger. The waters from thousands of swollen streamlets above are pressing behind it; wreckage and refuse are piling up against it; everyone knows that it must yield. But there is a danger that it may resist the pressure too long and break suddenly, wrenching even the granite quays from their foundations. . . But the patient mujiks are doing the right thing. The barrier, exposed more and more to the warmth of spring by the scores of channels they are making, will break away gradually, and the river will flow on beneficent and beautiful.'[44]

With the publication of *Lux Mundi* in 1889 and of Driver's important study of the Old Testament literature in 1891 it could be said that the battle for acceptance of critical principles was won at last.[45] 'The Doctrine' was, for practical purposes, gone. Geddes had been instrumental in making at least one channel which contributed towards the final result. Indeed, Professor White considers Geddes as one of the two men who most influenced biblical interpretation at the end of the eighteenth century. The other was Herder — utterly different though the two men were. 'Although,' he writes, 'there was a fringe of doubtful theories about them [Geddes's views] these main conclusions [on the composition of the Pentateuch] supported as they were by deep research and cogent reasoning are now recognised as of great value. But such was not the orthodox opinion then. . . he was suspended by the Catholic authorities as a misbeliever, denounced by Protestants as an infidel and taunted by both as "a would-be corrector of the Holy Ghost".'[46]

In spite of the opinion held by a number of his contemporaries that he was a vain man, Geddes had no illusions as to his limitations. His only concern was to make the best use of such talents as he possessed and the opportunities which came his way. And in so doing he was conscious of accomplishing something which not all of his contemporaries similarly, and even more generously, endowed with talent were attempting. 'I am hopeful,' he wrote, 'that I shall ultimately be found to have done more in that branch of literature which I have especially cultivated, than any of my contemporaries, at least in this country. Nor is this advanced as a boast. With half the labour and time which I have bestowed on Scripture criticism, there are many persons in this country capable of going a much greater length, than ever my mediocrity of genius can attain. Superiority of talents I never claimed, because I was conscious I could not claim it with justice: but in patient industry and persevering indagation, in an eager desire to discover truth and an honest candour to acknowledge it in whatever guise it appear, I will not yield the palm to any man.'[47]

Perhaps that passage may serve both as a summary of his aims and as a fitting epitaph on his life's work.

> *Tu enim fere unicus es, quem, si liceret, judicem mihi expeterem; quandoquidem tu in litteris biblicis habitas, in eodem stadio magna cum laude decurris, omnesque difficultates et molestias, quae talem cursum impediunt, ipsa experientia edoctus, nosti, ut adeo nemo facile ad judicium tam aequius quam rectius ferendum cogitari possit.*

You are almost the only man whose view on my work I would seek out, if I may, since you live only for biblical studies and have made a name for yourself in that field, knowing from experience all the difficulties and harassments that block one's path. Consequently, it would not be easy to think of anyone whose judgment would be fairer or more balanced than yours.

J. G. EICHHORN to GEDDES
1st September, 1800

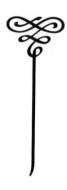

NOTES & LISTS
BIBLIOGRAPHY

NOTES

Foreword

1. T. K. Cheyne, *Founders of Old Testament Criticism*, 1893, p. 3
2. J. Geddes Macgregor, *The Bible in the Making*, 1961, p. 200.
3. A generation later, things were no better. In 1832, Dr Thomas Arnold wrote: 'As things now are, a man cannot prosecute a critical inquiry as to the date and authors of the books of Scripture, without the fear of having his Christian faith impeached, should his conclusions, in any instance, be at variance with the common opinion,' *Essay on the Right Interpretation and Understanding of the Scriptures*, in *Sermons*, Vol. 2, p. 477, London 1832, reprinted in *Sermons*, 2nd edition, 1874, p. lv.
4. For a stimulating account of Dr Geddes as a liberal Churchman before the ultramontane developments of the nineteenth century, see Bernard Aspinwall, 'The Last Laugh of a Humane Faith' in *New Blackfriars*, 58 (1977) 333-340. Again, though 'poetising' was a consuming passion of Geddes throughout his life, it must be admitted he was no Robbie Burns. 'His practical effusions are rather to be considered as the relaxations of a severe student than as the compositions of an author ambitious of poetical distinction. They discover what he might have effected; but are not sufficiently elaborated to be classed among finished productions,' David Irving, *The Lives of Scotish Writers*, vol. 2, 1804, p. 404. As to his priestly career, no attempt has been made to deal with this in detail or to give any assessment of it in the present study. This would be more appropriate to a biography portraying the whole man. And in that connection, since his aberrations have received more publicity than his more commendable qualities, it may be as well here to underline, as Charles Butler did soon after his death, the unflagging generosity with which Geddes was always prepared to help anyone in need. The most noteworthy of such instances was that of Sir George Chalmers, the painter, whom Geddes saved from a debtor's prison. In gratitude for this, Chalmers painted Geddes's portrait, the only one we can identify with certainty. It was Geddes's inability to turn a deaf ear to anyone in need that was as much the cause of his frequent indebtedness as his propensity to launch out on imprudent enterprises.

Chapter One

1. *Bishop Douglass's Diary*, Westminster Cathedral Archives, Z. 1, p. 82. Bishop Douglass was Vicar Apostolic of the London District, 1790-1812.
2. *Gentleman's Magazine*, 72 (1802) 279.
3. William Van Mildert, Bishop of Durham, *An Historical View of the Rise and Progress of Infidelity*, Boyle Lecture, 1802-4, Sermon 11, 3rd edition, 1820, p.411.
4. *Monthly Review*, 41 (1803) 376-384.
5. The Rev. James Augustine Stothert, whose Life of Bishop Hay is a source of much information, was born near Dumfries in 1817. He was ordained priest in 1848 and contributed his life of Hay to the 'Journal and Appendix' of the Rev. Dr Gordon's *Scotichronicon*, a work in three volumes. The 'Journal and Appendix' is for convenience referred to as volume 4 of *Scotichronicon*. Some confusion is caused by the fact that it bears the indication—volume 1. It was originally intended to be the first volume of an additional series but in fact was the only volume to be published of this series.
6. J. F. S. Gordon, *Scotichronicon*, 4, p. 38.
7. The figures for the various religious denominations in the parish of Rathven in 1720, as given in the *Statistical Account*, are: 1,700 adult Presbyterians, (i.e. over

10 years old); 600 Catholics. In 1793 the corresponding totals were: 1,766 Presbyterians, 950 Catholics and 303 Episcopalians.

8. In 1670 the Privy Council ordered that sons of Catholic nobles be handed over to 'Episcopal ' bishops for education. See P. F. Anson, *The Catholic Church in Modern Scotland*, p. 53. W. Forbes Leith, *Memoirs of Scottish Catholics*, 2, p. 132. Conditions in Scotland had changed since that time but the policy had a continuing influence.

9. *Dr Geddes's General Answer*. . . 1790, p. 2.

10. G. D. Henderson, *Religious Life in Seventeenth Century Scotland*, 1937. In chapter 1, The Bible in Seventeenth Century Scotland, the author describes the importance given to family worship and notes how the Geneva Bible continued in general use long after the appearance of the Authorized Version. But by Geddes's time the Authorized Version would have supplanted it. Cf. also W. J. Anderson, 'Catholic Family Worship on Deeside in 1691', in *The Innes Review* 18 (1967) 151-156. Robert Burn's poem 'The Cotter's Saturday Night' gives us a picture of his time. As to Roman Catholic use of the Authorized Version, there were not then the rigid restrictions on the use of 'Protestant' versions such as existed in the nineteenth century; possibly because of the more rudimentary Church organisation in Britain in the earlier period, cf. Dr. A. Geddes, *Letter to the Bishop of Centuriae*, 1794, p. 33.

11. Preface to Dr Nary's *New Testament*, 1718.

12. *Dr Geddes's Address to the Public*. . . 1793, p. 3.

13. Burton, *The Life and Times of Bishop Challoner*, 1, pp. 270-289.

14. *Scotichronicon*, 4, p. 31.

15. *Dr Geddes's Address to the Public*. . . p. 3.

16. *Roll of Alumni in Arts at King's College*. . . ed. P. J. Anderson, 1900, p. 74, has an entry of a student of this name in the class of 1745-49. Cf. also *Scotichronicon*, 4, p. 21 and D. Irving, *The Lives of Scotish Writers*, 1804, 2, p. 355 ('Mr Shearer, a student of Aberdeen').

17, Geddes succeeded him as priest-in-charge on his death in 1769, *Scotichronicon*, 4, pp. 39, 62.

18. Cf. *Innes Review* 18 (1967) 'The Autobiographical Notes of Bishop John Geddes' by William James Anderson, pp. 36-57.

19. *Scotichronicon*, 4, p. 11.

20. *Scotichronicon*, 4, pp. 275-6.

21. W. J. Anderson, 'A Brief Historical Account of the Seminary of Scalan', *Innes Review*, 14 (1963) 93ff; and Appendix I. 'Bishop Gordon's Rules for Scalan', ibid., p. 107.

22. *Dr Geddes's General Answer*. . . p. 3.

23. Dr J. M. Good, *Memoirs of Dr Alexander Geddes*, 1803, p. 11-12.

24. Letter of Dr A. Geddes to Bishop John Geddes, 14 August 1784, Scottish Catholic Archives, Edinburgh. (SCA)

25. See pp. 147, 164.

26. The outstanding work of the *philosophes* was of course the famous *Encyclopédie*, ou Dictionnaire raisonné des sciences, des arts et des métiers, par une societé de gens de lettres, mis en ordre et publié par Denis Diderot, et quant à la partie mathematique par M. D'Alembert, 1751-65.

27. The purpose of the *Encyclopédie* was 'pour changer la façon commune de penser', A. M. Wilson, *Diderot (1713-1759)*, p. 334.

28. Encyclopédie,, Discours Préliminaire.

29. Leslie Stephen, *English Thought in the 18th Century*, 1, p. 89.

30. William Cole, *A Journal of my Journey to Paris in the Year 1765*, ed. F. G. Stokes, London 1931.

31. Alfred Noyes, *Voltaire*, p. 104.

32. Op. cit., p. 491. There seems little doubt however that Voltaire was much more the sceptic than the believer, cf. p. 555. Geddes was never an unbeliever. He continued to celebrate Mass long after being dismissed by his bishop as is clear from his letters to his cousin Bishop Geddes. Thus on one occasion he wrote, 'I

must away to dinner—for as you know, meat and Mass are never to be omitted', Geddes to Bishop Geddes, 20 June 1784, SCA. Furthermore Geddes maintained a genuine devotion to the person of Jesus Christ, cf. his *Critical Remarks on the Pentateuch*, pp. vi, 474, and the epitaph on his tombstone, cf. p. 151.

33. Scotichronicon, 4, pp. 247-48.

34. William Cole in his *Journal* thus describes the College:'I drove to the Scotch College of St Andrew situated in a street pretty steep of ascent, called Les Fossez de St Victor, just without the limits of the University. . . The House was so loftily situated on the side of a hill that when I had ascended one pair of stairs up to the Principal's lodgings I was upon a level with their gardens and on the same floor with their chapel', p. 192. The chapel still retains much of its ancient appearance but there is little else left in the interior of the College, except the great staircase, to remind one of bygone days. The building is now a school for girls directed by Dominican nuns. The address is 65 rue du Cardinal Lemoine, not far from the Panthéon.

35. The Universities under the Ancien Régime and established by Letters Patent registered in the Parlement had a monopoly of conferring degrees and only admitted to degrees those who passed through their system, Louis Grimaud, *Histoire de la liberté de l'enseignement en France*, 1, L'Ancien Régime, Paris 1944, p. 18. Charles Jourdain, *Histoire de l'Université de Paris aux 17e et 18e Siècles*, 1862.

36. The first Vicar Apostolic, Bishop Nicolson, was appointed in 1695.

37. Pierre Coste, *St Vincent de Paul*, (English trans. of *Le Grand Saint du Grand Siècle*), 1935, 2, pp. 170ff, describes the seminaries founded in the years 1640-60.

38. In 1789 there were 562 Colleges in France with 72,747 pupils. Those Colleges aggregated to Universities had to have a staff with university degrees and the pupils were subject to university laws. The Faculty of Arts saw to their observance. Only pupils of such Colleges could proceed to degrees. The universities were jealous of their rights and never surrendered them or shared them with the religious orders, least of all with the Jesuits, who were in fact suppressed in France (1763) while Geddes was in Paris, Grimaud, op. cit., p. 26.

39. David Irving, *The Lives of Scotish* (sic) *Writers*, 1804, 2, The Life of Alexander Geddes (pp. 353-410), p. 357. A valuable addition to Good's *Memoirs*. This Life is omitted from subsequent editions of Irving's work.

40. *Prospectus*, p. 120, footnote; J. M. Good, *Memoirs of Dr A. Geddes*, pp. 13, 21 and 25. Resident in the Scots College at this time was an elderly priest named Robert Gordon who had made a translation of the New Testament from (presumably) the Vulgate. Geddes had a copy and refers to Gordon in the *Prospectus*, p. 111. The version for some reason failed to secure Rome's approval and was never printed. Gordon visited England at the time of the '45, was arrested for suspected complicity in the revolt, was deported and told never to return. He died at the Scots College, Paris, a year before Geddes was ordained. It is probable that Gordon too had an influence on Geddes in inclining him to biblical study.

41. R. Klibansky-E.C.Mossner, *New Letters of David Hume*, 1954, p. 74, Hume to William Robertson, 1 December 1763, from Paris. James Stanier Clark's *The Life of James II*, published in 1816 in two handsome leather-bound volumes, consists largely of long extracts from these very *Memoirs*, made before the French Revolution. The extracts were made by the abbé Waters and brought to England in 1788.

42. *Scotichronicon*, 4, p. 249. Most of those who defected were not priests but students who gave up before ordination. It must not be overlooked moreover that not all the inmates of the Paris College were church students. There were also a number of priests who abandoned their priesthood on return to Scotland and in some cases their faith as well. A few became ministers in either the Presbyterian or the Episcopal Church. Much information can be gathered from the Clergy Lists for the eighteenth century, cf. Gordon, *Scotichronicon*, 4, pp. 627-636; F. Forbes and W. J. Anderson, 'Clergy Lists of the Highland District, 1732-1828' in *The Innes Review* 17 (1966) 129-184. These of course concern only secular priests and take no account of Jesuits. Another serious criticism of the Paris College was

that for many years it produced hardly any priests at all. This lack of production however, was due, in the 1770s to another cause, namely the unwillingness of the bishops to send students to that College, because they disapproved of the way in which it was run.

43. *Letter to the Bishop of Centuriae*, p. 8, footnote.
44. Letters of Thomas Innes 1714-1728, preserved in the Scottish Catholic Archives. Forty years later the attitude of the Church had changed. Writing to His Majesty's Secretary of State, from Paris, David Hume observed that the Clergy had voted an Address to the King of Seven Articles. They asked that the silence imposed about *Unigenitus* be removed; that the Bull be made obligatory and of faith; that those who refuse acceptance should be refused the sacraments; that the Jesuits should be reestablished; that the Civil Tribunals should not interfere in Church matters. . . Hume to H. M. Secretary of State, August 1765. Klibansky-Mossner, *New Letters of David Hume*, Letter 47, p. 97. It would seem that little of this new trend had penetrated the Scots College, Paris, during Geddes's residence there.
45. Preserved in the library of Blairs College, Aberdeen, where many of the books and manuscripts from the Scots College, Paris, have been lodged.
46. Fliche-Martin, *Histoire de l'Eglise*, 19, Paris 1956, p. 259. Throughout the whole of Noailles's episcopate and even for some years after his death, Lercari, the Vatican Chargé d'Affaires in Paris, could gain no access at all to the Scots College to conduct a Visitation of any kind. Not surprisingly his Report when eventually it appeared was strongly biassed against the College, Bellesheim, *History of the Catholic Church of Scotland, from the Introduction of Christianity to the Present Day*, Edinburgh, 1887, vol. 4, p. 409.
47. A great deal of Jansenism had little or nothing to do with theology. It was mixed up with Gallicanism and rivalries within the Church. The Scots College, Paris, likewise, was more interested in allegiance than in theology. Archbishop Beaton, who died in 1603 had probably meant to put the Jesuits in charge of the Scots College, Paris, but at that time they were out of favour, accused of regicide, and had been banished from Paris. Beaton put the Carthusians in charge. Later, when restored to favour, the Jesuits tried to get control of the College, as they had control over most of the national Colleges around Europe. However, the Carthusians stoutly resisted and the Jesuits failed to oust them. Many attempts were made later with the inevitable result that the Scots College, Paris, became one of the most anti-Jesuit places in Europe. Much of the enmity between the Jesuits and Port-Royal was due to rivalry in the field of education. The Jesuits won for a time, but were later, in their turn, suppressed. Thus, a good deal of so-called Jansenist sentiment was in fact nothing more than anti-Jesuit feeling, and, since the Jesuits made public profession of their special loyalty to the Holy See, those who differed from them tended towards Gallicanism.
48. This copy of the anti-Jansenist Formula with its appended signatures is preserved in the Scottish Catholic Archives, Edinburgh. A photography (and a translation) appears in the review, *Claves Regni,* published by St Peter's College, Cardross, Dumbarton, vol. 22 (1955), pp. 24-25.

THE ANTI-JANSENIST FORMULA

Signed by the Scottish clergy in the eighteenth century. The text in this document was written out by Charles Cruikshank, Notary, in 1770. It was signed by Alexander Geddes, after a delay, in 1771. Here is a translation from the Latin text:

I, ... submit myself to the Constitutions of St Pius V, Gregory XIII and Urban VIII, supreme Pontiffs, condemning certain propositions of du Bay; also to the Apostolic Constitution of Innocent X, promulgated on 31 May 1653, the Constitution of Alexander VII of 16 October 1656 and the Briefs of Innocent XII, published on 6 February 1694 and 24 November 1696 to the Bishops of Belgium, also to the Constitution of the same Pontiff issued on 12 March 1699 against the book, entitled *Maximes des Saints*, as also to the Constitution of Clement XI of 15 July 1705. And the five propositions taken from the book 'Augustinus', written by Cornelius Jansen, and in the sense intended by that author, just as the Apostolic See has condemned them through the said Constitution, I reject and condemn with a sincere heart.

In particular, I submit myself sincerely to the Constitution *Unigenitus*, issued by Clement XI, 8 September 1713, against 101 propositions taken from the book of Moral Reflections by Pasquier Quesnel; also to all those other Constitutions, Decrees and Briefs of the Apostolic See, both before Clement XI and also, those issued by him on these matters or against propositions concerning morals.

Likewise, I expressly reject and condemn those books in English, publicly condemned through decrees of the Holy Inquisition, 7 December 1734 and 12 January 1735, of which the titles are: Catechism, or Abridgement of Christian Doctrine, 1725; 'Instructions and Prayers for Children with a Catechism for Younger Children', printed in 1724 and a Catechism for those more advanced in years and knowledge, 1724.

Moreover, I promise that I shall never make use of the Montpellier Catechism in instructing the faithful nor allow it to be used by others, wherever and whenever and in whatever manner it may be published and translated. Its title in French is: 'Instructions Générales en forme de catéchisme ou l'on explique en abrégé par l'Ecriture Sainte et par la Tradition, l'Histoire et les Dogmes de la Religion'. Printed by command of Charles Joachim Colbert Bishop of Montpellier. So I vow and swear. So help me God and these his holy Gospels.

49. Bishop Grant to A. Geddes, 3 March 1771, SCA.
50. Geddes to Bishop Grant, 7 March 1771, SCA. 'It is probable,' wrote Geddes later, 'that I shall think myself obliged to make a sacrifice to Friendship and the love of Concord of what I cannot esteem a tribute due to Religion and Conscience.' Geddes to Bishop Grant 27 March 1771.
51. Geddes to Bishop Geddes, 12 September 1786, SCA. During A. Geddes's ministry in the Enzie, his cousin John Geddes was in Spain, 1770-1780, as rector of the Scots College there. It is strange that among the hundreds of letters preserved in the archives of that College there is not one from Alexander to his cousin although there are references in later correspondence to his letters of this time. The correspondence of the following decade, 1781-1791 which is preserved in the SCA is one of our chief sources for those years, yet this too is defective, consisting as it does only of Alexander's letters and containing not even one of his cousin John written to him, though there are many of John Geddes's letters to other correspondents. It is to the credit of both that their correspondence continued as long as it did, in spite of the circumstances in which Alexander lived. John could have been pardoned for exercising less patience than he did with so difficult a priest; Alexander could very easily have visited on John's head some of the bitterness he felt against others on the episcopal bench, but in fact refrained. He wrote freely to his cousin on every topic of interest to him, and John in spite of his many labours in the mission field kept up his contact with him.
52. Preface to the Rheims New Testament, 1582.
53. Denzinger-Schönmetzer, *Enchiridion Symbolorum*. Of the 101 propositions of Pasquier Quesnel condemned in *Unigenitus* those referring to Scripture are nos 79-85. The reference in the *Enchiridion* is 2479-2485.
54. Geddes to Bishop Geddes, 10 April 1782, SCA.
55. Geddes to Bishop Geddes, 6 May 1783, SCA. It will be seen that these recorded thoughts date from his early years in London. All the extant letters of his Scottish period are confined to practical matters mostly connected with his ministry.
56. The library at Traquair House where Geddes must have spent many hours, contains a varied collection of books of the 17th and 18th centuries, historical, literary, topographical, doctrinal, biblical and devotional. In the matter of Scrip-

ture however, it is less comprehensive than the splendid library which Geddes built up in London, at Lord Petre's expense during twenty years' residence there. After Geddes's death, his library was sold by auction at Sotheby's and a catalogue of the sale is preserved in the Bodleian Library, Oxford. See p. 164.

57. Writing some years later and referring to himself in the third person Geddes observed to his cousin John Geddes: '(The Bible) has always been his favourite study, though from the idea that he should never be called forth to exert his abilities in that line, he has divided his applications with four other branches of literature much less to his taste', Geddes to Bishop Geddes, from London, 26 January 1782.

58. 'The Duke of Gordon,' wrote Lady Traquaire on one occasion to Dr Geddes, 'does not forgive the Dr for not visiting him at Gordon Castle when last in Scotland', Lady Traquaire to Dr Geddes, 24 October 1783, SCA.

59. Beattie wrote his *Essay on Truth* in 1770 as an answer to Hume. This secured him a niche in the contemporary Hall of Fame and a pension from King George III. He increased his reputation the following year with the publication of his poem *The Minstrel*, 1771. Strangely enough, however, it was in England rather than in Scotland that his fame was made. He was lionised in London and met famous people, including Dr Johnson, cf. R. S. Walker, *James Beattie's London Diary*, 1946, and H. G. Graham, *Scottish Men of Letters in the Eighteenth Century*, 1901, pp. 259-272.

60. At that time the allowance amounted to £8 a year in the country and £11 in the town, paid from the Common Fund, supplemented by a small amount contributed by the Congregation de Propaganda Fide in Rome and such financial help as the few wealthy Roman Catholics in Scotland could provide. Sometimes the priest kept a cow and grew vegetables to supplement his income.

His financial difficulties began fairly soon (1767) after his return from Paris and involved him in trouble. He could not pay the charges for the transport of his books from Paris and Hay proposed that it should be deducted from his stipend. Geddes strongly objected to this suggestion. A year or two later Geddes was busy erecting a small chapel at Auchinhalrig and by October 1771 (see Letter of Geddes to Grant, 2 October 1771) it was almost finished. Then, finding himself unable to pay the cost of erection, he bought a small farm hoping to make money from its produce with which he could pay for the chapel. But the farm proved to be a liability instead of an asset and he found himself more in debt than ever.

In 1776, he began to build a chapel at Fochabers, at the gates of Gordon Castle. 'I am in the greatest hurry,' he wrote to Hay, 'with my building; being obliged to be at least once every day at Fochabers', Geddes to Hay, 10 September 1777. For this project Geddes borrowed money (£22) from a Mrs Gordon and then as usual found himself unable to repay her. Writing to his cousin, Bishop John Geddes, some years later, he said he was afraid that Mrs Gordon 'will attack the chapel unless she gets paid'. This was in 1782 when Geddes had already left Scotland and was resident in London. The only solution he could think of was that the Church authorities should sell the books he had left behind in order to pay his debts, Geddes to Bishop Geddes, 7 May 1782.

61. Geddes to Bishop Geddes, 14 September 1782, SCA.

Writing to his friend J. Reid, Geddes spoke of his prospects. 'I am very busy writing a fair copy of my Satires for the Press. Dr Johnson (who is just what Lord Chesterfield calls him—a respectable Hottentot)—has strongly advised me to run the risk of the first impression myself and assures me that, if it have the sale he expects, the booksellers will give me more for the second edition than they would probably be willing to venture for the first' (Geddes to J. Reid, 3 April 1779).

62. P. J. Anderson (ed.) *Officers and Graduates of University and King's College, Aberdeen*, (Aberdeen 1893), p. 111; J. M. Good, *Memoirs of Dr Alexander Geddes*, pp. 38, 53. The full text in the Minutes of King's College is as follows: 'King's College May 20 1780. Conveened the principal and masters. The said day the University conferred the Degree of Doctor of Laws on Mr James (sic) Geddes author of some Translations and imitations from Horace, recommended by Mr

Baron Gordon, Dr Beattie, Mr George Grant, Minister at Raffan and Mr James Gordon, Minister at Bellie, and appointed a Diploma to be made out and subscribed'. MS. K. 47, p. 111.

In MSS K.13 and K.15 which both contain lists of LL.D's, the name is given as Alexander Geddes in both cases under this date, 20 May 1780.

The award is not mentioned in the Minutes (for 1780) of Marischal College, then a separate University, and this no doubt accounts for the apparent discrepancy in the names of the recommenders. J. M. Good mentions that Dr Geddes was recommended by Messrs Crawford and Buchanan, Ministers of Bellie and Cullen respectively. These may have been recommenders of Dr Geddes at Marischal College, as well as Dr Campbell, Principal of that College. The Ministers would appear to have been of the Episcopal Church, as their names do not appear in the lists of the Established Kirk. Unfortunately, records of the Episcopalians are incomplete.

For many of these details I am indebted to the kindness of the University Archivist and Keeper of Manuscripts, Mr Colin A. McLaren.

63. P. J. Anderson, loc. cit., and P. J. Anderson, (ed) *Fasti Academiae Mariscallanae Aberdonensis,* vol.2 (Aberdeen 1898), p.99. Only the year 1780 is noted in the latter work. Geddes's letters however, written at this time, make it clear that he spent some time (May 29th to about June 15th) in Aberdeen before proceeding south to Edinburgh. It is possible that he received the degree from Marischal during this period, though it was not necessary to receive it in person.

64. Thus, for example, in 1775 Geddes wrote a rather impolite letter to Bishop Hay demanding an explanation for the bishop's undemocratic manner of appointing new administrators of the Clergy Fund.

65. 'Banff Affair' Correspondence, SCA.

66. It was at this time of enforced leisure and of frequent visits to the Traquaires that Geddes celebrated the birth of their eldest son, Lord Linton, by composing a panegyric in verse — 'Linton, a Tweed-dale Pastoral'. In this, the trend of his thoughts, influenced by current events, may be discerned. Hardly a year had passed since the riots, occasioned in Scotland by the passing of the Catholic Relief Act, had taken place,

No more religion with fanatic hand
Shall fan the fire of Faction in the land
But mild and gentle like her heavenly Sire
No other flames but those of Love inspire
Papist and Protestant shall strive to raise
In different notes one great Creator's praise
Polemic volumes on their shelves shall rot
And Hays and Abernethies* be forgot.

* Dr Abernethy Drummond, an Episcopalian preacher had also entered the lists against Catholics in 1779.

67. Reporting to Bishop Hay about Geddes, John Reid, his near neighbour at Preshome, wrote as follows: 'He left the country on Monday last and before he left, visited everyone, saying he would be 'back in two years', Reid to Hay, 31 May 1780. The stage coach carrying Dr Geddes south actually passed the coach bringing his cousin, John, newly consecrated bishop, north to Edinburgh. 'It was unlucky,' Dr Geddes wrote, 'that we missed one another at York. I had written that I was to meet you there, but you were gone (from London) before my letter arrived', Geddes to Bishop Geddes, 5 June 1781. An opportunity for reconciling Alexander with Bishop Hay had thus been missed.

Chapter Two

1. Letter of Geddes 'to a friend', 5 June 1781, SCA. The friend was his cousin Bishop John Geddes as appears from the letter next quoted.

2. Geddes to John Reid, 8 June 1781, SCA. Throughout most of the eighteenth century the Imperial Embassy was at no. 5 Portman Square, (east side). The am-

bassador with whom Geddes had contact was Karl Ludwig Graf von Barbiano und Belgiojoso, whose term of office in London was 1770-1782. At this time the principal chaplain was Dom Placid Hamilton, formerly abbot of the Scottish Benedictine Abbey in Würzburg and it was doubtless through him that Geddes eventually got his chaplaincy there. In 1774 the Empress Maria Theresia resolved to increase the number of chaplains to six and allocated a sum of fl. 3,000 a year for the support of the chapel, (see report of the Ambassador with consequent resolutions in *Staatskanzlei Vorträge*, Kart. 114, *Vortrag Kaunitz*, on 12 February 1774). The names of the chaplains are given in Belgiojoso's reports of 19 September 1775 (*Staatenabteilungen England* Kart. 117) and of 12 February 1779, but of course this was before Geddes's time. It was further decided to build a much larger chapel; and in 1778 a building to seat 550 persons was erected at the rear of the embassy in the area of the stables, see report of Belgiojoso, 22 December 1777, *Staatenabteilungen England* Kart 118 and report of 17 November 1778, ibid., Kart. 119.

In 1781 however, perhaps as a result of the First Catholic Relief Act of 1778, Belgiojoso decided that the existence of a chapel at the Imperial Embassy was no longer necessary for the maintenance of Catholicism in London. He wished to close it to the general public and reduce the number of chaplains to one, namely Dom Placid Hamilton. Though Chancellor Kaunitz did not agree, he was overruled by Emperor Joseph II, see *Staatskanzlei Vorträge* Kart. 134, *Vortrag Kaunitz, 7 July 1781,* and the chapel was closed before the end of 1781, see report of Belgiojoso, 2 October 1781, *Staatenabteilungen England* Kart. 120.

For these details I am indebted to the Archivist of *Oesterreichisches Staatsarchiv,* Wien 1, and to the Westminster City Librarian, Archives Dept., Public Library, Marylebone Road, London, N.W.1.

3. Robert Edward, Baron Petre, was a wealthy and liberal-minded Roman Catholic, and Chairman of the Catholic Committee. His principal residence at this time was Thorndon Hall in Essex.   See M. D. Petre, *The Ninth Lord Petre,* London 1928.

4. The *Dictionary of National Biography* states that Geddes went to London in 1780, that the Imperial Chapel was closed at the end of 1780 and that Geddes gave up his ministry at Easter 1782. It will however be clear from the letter above that Geddes came to London in 1781. Correspondence of Lady Traquaire with Geddes, preserved in the SCA, shows that the Imperial Chapel was closed towards the end of 1781; and the Baptismal Register of the Sardinian Chapel, Lincoln's Inn Fields, preserved at the Church of St Anselm and St Cecilia, Kingsway, records that Geddes was exercising his ministry there in September and October, 1782.

5. *Idea of a New English Catholic Edition of the Holy Bible for the Use of the Roman Catholics of Great Britain.* Geddes's biographer, J. M. Good, gives 1780 as the date of this pamphlet (*Memoirs. . . p.* 61). This is because it was written soon after Geddes's arrival in London, and Good thought he arrived in 1780. The actual date of the pamplet was probably February, 1782. See next note.

6. Geddes to Bishop Geddes, 26 January 1782, SCA.

7. Geddes to Bishop Geddes, 12 February 1782.

8. Geddes to Bishop Geddes, 17 November 1782.

9. Geddes to Bishop Geddes, 7 May 1782.

10. Geddes to Bishop Geddes, 14 September 1782.

11. Geddes to Bishop Geddes, 17 November 1782.

12. Geddes to Bishop Geddes, 18 July 1783. The young Mr Howell was but 15 years old, according to Lady Traquaire's Diary, preserved in the archives at Traquair House. On returning from the tour, they travelled north and arrived at Traquair on 30 July 1783. Although Geddes gives few details of his tour, the nine countries he refers to clearly include Italy, Germany and France. It is interesting to speculate about whom he might have met on this tour: Michaelis at Göttingen? Some of his old professors at the Sorbonne? Not, at any rate, de L'Advocat, his revered professor of Hebrew, for he died in 1765, not long after Geddes left Paris as a student. Geddes pays a warm tribute to him in his *Prospectus*: 'He had a pene-

trating genius, an astonishing memory, a correct judgement and exquisite taste. He was the most universal scholar, the most pleasant teacher, the most benevolent man and the most moderate theologian I ever knew. . . A weakly constitution and too constant application to his professional duties hurried him away in his 56th year to the great regret of all who knew him but of none more than of him who dedicates these lines to his memory', p. 120, footnote. J. M. Good, with some disregard of accuracy, says that de L'Advocat died 'about 1780', *Memoirs of Dr Geddes*, p. 21.

13. Geddes to Bishop Geddes, 25 December 1783.

14. Geddes to Bishop Geddes, 8 April 1784. It seems reasonable to conclude that Geddes's rather sudden desire to learn German was, in part, the consequence of his visiting Germany on his tour, during the previous summer.

The year 1784 was a momentous one for Geddes. His dear friends the Traquaires had come south to London at the end of 1783 having found that they could no longer afford to live in their ancestral home and now had thoughts of going to live somewhere on the Continent. They were a generous but improvident pair and could never manage their affairs. They stayed in London throughout the whole of 1784 and part of 1785, eventually leaving England in March of that year. They were never to return as a family. After staying at various places in France they finally settled in Madrid, where, after years of penury and much suffering, Lady Traquaire died in 1796.

During the early months of 1784 the President of the Scots College at Douay, Mr Grant, was sick in London and was staying with Dr Geddes at his home in New Road, Marylebone. Geddes had visited him the previous year at Douay while on his European tour with the young Mr Howell. Dr Grant died on 26 March at Geddes's house.

15. Geddes to Bishop Geddes, 27 February 1784. Bishop Hay was becoming increasingly intolerant of his clergy and was especially critical of the situation in the Scots College in Paris. He wrote a long report on the College to the Prior of the Carthusians in Paris, the ecclesiastical superior of the College, and severely criticised the Principal, Alexander Gordon. The Prior however rejected the report. Principal Gordon went further. He produced and printed a very violent reply in French, dated 20 April 1785, in which he had the help of Dr Geddes. When criticised for his part in it, Geddes claimed that he had only helped with the French and in fact had tried to get Gordon to tone down some of his more forceful expressions. In view of his failing health and the increasing hostility of some of his clergy, Hay now thought of resigning, but eventually was persuaded by his advisers, including Bishop Geddes, to carry on. This he did, and continued as bishop for another twenty years.

16. Geddes to Bishop Geddes, 3 March 1785.

17. Geddes to Bishop Geddes, 31 March 1785.

18. Geddes to Bishop Geddes, 5 October 1785.

19. Geddes to Bishop Geddes, 23 October 1785.

Geddes also found time for a little pastoral work. He said Mass at the house of the Misses Fletcher for a group of local Catholics. 'Your little flock here,' he wrote to his cousin, 'will get into a *bad* habit of hearing Mass every Sunday and will take ill with their old period of six months', Geddes to Bishop Geddes, 15 October 1785. During this stay in Glasgow, Geddes took the opportunity of getting himself elected a Corresponding Member of the recently founded Scottish Society of Antiquaries. Bishop John Geddes had been elected a Corresponding Member very soon after its foundation, and it may be assumed that the bishop was instrumental in securing the election of Dr Geddes. From the moment of his election, 1 November 1785, Geddes showed that he had no intention of remaining inactive and contributed numerous articles to their periodical, *Transactions of the Scottish Society of Antiquaries*. Writing to his cousin again, in January 1786, still from Glasgow, Geddes was busy giving instructions as to how the bishop was to dispose of and publicize the copies of the *Prospectus* now being sent to him in Edinburgh. 'The price is seven shillings and sixpence—and in the Advertisement, after LL.D., he (Mr Elliot the publisher) may add 'and correspondent Member of the Scotch Antiquarian Society'. Geddes to Bishop Geddes, 12 January 1786. Geddes returned to London in February to promote the sale of his book in the south.

20. Geddes to Bishop Geddes, 28 February 1786.
21. Geddes to Bishop Geddes, 25 April 1786.
22. *Prospectus*. . . pp. 47-48.
23. *Address to the Public*. . . pp. 5-6.
24. *Prospectus*. . . p. 4.
25. Ibid., p. 8.
26. Ibid., pp. 3-4.
27. Ibid., p. 119.
28. Cf. his *Arcanum Punctationis Revelatum*, Leyden, 1624; and his later *Critica Sacra*, Paris, 1650. In his *Critica Sacra* Cappellus initiated the science of examining and comparing Variant Readings in order to reach a more reliable text—that is, textual criticism.
29. *Prospectus*. . . p. 9.
30. *Critical Remarks*. . . p. v.
31. *Exercitationes Ecclesiasticae in utrumque Samaritanum Pentateuchum*, Paris, 1631. The 'two Pentateuchs' were (1) the Pentateuch in Hebrew written in Samaritan characters, (2) a Samaritan 'translation' or paraphrase, also written in Samaritan characters.
32. *Histoire Critique du Vieux Testament*, Rotterdam, 1685, p. 464. Simon was not only a textual critic like Morin but expert in historical criticism as well. It is strange that Geddes did not appreciate him, though he did describe his *Histoire Critique* as a capital work, (*Prospectus*, p. 6). But Simon was born before his time. At the instigation of Bossuet, the original edition printed in Paris was seized and burnt. It was printed subsequently at Rotterdam, J. Steinmann, *Richard Simon et les origines de l'exégèse biblique*, Paris, 1960, pp. 124-130.
33. *Prospectus*. . . p. 19.
34. *Orientalische und Exegetische Bibliothek* 4 (1787) 19.
35. Dr Herbert Marsh, professor of divinity at Cambridge, soon after Geddes's death reminded his readers that the difference in age between the oldest Hebrew and the oldest Samaritan MS was slight compared with the distance in time between the oldest existing MS and the original autograph. Hence both texts were subject to errors. *Lectures on the Criticism and Interpetation of the Bible*, new ed., 1828, p. 257.
36. Caroli Francisci Houbigant, *Notae Criticae in universos V. T. libros. . . cum integris eiusdem Prolegomenis*, Frankfurt, I, 1777, pp. xv-xvii. (Reprinted from the original edition of his *Biblia Hebraica, 1753*).
37. *Prospectus*. . . p. 15.
38. *Prospectus*. . . pp. 80-81.
39. Dr Bernard Hodgson, Principal of Hertford College, Oxford, wrote on Eccles. 6:9: 'Houbigant here, as in other passages which he finds difficult, makes the matter easy by altering the text. For *nps* he substitutes without authority *dbs* honey—'Paululum recreat oculos favus mellis'. I cannot but think that the liberties frequently taken by this learned father in the transposition of letters and the alteration of the original words, without any authority whatever, to be highly unjustifiable: by this method a person might with facility make almost any sense out of any words: in Hebrew more particularly, where the radical letters seldom exceeding three, a transposition or change of any one of them makes a new word with a new signification', *Ecclesiastes, a new translation*, Oxford, 1790, in loc.
40. Some time later, Dr Lowth explained why there had been such a delay: 'The knowledge of Hebrew manuscripts is almost a new subject in literature: little progress has been made in it hitherto, and no wonder, when they were esteemed uniformly consonant one to another and with the printed text, consequently useless and not worth the trouble of examining', *Isaiah, a new translation with a preliminary Dissertation and Notes Critical and Explanatory*, London, 1778, p. lxxi.

41. *The State of the Printed Hebrew Text Considered*, 1753, vol. 2, p. 247, i.e. from a false idea of the sacredness of the text.
42. Dr David Durell was one of the earliest — *The Hebrew Text of the Parallel Prophecies of Jacob and Moses*, Oxford, 1763, p. iv.
43. Ibid., pp. 8-9.   44. *Prospectus.* . . p. 11, footnote.
45. Bishop Patrick Torry, *A Few General Remarks on the Modern Plan of Correcting the Original Hebrew Scriptures*, with some critical remarks on the Rev. Dr Geddes's Specimens of a new Translation. . . of the Holy Bible, 1787, p. 24.
46. Kennicott, op. cit., 1, p. 272.   47. *Histoire Critique.* . . p. 354.
48. *Prospectus.* . . pp. 13-15.
49. *The Old Testament Text and Versions*, Cardiff, 1951, p. 19.
50. 1st edit., *The Cairo Geniza*, p. 146, and cf. 2nd edit., 1959, pp. 212-13, 257; and in F. Kenyon, *Our Bible and the Ancient Manuscripts*, ed. 4, 1964, p. 7. On the other hand Würthwein suggests that the Hebrew text which began to emerge after AD 100 was clearly based on forms of the Hebrew older than that of the popular texts like the Samaritan Pentateuch and the original underlying the Septuagint. Hence the more sparing use of *scriptio plena* is not necessarily a sign of late date or late editing, *The Text of the Old Testament: an Introduction to Kittel-Kahle, Biblia Hebraica*, trans. P. R. Ackroyd, Oxford, 1957.
51. *Prospectus.* . . p. 143.

APPENDIX: GEDDES'S TEXTUAL CRITICISM — SOME EXAMPLES

When quoting Hebrew manuscripts, Geddes usually contents himself with giving the number of manuscripts which support a particular reading, e.g. 1 Heb MS, or 17 Heb MSS, as the case may be. We know that he collated manuscripts at Lambeth Palace, the British Museum, the Bodleian Library and Glasgow University Library, but there is little evidence in his work, or indeed in that of his contemporaries, of the relative importance of individual manuscripts. A distinctive feature of his criticism is the use he makes of both the Samaritan Pentateuch and the Septuagint, and many of the choices of text which he made on the basis of these have stood the test of time. The Samaritan Pentateuch he used was that edited by Morin in the Paris Polyglot; the Septuagint manuscripts are frequently mentioned by name, Vatican, Alexandrine, Aldine, etc. Some comments by contemporaries have been added.

We give first a sample section, Gen 1:1—2:4, picking out the principal points treated.

Gen 1:6. Geddes transfers 'and so it was' from the end of verse 7 to the end of verse 6, on the analogy of verses 9, 11, 15, 24, 30. But the phrase does not occur in verse 20 where it should do, according to the pattern, and Geddes inserts it there too. Both insertions (6 and 20) are made on the authority of the Septuagint.

Gen 1:8. After 'heaven', Geddes inserts with Septuagint, 'This also God saw to be good', to keep the pattern. Houbigant,* in his Latin translation, also does this.

Gen 1:9. Geddes adds with Septuagint, 'For the waters below the expanse were collected into their places and the dry land appeared'. So also Houbigant. This too is to keep the pattern: command, execution, approval. Houbigant says it is not a doublet rightly omitted by Hebrew, but a passage rightly kept in the Septuagint and to be replaced in the Hebrew.

Gen 1:14. After 'heavens', Geddes adds 'to illuminate the earth, and'. So 1 Heb MS, Sam, LXX. Rosenmuller† specifies the MS as 'Cod. meus 76' and notes that though it has the passage the pointing is defective as if there were doubts of its authenticity. De Rossi notes that the words occur in the next verse. Houbigant says that if you insert this, verse 15 becomes redundant. Geddes seems to have nobody on his side.

Gen 1:15. Geddes says this verse 'has all the appearance of an interpolation' and puts it in square brackets. Naturally he thinks this, after his insertion in v. 14.

Gen 1:26. 'and in all the earth'. This fits awkwardly between 'cattle' and 'creeping things' as if it were another category. Houbigant notes that Pentateuchus Venetus in 4, 1566 drops the *waw* ('and') thus linking the phrase to the preceding. He prefers this reading and Rosenmüller approves this. Geddes prefers, with Syr. 'And all the wild beasts' in place of 'and in all the earth'. Kittel, in our time, also prefers Syr. in this passage.

Gen 1:28. After 'flying creatures of the air', Geddes adds 'with Sep, Syr and Targ', 'over the cattle and the wild beasts'. Long ago, however, S. Davidson** wrote 'Syr has merely "and over the cattle" and does not therefore agree with LXX as has been said'. (Had he read Geddes?). This is confirmed by Brooke-McLean.†† Moreover Targum Onkelos has none of this insertion, according to the text printed in Walton's Polyglot Bible, which Geddes probably used.

Gen 2:2. For 'seventh' Geddes reads 'sixth' (in the first instance) with Sam, LXX, Syr. Geddes says that the sense requires this reading, for God in fact stopped work on the sixth day and it would be forcing the text to translate with a pluperfect 'he had completed'. Houbigant also reads 'sixth' and quotes Ex 20:11 and 31:17 to show that God worked on six days and rested on the seventh. This reading perhaps came in, in order to remove doubt as to the day. But Houbigant follows Capellus in finding fault with MT.

Gen 2:4. Geddes sees no break here but divides after verse 6, though he maintains that both accounts of creation are by the same person.

Gen 4:8 is also of interest. After 'Abel' there appears to be a gap in the sense. Cain is said to 'speak' to Abel, but nothing is recorded in MT. Geddes quotes de Rossi, adducing Ex 19:25 as an indication that what is said is not always recorded. He comments that this proves nothing as it was not needed there in any case, since the words had just been put into God's mouth and Moses was to repeat them. Geddes rejects Dathe's suggestion that it should be translated 'spoke harshly'. He proposes, with LXX, Syr, Vulg and Targ the additon 'Let us walk out into the fields'. He notes that a space is left in 27 Hebrew MSS and nearly forty printed editions to indicate the omission of those words.

* F. Houbigant, *Biblia Hebraica cum notis criticis et versione latina ad notas criticas facta*, Paris, 1753. J. B. de Rossi, *Variae Lectiones Veteris Testamenti. . . ad Sam. Pent. ad vetustissimas versiones. . . examinatae*, Parmae, 1784-88.
† Rosenmüller, E. F. C, *Scholia in Vetus Testamentum*, Leipzig, 1795f.
** S. Davidson, *Treatise on Biblical Criticism*, 1854, p. 413.
†† A. E. Brooke–N. McLean, *The Old Testament in Greek, according to the text of Codex Vaticanus. . .* Cambridge, 1906-1935.
Other examples of Geddes's textual criticism may be found in the more extensive treatment of the original Dissertation (1968) in the Cambridge University Library, entitled 'Dr A. Geddes, A Forerunner of Biblical Criticism.'

Chapter Three

1. *Address to the Public*, p. 1; cf. *Bible*, 1, p. x.
2. Geddes to Bishop Geddes, 12 February 1782.
3. *Critical Remarks*, p. vi.
4. Geddes to Bishop Geddes, 10 April 1782.
9. Geddes to Bishop Geddes, 10 April 1782.
10. Geddes to Bishop Geddes, 12 February 1782.
11. Gal 1:8; *Bible*, 2, p. xi.
12. *Bible*, 2, p. xi, footnote.
16. *Critical Remarks*, p. 475.
17. *Critical Remarks*, p. 41.

5. *Critical Remarks*, p. vi.
6. Ibid., p. v.
7. *Bible*, 1, p. 1.
8. Ibid., 2, p. xii.

13. Ibid., p. iii.
14. Ibid., p. v.
15. Ibid., p. iv.

18. *Bible*, 2, p. xii.   Geddes does not seem to have envisaged the possibility of an effective divine influx which would nevertheless allow for the characteristics and defects of the human writer. The only inspiration of an all-embracing kind which he felt able to concede was that enjoyed by poets, dramatists, etc.
19. Ibid., p. xiii.

20. *Prospectus*, pp. 114-115.
21. *Analytical Review* 3 (1789) 289.
22. Geddes to Bishop Geddes, 12 February 1782.
23. *Address to the Public*, p. 2
24. *Bible*, 1, pp. ii-iv.
25. *Critical Remarks*, pp. 25-26.
26. Ibid., p. 29, and see above, pp. 99-100.

27. Ibid., p. 32.
28. Ibid., p. 33.
29. Ibid., p. 35.
30. Ibid., p. 37.
31. *Bible*, 1, pp. vi-ix.
32. See chapter 4, p. 000.

33. *Bible*, 1, p. xi. It is strange that Geddes criticizes Eichhorn's early view as found in the original edition of his *Urgeschichte*. That appeared in 1779 when Eichhorn was at Jena. Much had happened since then. Not long after Eichhorn's arrival at Göttingen, his pupil Gabler had brought out the first volume of the new edition in which the mythological principle is consistently applied. Geddes says not a word about this, though the first volume of his *Bible* appeared two years later. See chapter 4, p. 78 and note 50 (p. 141).
34. *Critical Remarks*, p. 44.
35. Ibid., p. 59.
36. Ibid., p. 62.
37. Ibid., p. 62.
38. Ibid., p. 72.
39. *Bible*, 1, p. xi.
40. *Critical Remarks*, p. 117.
41. *Bible*, 1, pp. xii-xiii.
42. *Critical Remarks*, p. 182.
43. Ibid., p. 191.

44. Ibid., pp. 212-213.
45. Ibid., pp. 224-225.
46. Ibid., p. 249.
47. Ibid., p. 251.
48. Ibid., p. 384.
49. Ibid., p. 375.
50. Ibid., p. 205.
51. Ibid., p. 205.
52. Ibid., p. 410.

53. Richard Watson, Bishop of Llandaff, Regius Professor of Divinity at Cambridge.
54. *Critical Remarks*, p. 422. See especially below, p. 155 (note 38).
55. *Bible*, 2, p. ii, footnote.
56. J. Astruc, *Conjectures. . .* ; J. G. Eichhorn, *Einleitung in das Alten Testament*. Cf. chapt. 4, p. 81.
57. *Bible*, 1, p. xxi. It is worth noting that F. A. Wolf published his *Prolegomena*, dissecting the Homeric authorship, in 1795.
58. Ibid, p. xviii.
59. Ibid, p. xix.
60. *Critical Remarks*, p. 29. Even more curiously, Geddes wrote in the first volume of his *Bible*: 'The first six verses of ch. 2 evidently connect with what precedes and should make a part of chapter 1.' On verse 4 he added: 'This and the following two verses are the epilogue if I may so call it, of the first chapter and not the beginning of a new historical fragment, as some moderns have imagined.' *Bible*, 1, in loco.

Referring to Exodus 3 Geddes discussed the question of whether the divine name Jehovah (or Yahweh) was known to the Patriarchs before Moses. The mention of the name in the historical narrative of Genesis could perhaps be explained by later editing. But what of the use of the name in the mouths of the Patriarchs themselves? There could have been a substitution or an insertion at a later date. Need we be surprised if, after the name Jehovah had been made known, later historians put it in, as a substitute for the name Elohim? The blessing of the Patriarchs suggested the same conclusion. El Shaddai was their usual name for God. 'It matters not whether these were the very words of Jacob and Isaac or of the poetical historian who put them in their mouths. The poetical historian must have made them speak something like the language of their age, and use terms that were then known. In short, unless we suppose the Pentateuch to be a compilation of jarring elements assemblaged by different hands, we must allow that the name *Jehovah* has been put in the mouths of the Patriarchs prior to Moses, and in the mouth of God himself, by some posterior copier; for the same person who wrote this third verse of Exodus 6 could not have been so inconsistent with himself, as to make the name Jehovah familiar to the Patriarchs before that period.' *Critical Remarks*, p. 179. The variety of explanations of the presence of the divine names in the Genesis narrative evidently assisted Geddes in rejecting the distinct-

ion of names as a criterion for distinguishing sources or documents.
61. *Critical Remarks,* p. 390.
62. Ibid., p. 393.
63. Ibid., p. 376; cf. J. G. Eichhorn, *Einleitung in das Alte Testament,* 2nd edition, vol. 2, p. 377.
64. *Critical Remarks,* p. 416, note.
65. G. von Rad, *Deuteronomy,* Old Testament Library, in loc.
66. G. von Rad, in loc.
67. *Bible,* 1, p. xxi.

Chapter Four

1. See chapter 1, p. 15.
2. Chapter 3, p. 38.
3. J. Leclerc, *Letters on Inspiration,* Eng. tr. 1690. Foreword by the Translator.
4. A modern writer, H. Robinson, describes Bayle thus: 'Like Erasmus before him and Voltaire afterwards, Bayle was European in his influence, the first really cosmopolitan figure in French literature', *Bayle the Sceptic,* New York 1931, p. 246. Another critic sees him differently: 'To doubt without openly denying; to argue without hope or desire of reaching the truth; to look for difficulties and multiply objections; to confuse one's opponent with subtle or sophisticated arguments, for which he dare not always take responsibility; there you have the work and method of Bayle', V. Oblet in *Dictionnaire de Théologie Catholique,* s. v. Bayle, col. 490. Geddes was well acquainted with Bayle and had at least three of his works in his library, namely, *Pensées diverses. . . à l'occasion d'une comète. . .* 4 tom. 1683; *Critique générale de l'histoire du Calvinisme* du Père Maimbourg, 1682, and especially the *Dictionnaire historique et critique,* 4 tom., Paris 1781 (first published in 1695-97). It was above all through the *Dictionnaire,* written after he was removed from his professorship (1692), that Bayle's influence spread.
5. *Letter to the Bishop of Centuriae,* p. 38.
6. See chapter 4, p. 65.
7. Charles Butler, *Historical Memoirs of the English, Irish and Scottish Catholics since the Reformation,* 3rd edition, 1822, vol. 4, pp. 417-18.
8. Chapter 3, p. 43.
9. Hume's *Essay on Miracles,* Part 1, originally written as part of his *Treatise of Human Nature* (1739-40) but not published until 1748 in his *Inquiry concerning Human Understanding.* It is interesting to note that in the same year Conyers Middleton published his *Free Inquiry into the Miraculous Powers which are supposed to have subsisted in the Christian Church from the Earliest Ages through Several Successive Centuries,* London 1749.
10. *Some Cursory Reflections on the Dispute or Dissension which happened at Antioch between the Apostles Peter and Paul,* Middleton's Works, 2nd ed. 1755, p. 290.
11. Op. cit., p. 292. It may be recalled that this work was never published in Middleton's lifetime. For a similar view, see Eichhorn-Gabler, *Urgeschichte,* vol. 3, p. 7, Anm. 2. No doubt too the exaggerations of the Deists were partly responsible for the continuance of the rigid doctrine of Inspiration throughout the eighteenth century and its revival in the nineteenth, after having been the 'unshakable foundation' of orthodox theology for the previous 150 years, G. Hornig, *Die Anfänge der historisch-critischen Theologie,* Göttingen–Lund 1961, p. 56.
12. L. Zscharnack, *Lessing und Semler,* Ein Beitrag zur Entstehungsgeschichte des Rationalismus und der kritischen theologie, 1905, p. 26.
13. H.-J. Kraus, *Geschichte der historisch-kritischen Erforschung des Alten Testaments,* 2te Auflage 1969, p. 94.
14. D. F. Strauss, *Life of Jesus,* Eng. tr. by George Eliot, new ed. 1892, Introduction by Georg Pfleiderer, p. viii.

15. J. S. Semler, *Apparatus ad liberalem Veteris Testamenti interpretationem*, Halle 1773, Praefatio. Though Geddes's thought was so similar yet there is no book of Semler's in the catalogue of Geddes's library.

16. Ibid.

17. G. Hornig, *Die Anfänge der historisch-kritischen Theologie*, Göttingen-Lund 1961, pp. 88-89. Semler's 'Freieuntersuch' aimed at finding what Scripture meant to its first hearers. That was the real meaning and actuality of God's Word. The Word of God, for Semler, was the Absolute and the Ever-Present: Scripture, however, was the Relative, the Past, the Human. In confrontation with the Bible, man is the authority; he decides where the historical past and the divine present are to be sought. This led on to another distinction — that between Theology and Religion. The former is the raw material examined by the critic: the latter is the Absolute, the obligatory Authority of Conscience and Morality, Cf. H.-J. Kraus, op. cit., p. 111.

18. R. W. Mackay, *The Tübingen School and its Antecedents*, 1863, p. 98.

19. R. W. Mackay, op. cit., pp. 97-99. Cf. Zscharnack, op. cit., p. 103. E. B. Pusey, fresh from his studies in Germany of the previous year, laid at Semler's door the blame for much that he considered wrong in the contemporary trend of German theology. 'Semler,' he wrote, 'became the most extensive instrument of the degradation of Christianity.' But he hastened to add that Semler's error lay, not in adopting the historical interpretation but, in applying it too exclusively, failing to perceive the connection between Jewish and Christian as the completion of the earlier education of man—and an inability to distinguish between what was meant for contemporaries and what was of eternal value. E. B. Pusey, *An Historical Enquiry into the Probable Causes of the Rationalist Character lately Predominant in the Theology of Germany*, I, 1828, pp. 142ff.

20. G. Hornig, op. cit., p. 15.

21. *Uebersetzung des Alten Testament mit Anmerkungen für Ungelehrte*, Numeri, 2te Ausgabe, 1787, in loc.

22. Chapter 4, p. 73f.

23. H.-J. Kraus, op. cit., p. 93.

24. *Apologie oder Schutzschrift für die Vernünftigen Verehrer Gottes*. As son-in-law of Johann Albrecht Fabricius, Reimarus could not afford to risk his reputation in this way.

25. H. Chadwick, *Lessing's Theological Writings*, p. 52ff, On the Proof of the Spirit and of Power; J. Sime, *Lessing, His Life and Writings*, 1877, vol. 2, p. 212; G. E. Lessing, *Sämmtliche Schriften*, X, p. 40. Actually, Lessing declared the Resurrection to be a conclusion against which his reason rebelled. Hence it would seem that, even if history could 'prove it', he could never accept it.

26. Zscharnack, *Lessing und Semler*, pp. 318-320. In *Nathan the Wise* (1777) Lessing stressed the relative and subjective character of positive religions, while asserting that the only absolute religion was Natural Religion.

27. *Urgeschichte—Ein Versuch*, in *Repertorium für biblische und morgenländische Litteratur*, 1779, Th. 4, pp. 129-172 and 172-256. Eichhorn attacked the view of Reimarus that the Old Testament could not have been the vehicle of a revelation. He argued that there was on the contrary no difficulty in admitting this provided one recalled the conditions of the *infantia generis humani* and that such a revelation was gradual and conditioned by successive ages. It was Eichhorn's life-work to destroy the extreme rationalist position as well as the old orthodoxy by putting in place of their basic assumptions his own concept of the *infantia generis humani*. Thus the fierce attacks on the Old Testament lost their force when faced with Eichhorn's contention that the Old Testament was neither a catechism, nor even itself a revelation. And even if it were a revelation, should the dawn-light be equal to that of midday? Cf. J. G. Eichhorn's review of *Uebrige noch ungedruckte Werke der Wolfenbüttlerischen Fragmentisten, Ein Nachlass von G. E. Lessing'*. Herausg. von C.A.E. Schmidt, 1787; reviewed in *Allgemeine Bibliothek der biblischen Literatur* 1 (1788) 261-311.

28. Op. cit., p. 193.

29. Op. cit., p. 194.

30. Reviewing Michaelis's *Einleitung in die göttlichen Schriften des Alten Bundes* some years later, Eichhorn noted that Michaelis envisaged Man in the first Age of the World as existing in a state of great enlightenment and thought that a large part of the Herbew Scriptures were written under the influence of exceptional knowledge. Eichhorn found no trace of this enlightened early world and thought that the Scriptures were produced at a much lower level of mental development, *Allgemeine Bibliothek der biblischen Literatur* 1 (1787) 430ff.
31. *Urgeschichte*, pp. 195-96.
32. Ibid., p. 256.
33. See Chapter 4, p. 82.
34. R. W. Mackay, op. cit., p. 138. Eichhorn was not especially concerned to work out a theory of inspiration which fitted the new interpretation of the Bible. He was content to demolish the old theory and then let the facts speak for themselves. He regarded himself as the critic rather than the theologian, *Einleitung in das Alte Testament*, 1803, 3rd ed., vol. 2, p. 615, note.
35. Stendal, *Die Ältesten Urkunden der Hebräer im ersten Buch Moses für freymütige Altertumsforscher, neu übersetzt und erläutert*, reviewed by Eichhorn in *Allgemeine Bibliothek der biblischen Literatur* 1 (1788) 984-999.
36. Loc. cit., p. 994.
37. C. Hartlich-W. Sachs, *Der Ursprung des Mythosbegriffes...* 1952, p. 1.

ADDENDUM: GIAMBATTISTA VICO

Al though the whole framework of the mythological interpretation was the work of Christian Gottlob Heyne, some of the leading ideas can be traced back a long way. Thus Giambattista Vico (1688-1744), the philosopher and author of the *Scienza Nuova*, had elaborated certain notions concerning human development. Primitive man not only ascribed physical phenomena to the gods and indeed identified such happenings with them but went further and attributed many experiences of society and personified them in the same way. Physical and social experiences thus became inextricably intermingled. Then came the age of myth or legend which described widely experienced truths, not just isolated facts, historical or physical. With the growth of abstract reasoning came a diminishing of the status of the gods. To the gods succeeded the heroes and every nation had its heroes. The earliest forms of expression were poetic and Homer would have written at the end of the heroic age. By this time the legends were becoming frankly immoral but it was impossible that they could have started in that way. Legend or myth was originally austere and moral, expressing facts of human experience. Vico rejected any explanations of human life involving fraud. The superstition of the hero was not imposture but the first stage in interpreting nature. G. Vico, *Principii di Scienza Nuova*, 3rd ed. 1744, Book III, 873-879. Eng. tr. 1948; H. Adams, *The Life and Writings of Giambattista Vico*, 1935, p. 129.

38. This quotation from Gabler refers, strictly speaking, more to the principle of the *infantia generis humani* than to the mythological principle, but the former led to the latter. Gabler, of course, may well have been referring to Eichhorn's book-review as well.
39. J. G. Eichhorn's *Urgeschichte*, herausgegeben mit Einleitung und Anmerkungen von D. Johann Philipp Gabler, ordentlichen Professor|der Theologie zu Altdorf, 1790. An unmistakable connection will also be seen between Heyne and Hume's *Natural History of Religion*, 1755, which was translated into German by J. G. Hamann. Heyne began to teach in 1763, cf. Hartlich-Sachs, op. cit., p. 169 and Beilage II, p. 169.
40. Thus Dathe argued that to abandon the literal sense in this way was a most dangerous step. See J. A. Dathe, *Pentateuchus ex recensione textus hebraici et versionum antiquarum latine versus, notisque philologicis et criticis illustratus*, editio 2a, 1791, p. 36, and see above p. 101.
41. See Chapter 4, p. 70.
42. Paradoxically, the use of allegory by an 18th century Deist, Thomas Woolston, had a link with the new mythical interpretation. Woolston found that the Gospel

accounts of miracles were, taken literally, absurd, inconsistent and inherently incredible. In his work *Discourses on the Miracles of our Saviour*, 1727-29, Woolston professed to revive the allegorical method of interpretation as a way out of his difficulty, and argued that this interpretation could be used as a valid argument for Christ's claims. He denied any intention of impiety. Nevertheless his contempt for the accounts taken literally and the frequent parallels with mythology which he gave, suggested that he was really trying to destroy the historical sense and reinterpret mythically. But he could not do this openly and had to camouflage his thoughts for fear of reprisals. His concealment was in vain. He was eventually imprisoned for his opinions and died there in 1733. 'It is possible,' wrote G. Pfleiderer, 'to find in Woolston's theory an anticipation of the mythical principle which Strauss opposes to the rationalistic one'; see Strauss, *Life of Jesus*, 1892, Introduction, p. viii.

43. As Mackay has pointed out, for those who felt unable to accept the Bible miracles and other supernatural interventions, two courses were basically open: (1) they could deny the supernatural character and retain the event as historical, but reinterpreted as a natural occurrence, or (2) they could deny the event as historical while retaining all its wonderful and supernatural characteristics. The latter alternative involved the interpretation of the event either as allegory or as myth. In the eighteenth century the use of allegory was discredited; myth had not yet been applied—and most people felt (until Eichhorn began to change the climate of opinion) that, however appropriate myth might be in the ancient traditions of pagan peoples, it could not be admitted in the interpretation of the inspired word of God. Much work remained to be done before it could be generally accepted. Cf. R. W. Mackay, op. cit., p. 137.

44. Mark Pattison, *Essay on Friedrich August Wolf*, in *Essays*, vol. 1, ed. H. Nettleship, 1889, reprinted from the *North British Review*, June 1865. Much of Heyne's work is published in the *Commentationes Societatis Regiae Scientiarum Gottingensis*, 1763-.

45. Dr Robert Lowth made an important contribution to the study. Not that Lowth was specially interested in myth or historical criticism. But his penetration into the structure of Hebrew poetry and the background to biblical literature was so thorough that it served as a useful starting point for later inquiries into the nature of myth. Lowth embarked on the task of studying and analysing the literature of the Bible as he would any other secular literature yet without ignoring its divine origins. It was a serious and effective attempt to penetrate the world in which the literature arose. He stressed that the more remote the period in which the literature took its origin the more difficult it was for us to understand the habits of the time. We should, at all costs, he said, avoid judging them by our own standards. We should know their language, customs and even thoughts and try to read the Hebrew as the Hebrews themselves would have read it. We should place ourselves in the position of the persons for whom it was written or who did the writing. Cf. R. Lowth, *Lectures on the Sacred Poetry of the Hebrews*, Eng. tr. by G. Gregory, with . . . notes by Prof. J. J. Michaelis, by the Translator and by others, 1787, Vol. 1, p. 114.

Lowth stressed not only the inspiring and refreshing nature of poetry but also its power to instill into the soul the principles of morality itself. This, he said, was specially true of Hebrew poetry. Why read Homer and neglect Isaiah, he asked. In that inspired book we might contemplate poetry as an emanation from heaven, op. cit., pp. 35-44.

46. Hartlich-Sachs, op. cit., pp. 13-14; C. G. Heyne, *Apollodor*, I, xvi-xviii.

47. Hartlich-Sachs, op. cit., pp. 14-19.

48. Gabler specified the responsibility thus: 'In October of last year I received from him full permission to prepare a new edition of his *Urgeschichte*, only he took no part in it'; Eichhorn-Gabler, *Urgeschichte*, vol. 1, p. viii.

49. Geddes refers to the author of the *Urgeschichte* as 'an anonymous writer supposed to be Eichhorn himself' (*Bible*, vol. 1, p. ix). If he had seen Gabler's edition before he published this statement, he would have known at once who the author was as it is stated on the title-page. Even more strangely, there is no refer-

ence to Gabler's edition in Geddes's *Critical Remarks on the Pentateuch*, published in 1800.

50. Geddes's ignorance at the time of the publication of the first volume of his Bible can be explained by the fact that the work had been written some time before it was published—in fact before Gabler's edition appeared in 1790. At this time Geddes was much preoccupied with religious and political matters connected with the Second Catholic Relief Act of 1791; see chapter 5, p. 88. Also, Geddes's known sympathies with the cause of the French Revolution and his acquaintance with Tom Paine, made him fear the possibility of imprisonment at this time, remote though it may have been; see chapter 5, notes 1 and 42. To some extent in consequence, he fell seriously ill. No satisfactory explanation however can be offered for the omission in *Critical Remarks.*

51. *Urgeschichte*, 1, p. xxx. Eichhorn gave his full approval and, in general, endorsed Gablers's conclusions, cf. *Allgemeine Bibliothek der biblischen Literatur* 3 (1790) 72.

52. Hartlich-Sachs, op cit., p. 38.

53. Ibid, p. 27.

54. Ibid., p. 30. It will be clear by now that this book *Der Ursprung des Mythosbegriffes in der Modernen Bibelwissenschaft* has been of crucial value to the present author.

It is worth noting that Geddes published volume two of his *Bible* (1797) two years after F. A. Wolf brought out his *Prolegomena* to Homer, in which he distinguished between unconscious creative imagination and conscious poetic expression. Wolf regarded the conscious poetic product of one writer as quite different from the genuine and unconscious product of creative imagination in the course of successive generations. Homer, he said, was a work of rhapsodic origins of this kind.

55. Eichhorn-Gabler, *Urgeschichte*, p. 260.

56. Ibid., 3, p. xxx.

57. Ibid., 1, p. xvii.

58. Richard Simon, *Histoire Critique du Vieux Testament*, Rotterdam, 5th ed., 1685, Book 1, ch. 1-2.

59. In Simon's time the prevailing view was that if Genesis was inspired it must be by Moses and taken as strict history. To counter this view he proposed collective inspiration to embrace primary authors and later redactors. But even more important, it was made to cover later additions and corrections. It has been said that Simon spread inspiration further than his contemporaries, but he spread it more thinly.

60. 'Tout est écrit pesle-mesle dans les cinq livres du Pentateuch, qu'il n'est ni histoire, ni narration, qui y soit en son lieu,' quoted by Astruc in *Conjectures*, Part XVI. A second good reason for the delay in Pentateuchal analysis was the fact that both textual and literary criticism were still in their infancy.

61. It is perhaps unnecessary to add that Astruc was not the first in the field. A. Lods in 'Un précurseur allemand de Jean Astruc; Henning Bernhard Witter,' in *Zeitschrift für die Alttestamentliche Wissenschaft* 1925, pp. 134ff, revealed that the scholar of that name had first distinguished the sources on the basis of the different use of the divine names, in his book *Jura Israelitarum...* published in 1711.

62. Dathe in his opusculum *De Ordine Pericoparum Biblicarum non mutando* is mainly occupied with Harenberg's suggestion that the sheets of the codex got mixed up at some stage of the transmission and this resulted in the present order. Dathe warns that if we are prepared to admit mistakes of this kind, we may soon be obliged to admit errors in doctrine. There is as little evidence for this dislocation, he maintains, as for conjectural emendation of the text. *De Ordine Pericoparum...* is published in *Opuscula ad Crisin et Interpretationem Veteris Testamenti spectantia*, ed. E. F. C. Rosenmüller,1797, but originally published in 1769.

63. Eichhorn followed Astruc in this: 'Die beyden ersten Kapitel des zweyten Buchs Mose's bestehen aus den letzen Abschnitten der Urkunde mit dem Nahmen Elohim,' *Einleitung in das Alte Testament*, Vol 2 (1803), 3rd ed., p. 385. Eichhorn's treatment is known as the Older Documentary Hypothesis. He thoroughly

analysed Genesis and Exodus 1—2. But for the rest he merely said the legal material was Mosaic and the narrative was Moses' *Reisejournal.* There were of course some later interpolations, e.g. the account of Moses' death. When later Vater began to analyse the other books in the same way he was at once up against a difficulty because he could find no parallel strands of J & E in the laws (Leviticus) and hence arose the Fragment Theory, see above, p. 105.
64. See chapter 5, p. 99.
65. *Vom Geist der Ebräischen Poesie,* vol. 1, p. 310.
66. *Einleitung,* 2nd ed. (1787), vol. 2, p. 256. Eichhorn stuck to his view of the Mosaic authorship in spite of the fact that Semler had already expressed his dissent some years earlier, and for reasons that should have appealed to Eichhorn: 'I share the view of those who hold that the Pentateuch, long after the time of Moses, was put together from a variety of words and passages and arranged as a continuous narrative.' J. S. Semler, *Apparatus ad liberalem Veteris Testamenti interpretationem,* Halle 1773, ch. 2, p. 67.

In Eichhorn's fourth edition (1823), he conceded that the editing might have been as late as Samuel. Eichhorn never wavered in his attachment to the Mosaic authorship, apparently because he took the evidence of Deuteronomy as proving beyond all shadow of doubt that Moses personally composed it. The warmth and vitality of Deuteronomy convinced Eichhorn that it was Moses' work. But if he composed Deuteronomy then he must have composed Exodus—Numbers of which Deuteronomy was the continuation. Once the barrier of Deuteronomy was removed (by W. M. L. de Wette) Eichhorn's case collapsed.

APPENDIX: HERDER AND THE MYTHOLOGICAL SCHOOL

Johann Gottfried Herder cannot be said to have belonged to any critical school but his influence in the world of literature was so great and his contacts with Heyne and Eichhorn so close that a consideration of his position is essential. Herder was convinced that it was necessary to put oneself as far as possible into the circumstances and ways of thought of those about whom one was writing. This was especially true of the ancient Hebrew prophets and writers.[1] He urged that in order to understand the New Testament one must fully appreciate the Old; and this was in striking contrast to Semler, who had an almost Marcionite distaste for the Old. In his *Die Ältesten Urkunden des Menschengeschlechtes* (1774) Herder looked on Genesis as the record of a primitive revelation, handed down from our first parents, and the first age of man as one of enlightened intelligence and of developed sensitivity. He further suggested that the original records were poetic in character. This was what Lowth had said. No distinction was made between the original tradition or raw material and the later developed poetic form. Herder was convinced that primitive man had a gift for lyrical poetry in which he expressed his deepest aspirations.

By the time Eichhorn wrote his *Urgeschichte* Herder was already changing his view of the primitive Golden Age as a time of developed culture, and came to the same conclusions as Eichhorn. Thus he now envisaged the first age of man in terms of innocence and unsophisticated simplicity. It was still a culture but a pastoral culture, to be clearly distinguished from savagery as that of Hurons and Iroquois.[2] Men thought and expressed themselves in terms of concrete objects and personifications. They used Bildersprache and tended to interpret inanimate objects as living beings or animals with human personality. Herder now thought that poetry might be attributed to the youth rather than to the childhood of the human race; to the second rather than to the first age of man. The primitive sagas came before the developed poetical structures, and the original form of these sagas came to be overlaid with more or less fabulous detail — the marvellous was added to the ordinary.

Herder was reluctant to commit himself as to the historical content of these sagas. They must have had some historical fact at their base, but he confessed that he was no saviour of history. He was not interested in intricate critical questions and concerned himself only with the poetry and spirit of the ancient literature. Herder would exhaustively study the historical and cultural background of the literature he was considering but he did this not with a view to any clinical analysis of that literature; rather was it so that he could get inside it and live it. Eichhorn studied it as a modern man studies an ancient document; Herder became a contemporary of the author, in order that he might feel and appreciate the divine spirit which lived in those writings. He did however make some attempt to draw a line of distinction between history and fiction.[3] Saga was primitive history — basic fact mixed with fictitious accretions which grew and accumulated with the passage of time. Saga was the type of primitive history common to all nations and they all had their admixture of fable. He cited a large number of fables in the early traditions of many nations showing how there were striking parallels in the early Hebrew records. Herder insisted that when he admitted a fictional element he did not mean lies. The imagery of the fable, the meaning of the symbol, was indeed truth. Every nation had these in recognisable form. Thus the cherubim of Genesis 3 were to be found in the ruins of Persepolis and in the Sphinx of Egypt. Herder dissociated himself entirely from the attitude of Reimarus and the Deists who accused the biblical writers of practising deception on a large scale.[4]

While Herder's ideas therefore so closely resembled those of Eichhorn and of Heyne, they were not so clear-cut, and, for the most part, not so early. Herder was the poet, not the critic. He stands beside both Heyne and Eichhorn in his insistence on the need for the thorough historical study of the records, but then he parts company from them in the use he makes of his information in order to 'live' the literature he is reading. It has been said that Herder made no distinction between the primitive tradition or saga and the later, developed poetical form which it assumed. It will be seen however from the above account that the elements of a distinction did exist (e.g. in his later work, *Vom Geist...*), even if not worked out so clearly as in Heyne. Again, the extraordinary profusion of legend and fable produced by Herder as parallels to the biblical narrative might lead the reader to conclude that there was little, if anything, historical in the Bible account. This however would be to misjudge him. Herder did not feel obliged to undertake the task of a literary critic. He was content to state the way in which the primitive traditions took their rise, by analogy with those of every other nation of which any records survived. There was historical fact but it was primitive history; basic fact mixed with fabulous detail. It was these primitive traditions, irrespective of any precise distinction between what was or was not strictly historical, in which Herder took his greatest delight. In such productions, he felt, one could approach most closely to the very spirit of earliest unspoilt man and imbibe something of his direct, unsophisticated outlook on life and receptiveness of divine revelation.

Herder played a real part in the general development of biblical criticism, but he certainly could not be called a critic in the usual sense. The real predecessor of Eichhorn was Heyne, the classical critic, and Eichhorn was his faithful disciple in the application of critical principles to the Bible literature.

It has been said: 'If you ascertain the great principles on which you must judge

Hebrew poetry. . . study Lowth; if you desire to know more of the idea intended
. . . and trace it with philological accuracy. . . . follow Michaelis; but if you would
lay aside the philosopher and critic and give yourself up to intellectual enjoyment,
if you would have the same sensations and the same thoughts while chanting
Hebrew poetry, which the Hebrews themselves had, catch the tuneful notes of
Herder.' Cf. Calvin E. Stowe, in his edition of Gregory's translation of Lowth's
De Sacra Poesi Hebraeorum, with critical notes of Michaelis, quoted in R. T. Clark
Jnr, *Herder, his Life and Thought*, 1955, p. 294.

Notes to the Appendix:
1. Herder expressed it thus: 'The Bible must be read as a human book. It is a
book written by men and for men.' *Briefe das Studium der Theologie betreffend*,
Suphan, Band 10, Seite 7, quoted in Hartlich-Sachs, *Der Ursprung des Mythosbegriffes*, p. 50. Herder's original interest in the literature and traditions of ancient
peoples had been stimulated by Rudolf Erich Raspe, who introduced him to the
poems of Ossian. Raspe, a German savant, came to England about the year 1775,
where he took a job as a mining prospector in the copper mines of Cornwall.
When these failed, he came to London where he met many Scotsmen, including
Geddes. He tried various occupations, including writing, and it was at this time
that he wrote *The Travels of Baron Münchausen* to earn his bread and butter. The
book was a great success though he personally did not get much for it, and it was
translated into many languages. At this time he also compiled his impressive
Catalogue of Gems for Tassie. Eventually he moved to Scotland where he once
more undertook prospecting but it was a failure. There exists a letter from Geddes
to Raspe in the National Library, Edinburgh, see p. 162.
2. 'Kein kriegender Irokese, kein jagender Hurone dichtete so,' *Vom Geist der
Ebräischen Poesie*, 1782-3, edited by Dr K. W. Justi, Leipzig 1825, vol. 2, p. 37.
3. Herder is at pains to make clear that, e.g. the Crossing of the Red Sea did not
originate in the Song in Exodus 15, cf. *Vom Geist*, 2, p. 100.
4. Cf. Herder, *Vom Geist*, 2, p. 16: 'ich brauche Dichtung nicht für lüge.'

APPENDIX: LETTER TO PROFESSOR PAULUS

A hitherto unpublished letter written by Geddes to Professor H. E. G. Paulus
(see p. 163)

London, Alsop's Buildings
July 15th 1801
My dear friend,

You must now deem me a bad correspondent and an ungrateful man not to
have sooner answered your most polite and friendly letters. The truth is, I wrote a
pretty long letter to you on the 20th of September of last year, which lies now
before me; and a part of which I am just going to rewrite. — It was to this purport
'I am at length gratified with a very kind elegant Latin letter from you: but as you
wish me to answer it in plain English, I will humour your wish. I was truly somewhat angry with you, my dear Paulus, and in a letter to Eichhorn, some time ago,
had complained that I never heard from you. However, your present most
welcome Epistle has quite disarmed me of mine ire; and I am at this moment as
tame and pacific as a lamb. How the first two volumes of my Bible have never
reached you, I cannot possibly conceive; as they were sent at the same time as
Eichhorn's copy. — You shall now have them both, together with a huge volume
of Critical Remarks just about to be published; and which will, most probably
draw upon me a new torrent of illiberal censure here: for we are all mainly
orthodox in this land of holiness.

'I wonder that Holmes did not send you his Genesis, which is all that is yet published of his work. Both his prior specimens (for he gave two) were certainly liable to censure: and he has removed some of the most objectionable things in his last *Cura*, yet still there are some defects in his plan: particularly in his manner of arrangement. He should, in my oppinion distribute his page in method of Kennicott. I shall have occasion to write to him in a few days hence and will not fail to communicate to him that part of your letter which concerns him.

'Dr Ford continues to labour slowly on the *Coptic Fragments* left unfinished by Woide. — Winstanley has been preferred to the mastership of a College, and become idle in consequence — Dr White is a Canon of Glocester, and generally resides in that city; where he has a private press of his own, in which he has lately printed a neat *Diatessaron* — The Clarendon Press has been for a long time big with new editions of Strabo and Plutarch: but when the birth will be completed, no mortal can say. I shall impatiently wait for your present, which Timaeus tells me is on the way, and perhaps may at this moment be arrived. — I trust, now that our long interrupted correspondence is recommenced, that it will henceforth be more regular. I think you should write in English, as you once wrote so well: were it only to keep yourself in the habit. Could I write German but half so well, I would often plague you in that language. — I find I am drawing to the end of my paper — so I must in two words tell you that I ever am

D^r friend &c.

So far my first letter, which was sent to Hamburg at the time of the date, but came back to me six months after, through some unaccountable mistake of the ship-master: and has lain by me ever since. — I now come to answer your second letter, written in good English, and full of that friendship which might be expected from a Paulus. What thanks, my dear friend, have I not to render you for the very liberal and kind manner in which you express yourself in my regard and for the very valuable presents which, through Timaeus, I have received. — It is to me astonishing how amidst so much public employment, you can find leisure to compose so many volumes, replete with so much erudition and sound judicious criticism. — I consider it as a singular honour to have my *Apology* translated by *you* into German; which must greatly enhance its value on the continent, and make it more widely known that it could ever be in its natural dress. — Your intention to give a retrospective review of my biblical work gratifies me much. That you may the better understand my plan, I have sent you, together with the three Quarto vol. of *Translation* and *Remarks*, 5 smaller pieces relative to them; boarded up together. They were sent to Mr Huttener in March last; and I doubt not of your having received them long before this. — A long series of bad health has greatly retarded the printing of the work: but I hope the following volumes will succeed one another with less interruption.

I have had a letter from Holmes. He declines sending you a copy of his Septuagint, as he says he is accountable to the University for every copy that is printed. This I think a poor reason: but as it satisfies him, we too must be satisfied.

His Exodus has just appeared: but I have not yet had leisure to dip into it. — I am busy at present in printing a small edition of my Version of the Psalms, at the earnest request of some friends, who are unwilling to wait for that part of the larger work in which the Psalter is to be printed: namely the last vol. of the O. Testament. — I shall have the pleasure of transmitting to you the smaller volume, as soon as it comes from the press.

Although my *Apology* has operated strongly on the minds of our Legislators in general: yet I fear *Catholic Emancipation*, as it is termed, is yet at some distance. The conscience of the King has been tampered with: and he has set his face against the measure, so the poor R. Catholics are likely to remain unemancipated during *his* reign.

I before said that I expected a torrent of injuries on the appearance of my *Critical Remarks*: my expectations have not been disappointed. Papists and Protestants vie with one another, which shall throw the first stone: so that I may say with Erasmus *Undique lapidor!* — My resolution, however, is to let them pelt on — for the blows I feel not, any more than Theodosius felt the dirt that was thrown at his statue. —

With you I regret that the *Analytical Review* has been dropt: as it was conducted on a more liberal plan than most of the others but it was this very cause that chiefly contributed to its being dropt. Its publisher, Johnson, was marked in the *Black Book* of our political Inquisitors, as a Jacobine, foresooth! and as they could not lay hold on him merely for his Review, he was persecuted, tried and condemned to a fine and imprisonment for accidentally vending a few copies of a pamphlet written by Wakefield (the editor of Lucretius) for which the author has also suffered two years imprisonment. — Johnson was so much hurt by this treatment, that he conceived a hasty resolution to give up the *Analytical Review;* especially as the Attorney General had alluded to it in vague accusations. — It was kept up for six months more by a young man of spirit: but not meeting with the encouragement which he promised to himself, he also dropped it. The *Monthly Review* is now the only one that has any merit: although, in some respects, it too has fallen off from its former celebrity. — We still want a *Literary Journal* conducted on liberal and extensive principles: and were I but 20 years younger, and could find 5 or 6 associates to my mind, I would make an effort to establish such a work. But, alas! I am fast verging to the eve of life: and now have no other wish but to finish the work I am engaged in.

I have just now lost the best of Patrons, in my dear departed friend Lord Petre. He has not, however, forgotten me in his Will: although I know not yet to what extent I am a Legatee. His successor is a good young man, who, it is to be hoped, will tread in his father's steps, and be a friend to learning as well as he.

This, you will allow, is a letter of length — perhaps too long for your patience. — It goes with a friend of mine Dr Joseph Wilks, who will either send it from Weimar or deliver it to yourself at Jena. I have urged him to see you, for his own sake. He is a Benedictine, learned and liberal: and has suffered here from the illiberality and bigotry of some of his brethren. — He will be glad to meet with a learned German, who speaks English: and I am certain you will shew him a kind attention.

I am but just recovering from a very severe illness, which has left me so weak that I can hardly wield a pen. — I wish you may be able to read what I have scrawled, rather than written. Let me hear from you, my good friend, as often as you conveniently can — and believe that you have not in Old England a more faithful or more affectionate friend than

Al. Geddes.

Chapter Five

1. In the early stages of the French Revolution Geddes had written to his cousin, John Geddes: 'The time is come when every Tyrant, whether spiritual or temporal, must tremble on his throne, however exalted, and soon may every such tyrant experience a downfall. The still, small voice of reason begins at length to be heard and rational religion will, I trust, in the end triumph equally over Fanaticism and Superstition.' Geddes to Bishop Geddes, 18 January 1790. But much more significant than this were the *Carmina Saecularia Tria* written between 1790 and 1793 in praise of the Revolution—the second of which was printed in Paris also and read aloud in French to the Assembly. This was dedicated to Dumourier.

Robespierre's reign of terror changed all this.

There is a letter in the Scottish Catholic Archives, Edinburgh, from Henry Dundas (later Viscount Melville), the Home Secretary, headed 'Whitehall, 19 June 1794' and addressed to Dr Geddes. In this Dundas refers to a letter written to him by Geddes assuring him of the loyalty of Roman Catholics in Britain to His Majesty King George the Third. Dundas replies that he has never had any doubt of their good disposition and loyalty to His Majesty. The letter is addressed to 'A. Geddie' (sic) and it is more than likely that Dundas had never heard of Geddes. Cf. W. J. Anderson, 'David Downie and the "Friends of the People"', in *The Innes Review* 16 (1965) 175. The explanation of Geddes's strange action is that he had been friendly with a David Downie of Edinburgh recently arrested and later condemned to death for high treason in view of his taking part in a revolutionary movement in Scotland. By 1794, many of those who were sympathetic in the early stages, had changed their minds as they saw how the Revolution was proceeding. Downie was one of those who did not; and who were active in supporting a Convention in Britain. Other friends of Geddes suffered some years later. In 1798 Gilbert Wakefield and his publisher Joseph Johnson (who also published Geddes's books) were imprisoned for the publication of a pamphlet in which Wakefield had expressed the view that the poor in Britain would lose nothing by a French invasion, cf. above, pp. 102, 149.

2. Geddes's friendship with Unitarians was not of long standing. As recently as 1787 he had published a *Letter* to Dr Joseph Priestley, in which he made a cogent reply to Priestley's arguments, basing himself on the evidence for the divinity of Christ in early Christianity. Priestly answered this in a series of letters and these in turn were replied to by the Rev. James Barnard (1789) who paid Geddes the compliment of using and developing some of his arguments. Geddes had not yet been suspended by his Bishop. Some years later however the situation had changed. Geddes's connection with Coleridge is referred to in a letter, Geddes to Paulus, 14 September 1798, *Universitätsbibliothek*, Heidelberg, see p. 164. Coleridge was setting out on his German tour and Geddes asked him to take a letter to Paulus, recommending the young man to the German professor. Coleridge spend some months at Göttingen in Bible study, before returning to England.

3. Geddes seems by this time to have given up any thoughts of returning to his native Scotland and to have entered fully into the scholarly life he had adopted. Cf. chapter 1, page 130. It is of interest to note that his name appears in the list of subscribers at the beginning of Dr Karl Woide's handsome edition of the Greek New Testament.

4. B. Blayney, *Jeremiah and Lamentations*, 1784, p. xi.

5. *Critical Review* 63 (1787) 45-46.

6. *Neue Orientalische und Exegetische Bibliothek* 4 (1787) 18.

7. Op. cit., p. 20.

8. Op. cit., p. 23.

9. Op. cit., p. 29. Some time had yet to pass before German Critical Theology was taken notice of in the Latin nations. The earliest occasion appears to be a review of Strauss's *Leben Jesu* in the *Revue des Deux Mondes* for December 1838 — and that was to warn its readers off it. No doubt the French Revolution accounted to a large extent for this lack of contact in the intellectual field.

10. *Annales Literarii (Helmstädt)* cura H. P. C. Henke and P. I. Bruns, 1786, vol. 2, p. 97. It is interesting to speculate whether the recommendation in the Würzburg periodical had anything to do with the presence of Geddes's brother, Father Andrew Geddes, a Benedictine monk, in the Scots Abbey in Würzburg. When Father Andrew wrote, years later, to inform H. E. G. Paulus of his brother's death, he added that there were several copies of Dr Geddes's Bible which he would be pleased to let anybody have at half price who might be interested in purchasing them! Andrew Geddes to H.E.G.Paulus, 19 March 1802, in the *Universitätsbibliothek*, Heidelberg: Heid. Hs 855, cf. above, pp. 15 and 164. This Latin edition of the *Prospectus* is of particular interest. Its existence came to light through a review of it in *Allgemeine Bibliothek...* 1 (1787) 694, and a reference to it by Geddes in a letter to the abbé Thomson in Rome, 3 October

1787 (*Scottish Catholic Archives*, Edinburgh). See list of Geddes's published works, p. 156. Application to the *Staatl. Bibliothek*, Bamberg, its place of publication, disclosed that a copy of it is preserved there of which a xerox copy has now been placed in Cambridge University Library. No other copy is known to me. The erudition and judgment of the German translator and editor are such that one is tempted to ask why he translated it at all rather than produce his own work. The answer (suggested in the Foreword) is that in those early days of Biblical criticism there was not enough inter-communion between scholars of different countries; and it was judged useful for German readers to have something from a British scholar conveying information about Biblical scholarship in his own country not readily available to those living elsewhere.

11. *Neue Orientalische. . .* 7, 8, 9 (1790) 88-96.
12. Op. cit., p. 88ff.
13. Geddes to Bishop Geddes, 15 April 1788, SCA, Edinburgh. There were other reasons for the delay in publication. During the previous year Geddes's services had been much in demand by the Catholic Committee who were trying to secure from Parliament a further measure of freedom for Roman Catholics. Mr Pitt said they must give more assurance that the Papal dispensing power was not recognised in this country by Roman Catholics. Lord Petre asked Geddes to prepare a paper on this subject which could be submitted to Pitt. This was in May 1788.
14. *Reisejournal* of H. E. G. Paulus; recording his visit to London, p. 234, 12 May 1788. The work has never been published and is preserved in the Universitätsbibliothek, Heidelberg, see p. 164.
15. *Reisejournal*, p. 377, 21 October 1788. At this time Paulus was a young man of twenty-seven. The following year he became Professor of Oriental Languages in Jena. On Raspe, see p. 144.,
16. Geddes to Bishop Geddes, 12 September 1788. SCA.
17. Geddes to Bishop Geddes, 13 November 1789. SCA.
18. The Catholic Committee was a body of Catholic laymen formed to secure the passage through Parliament of the Second Catholic Relief Bill. See below, p. 164.
19. Geddes to Bishop Geddes, 5 July 1791. This is the last of the letters from Geddes to Bishop Geddes which are preserved in the Scottish Catholic Archives, Edinburgh. Bishop Geddes's paralysis began soon afterwards.
20. A number of other publications from the pen of Dr Geddes appeared in that year, in spite of the upheaval of the move from his lodgings in Clipstone Street to his new house, 24 Alsopp's Buildings, New Road, Marylebone (now Marylebone Road). It was a pleasant two-storey terrace house with a front and back garden. Geddes busied himself not only with gardening but also carpentry, neither of which he had had much chance to indulge in since he left Scotland, more than ten years previously. He now began to make bookshelves for his ever-increasing library until there was scarcely a room in the house whose walls were not covered with shelves.
21. 10 July 1792, printed in the Appendix to *Letter to the Bishop of Centuriae*, 1794, p. 44.
22. *Gentleman's Magazine* 63 (1793) 888.
23. *Letter to the Bishop of Centuriae* quotes the relevant extracts on pp. 15, 19.
24. Bishop Douglass to Dr Geddes, 23 June 1793; Westminster Cathedral Archives, MSS Vol. 44, letter 165. Printed in Appendix to *Letter to the Bishop of Centuriae*. Stothert comments on this: 'Thus by resorting to the harshness of extreme measures the English Bishops drove into open rebellion a man of genius whom the accident of residence had placed in their power.', J. F. S. Gordon, *Scotichronicon*, 4, p. 349.
25. See Letters to Miss Howard, below p. 163.
26. Geddes described his Bible as his 'darling child', *Letter to the Bishop of Centuriae*, p. 19.
27. *Monthly Review* 11 (1793), new series, p. 299.
28. Op. cit., pp. 300-303.
29. *Critical Review*, 11 (1794), new series, p. 136.

30. *British Critic* 4 (1794) 156.
31. Abraham Ben Yizakeer, *A Second Address. . .* humbly presented to the Rev.
pious and learned Dr G- - - - s on his late edifying publications and especially on
the first volume of his excellent translation of the Holy Bible; in three parts with
notes. For Ephraim Levy in Whitechapel and sold by Robinson's and Debrett,
1794, Part II. A copy of this is preserved in the Library of Oscott College,
Birmingham.
32. *Allgemeine Bibliothek. . .* 5 (1794) 448.
33. Op. cit., pp. 448-456.
34. The volume contained Judges, 1 & 2 Samuel, 1 & 2 Kings, 1 & 2 Chronicles,
Ruth and the (apocryphal) Prayer of Manasseh. Bishop Douglass wrote in his
Diary under date 6 July 1797, 'Alexander Geddes sent me the second volume of
his Bible and a letter in which he says "I trust you will not be too ready to
censure, as I find the Bishops of the Established Church will probably anticipate
you",' *Westminster Cathedral Archives*, Z. 72.
35. *Monthly Review* 25 (1798) 405-7.
36. Op. cit., p. 408.
37. See above chapter 3, p. 54.
38. *Critical Review* 21 (1797) 363-68.
39. *British Critic* 14 (1799) 577-586.
40. *Monthly Magazine* 5 (1798) 503.
41. J. Earle, *Remarks on the Prefaces prefixed to the first and second volumes of
a work entitled 'The Holy Bible etc.' by the Rev. Alexander Geddes LL.D.* in four
letters addressed to him by the Rev. J. Earle, London, 1799, p. 15. This book is
extremely rare. A copy is preserved in the British Museum.
42. Op. cit., p. 39. More than once Geddes was accused of propagating the same
ideas as Tom Paine. It is probable that Geddes knew Paine, since Joseph Johnson,
the radical publisher (see p. 147) undertook to publish Paine's *Rights of Man*,
Part I. Johnson had been publishing Geddes's books since 1788. After printing
the *Rights of Man*, Johnson took fright. He was afraid of punishment for sedition.
Paine meanwhile went to Paris, to avoid trouble and had the book published
there. Part I appeared in 1791 and Part 2 in 1792, and, immediately, it became
the text book of the reforming parties. Paine was tried by the British authorities
and condemned in his absence. He then started work on *The Age of Reason*, and
had it published in Paris. This had much the same effect on Britain as the Reimarus *Fragments* had on Germany. Paine was a thorough-going Deist who spent an
enormous amount of energy in proving that the Bible was a tissue of contradictions, falsehoods, misstatements, forgery, imposture and downright immorality.
43. Op. cit., p. 48.
44. Op. cit., p. 55.
45. Op. cit., p. 69.
46. Bishop Douglass's *Diary*. 9 May 1799, Westminster Cathedral Archives, Z. 72,
p. 147.
47. Geddes to Dr Kirk, 6 December 1798, Birmingham Diocesan Archives, C. 1512.
48. *Allgemeine Bibliothek. . .* 8 (1797) 534-547.
49. *Allgemeine Bibliothek. . .* 10 (1801) 1005-1011.
50. Ibid, pp. 1011-1015.
51. *Neuestes Theologisches Journal* 9 (1802) 360-371. The review is signed 'G',
which probably indicates Gabler, as he was the editor of the periodical.
52. Op. cit., p. 364. Contrary to what Gabler says here, Geddes denied that he got
his interpretation from Eichhorn, see above chapter 3, p. 45.
53. Op. cit., p. 371.
54. Geddes's frequent references to his *Critical Remarks* on the historical books,
as if they already existed, suggest that they existed in manuscript, probably in
considerable quantity, at least until shortly before his death. Perhaps the hostility
of his critics delayed publication.When his friend Gilbert Wakefield was in Dor-
chester Gaol for sedition, Geddes wrote to him, 'My last volume has, by the
German critics been received with the greatest applause, but you will soon see me,

here, torn to pieces by the hands of bigotry and sciolism in a most nefarious manner.' Geddes to Wakefield, 14 April 1801, written from Allsop's Buildings, Marylebone; printed in *Memoirs of the Life of Gilbert Wakefield, B.A.,* formerly Fellow of Jesus College, Cambridge, vol. 2, p. 257, second edition, 1804.
55. *Critical Review* 32 (1801) 163.
56. *British Critic* 19 (1802) 3, 10, 283. The reviewer was Dr Samuel Horsley, Bishop of St Asaph.
57. *Monthly Review* 41 (1803) 378.
58. R. Findlay, *The Divine Inspiration of the Jewish Scriptures or Old Testament, asserted by St Paul, 2 Timothy III, 16, and Dr Geddes's reasons against this sense of his words examined, 1803.*

Chapter Six

1. One of Lord Petre's residences.
2. Geddes to Miss Howard, from London, Oct 24th 1800. National Library of Scotland, MS 10999, fol. 93-115.
3. See List of Published Works, p. 159.
4. Dr Geddes died in the house provided for him by Lord Petre at 24 Allsop's Buildings, New Road, now Marylebone Road, near Baker Street.
5. *Account of the Death of the Rev. Alexander Geddes by the Abbé de St Martin,* 1803. See the list of Unpublished Manuscript Material, p. 4.
6. Entry in the *Times* of Saturday, 27th February, 1802. The account in J. M. Good, *Memoirs of Dr Geddes,* is inaccurate. It was based on a conversation Dr Good had with de St Martin in the course of which the abbé related various conversations he had had with Dr Geddes over several years on matters of religion in an endeavour to bring him to a more orthodox frame of mind. Dr Good however appears to have imagined that these conversations all took place just before Geddes's death, and he published his account under this impression. It was for this reason that the abbé was asked to write down what actually happened.
7. *Bishop Douglass's Diary,* 26th February, 1802. 'Dr Belasyse has called upon me and said that a French priest, abbé de St Martin, did gain admittance to him before he expired, did get from him some symptoms of sorrow and half-uttered sentences and therefore gave him absolution. . . Dr B. pressed me, on the grounds that he had received absolution to admit that a Dirge and Mass might be sung for the deceased, which Lord Petre had suggested, but I resisted the petition.' Westminster Cathedral Archives. See List of Unpublished Material, p. 164. Bishop Douglass's opinion of Geddes was not shared by everybody. Perhaps the fairest assessment of him came from Charles Butler, secretary of the Catholic Committee. After referring to Geddes's 'denial' of the inspiration of the Scriptures and his adoption of 'the German scheme of rationalising the narrative of the Old Testament', Butler continued: 'The frequent levity of his expressions was certainly very repugnant not only to all the rules of religion but also to good sense. It gave general offence, but those who knew him, while they blamed and lamented his aberrations, did justice to his learning, to his friendly heart and guileless simplicity. Most unjustly has he been termed an infidel. He professed himself a trinitarian and believed in the resurrection, in the divine origin and divine mission of Christ in support of which he published a small tract. He also professed to believe what he termed the leading and unadulterated tenets of the Roman Catholic Church. From her — however scanty his creed might be — he did not so far recede as was generally thought', *Memoirs of the English. . . Catholics,* ed. 3, vol. 3, p. 417.
8. Dr Geddes was buried in a part of the cemetery to the south of the church. All the graves and remains in this area were removed in 1967 to make way for a new motorway. The coffins of a number of people considered to be of importance or interest were selected for reburial nearer the church while the rest were removed to another cemetery. Dr Geddes's grave with its handsome, horizontal stone of polished granite is now situated close to the south wall of the church. As the inscription indicates, there are buried with him Edward Holland Esq[re] formerly an officer in the Oxford Blues, died November 29th,

1814, aged 69, and his wife, Hester Holland, died April 5th, 1816, aged 67. They were presumably close friends of Geddes.
The inscription relating to Geddes reads as follows:

Rev. Alexander Geddes LL.D.,
Translator of Historical Books of the Old Testament
Died February 26th, 1802, aged 65
"Christian is my name and Catholic my surname,
I grant that you are a Christian as well as I,
and embrace you as my fellow disciple in Jesus,
and if you were not a disciple of Jesus,
still I would embrace you as my fellow man."

Extracted from his work.

Requiescat in Pace.
This stone is erected by his friend, Lord Petre, in 1804.

The quotation is taken from Dr Geddes's *General Answer*. . . The first line is from a letter of St Pacianus, Bishop of Barcelona,'Christianus mihi nomen est, Catholicus vero cognomen.' The passage continues: 'Illud me nuncupat istud ostendit,' *Epist. 1:4 ad Sympronianum* (Fourth Century). In the National Library of Scotland, Edinburgh, there is a sculptor's drawing for Dr Geddes's tombstone which however is quite different from that which was actually executed. The drawing also bears the epitaph (though it omits one line).

9. Writing to Dr Kirk, the Rev. J. Berington, a friend of Geddes, remarked: 'All his books and papers go to Lord Petre. What or whether anything was in the Press I have not heard,' Berington to Kirk, 12 March, 1802, Birmingham Diocesan Archives, C.1657.

10. Butler, *Historical Memoirs of the English. . . Catholics. . .* 3rd ed. 1822, vol. 4, p. 420. An earlier version of this passage is to be found in the Preface to the posthumous volume of Geddes's translation of the Psalms, published in 1807. M. D. Petre, in her life of the Ninth Lord Petre, writes (p. 54) that biblical manuscripts of Dr Geddes existed at Thorndon, one of Lord Petre's residences in Essex. Recent investigation however reveals no trace of these.

11. Henry Cotton, *Rhemes and Doway—an attempt to shew what has been done by Roman Catholics for the diffusion of the Scriptures in English*, Oxford, 1855, pp. 62ff.

12. In a fragment of verse preserved in the Petre archive (see p. 163), Geddes refers to his housekeeper as 'Betty'.

13. *Commentar über den Pentateuch von Johann Severin Vater*. See Bibliography.

14. See p. 114.

15. *Commentar. . .* vol. 3, section 90, Elohim- und Jehova-Urkunde in der Genesis, p. 717. H.-J. Kraus, *Geschichte. . .* 2te Aufl. p. 156.

16. Op. cit. vol. 3 pp. 673-681.

17. Alexander Westphal, *Les Sources du Pentateuch*, Étude de critique et d'histoire, I, Paris, 1888, p. 149.

18. *Die Urkunden des Jerusalemischen Tempelarchivs in ihrer Urgestalt*, 1798.

19. See Vater, *Commentar. . .* III, p. 700.

20. *Commentar. . .* I, p. 1.

21. Geddes's views were to have appeared in the *General Preface* which never reached publication.

22. G. L. Bauer, *Entwurf einer Hermeneutik des Alten und Neuen Testaments*. Leipzig, 1799, p. 1. Hartlich-Sachs, *Der Ursprung des Mythosbegriffes*, p. 71. Cf. J. Ernesti, *Institutio Interpretis Novi Testamenti*, 1761.

23. T. Sadler, *Diary, Reminiscences and Correspondence* of Henry Crabb Robinson, Barrister at Law, F.S.A., 1869, p. 156.

24. Bauer's two principles were: (1) He no longer interprets (as Eichhorn tended to do) supernatural events in natural terms — (or at least does so rarely) but relegates them to the realm of myth — as de Wette does. (2) In raising the question of the historical transmission, Bauer is, in effect, saying with de Wette that we have no proof of its accuracy or any means of recovering whatever historical basis may underlie the story. Hence one must treat the whole as myth.

25. Hartlich-Sachs, op. cit., p. 78. On these principles Bauer considered as myth, for example, narratives which attempted to describe the cause of things, the formation of the world, physical or moral evil on the earth, the communication of God or of heavenly spirits with men, the wonderful doings of the Patriarchs, the miracles of the Exodus. Of such accounts, Bauer thought the earlier were philosophical myths and the later, historical myths. Sometimes Bauer lapsed into the Naturalist explanation, in spite of Gabler's caution, but this, as Strauss noted, was mainly in the New Testament where Bauer was reluctant to deny the historical sense, op. cit., p. 86.

26. Rudolf Smend, *Wilhelm Martin Leberecht de Wettes Arbeit am Alten und am Neuen Testament*, Basel, 1957, p. 11.

27. *A Critical and Historical Introduction to the Canonical Scriptures of the Old Testament*, from the German of W. M. L. de Wette, 1843, vol. 2, p. 43. See Bibliography.

28. R. Smend, op. cit. p. 56.

29. Hartlich-Sachs, op. cit., pp. 95-97. Apparently, de Wette's only sure criterion for a historical basis was the existence of a parallel account, such as that of the death of Herod Agrippa in Josephus *Antiquities* XIX, ch. 7. But, clearly, parallels of this kind would be rare. In 1811 there appeared a defence of the historical basis against the purely mythical interpretation of the Old Testament books and especially the Pentateuch, G. W. Meyer, *Apologie der geschichtlichen Auffassung der historischen Bücher des Alten Testaments, besonders des Pentateuchs in Gegensatz gegen die blos mythische Deutung des Letzeren. Ein Beitrag zur Hermeneutik des Alten Testaments*, Sulzbach, 1811. The book was a penetrating analysis with clear rules. Without denying the mythical character, Meyer stressed that it was historical myth and the history could be recovered by the application of certain rules, Hartlich-Sachs, op. cit., p. 99.

30. R. Smend, op. cit., pp. 15-18.

31. R. Smend, op. cit., p. 30.

32. R. Smend, op. cit., p. 27. See above, p. 116.

33. See chapter 3, pp. 47ff.

34. See chapter 3, pp. 49ff.

35. De Wette, *Dissertatio critico-exegetica qua Deuteronomium a prioribus Pentateuchi libris diversum, alius cuiusdam recentioris auctoris opus esse monstratur*, 1805. Quoted in Smend, op. cit., p. 32. In this work, de Wette demonstrated the late date of Deuteronomy and assigned it to the seventh century B.C.

36. See chapter 3, p. 56.

37. On Vater, see above, p. 105. It should be recalled that Vater's long *Abhandlung* appeared in his *third* volume, i.e. shortly after the publication of de Wette's book on Deuteronomy. Nevertheless, while his *Dissertatio* was being printed, de Wette was able to insert a note about Vater's *Fragmentenhypothese* showing that he clearly favoured that theory, Kraus, op. cit., 2te Aufl., p. 156. Perhaps he had been able to see Vater's third volume in manuscript. In any case there was already sufficient material in vols 1 and 2, published in 1802. De Wette dealt with Vater's *Abhandlung* in his *Beiträge*, vol. 1, 1806, and vol. 2, 1807. Vol. 1 was entitled *Kritischer Versuch über die Glaubwürdigkeit der Bücher der Chronik mit Hinsicht auf die Geschichte der mosaischen Bücher und Gesetzgebung. Ein Nachtrag zu den Vaterschen Untersuchungen über den Pentateuch*, Halle, 1806. This work of Vater he considered the most thorough treatment 'Am vollständigsten ist die Untersuchung geführt worden von Vater', *Lehrbuch. . .*, 1822, 1, p. 233.

38. De Wette, *Lehrbuch der historisch kritischen Einleitung in die Bibel, Alten und Neuen Testaments*, Erster Teil, Die Einleitung in das Alte Testament enthaltend. Zweyte verbesserte Auflage, Berlin, 1822, p. 216.

39. Ibid.

40. *Lehrbuch. . .*, pp. 220-232.

Chapter Seven

1. A. O. J. Cockshut, *Religious Controversies of the Nineteenth Century*, 1966, pp. 33-35, quoting S. T. Coleridge, 'Lay Sermons'.

2. See page 87.

3. See Chapter 5, p. 100.
4. See below, note 20, a reference to Marsh's criticism.
5. See Chapter 5, p. 106.
6. E.g. Max Löhr, *Untersuchungen zum Hexateuchproblem*, I, Der Priesterkodex in der Genesis, Giessen, 1924.
7. J. E Carpenter–G. Harford, *The Composition of the Hexateuch*, 1902, pp. 70-71.
8. See Chapter 5, p. 109.
9. J. G. Eichhorn, *Einleitung*. . . 4th edition, 1823-4, vol. 3, pp. 219, 350. Whereas, in the third edition, only 50 pages or so were devoted to the books Exodus–Deuteronomy, no less than 200 are given to the subject in the fourth edition, mostly taken up with Vater's *Abhandlung*. On the question of the date of Deuteronomy, so decisively dealt with by de Wette, Eichhorn found himself unable to modify his earlier views to any significant extent, reasserting his previous statement that this book, more clearly than the others, pointed to Mosaic authorship, op. cit., pp. 220ff.
10. *Einleitung*. . . vol. 3, 4th ed., p. 347. On page 297 of this volume, there appears the only reference to Geddes which I have noticed. On the text Num 33:8 Eichhorn writes: 'Schon Geddes hat den Vers für ein anderwärts her erbogtes und nicht hieher gehöriges Fragment angesehen. Siehe Vater's *Commentar* bei d. St.' Evidently Eichhorn's notice was drawn by its presence in Vater's *Commentar* rather than in Geddes's own works which he certainly possessed.
11. See Chapter 5, p. 92.
12. See Chapter 5, p. 98; and a similar view expressed by Gabler, Chapter 5, p. 99.
13. Chapter 3, p. 49.
14. Chapter 3, pp. 46, 50, 51.
15. See Chapter 5, p. 110.
16. Once more it may be well to mention the relevant fact that Eichhorn had no part in writing the second edition of the *Urgeschichte*, see p. 140, note 48.
17. De Wette, *Beiträge zur Einleitung in das Alte Testament*, vol. 1, 1806. See above, p. 138, note 27.
18. W. Vatke, *Die Religion des Alten Testaments nach den kanonischen Büchern entwickelt*, vol. 1, Berlin, 1835.
19. Thus Edward Evanson, a graduate of Cambridge, raised a considerable outcry against himself by his criticism of the Anglican liturgy, his alleged denials of certain articles of belief and his critical views of the New Testament writings, most of which he regarded as 'spurious fiction of no authority and undeserving the attention of a disciple of Jesus Christ,' *The Dissonances of the Four generally received Evangelists and the Evidence of their respective Authenticity examined*, 1792, p. 287.
20. Herbert Marsh, after graduating at Cambridge, went to Leipzig in 1785 to study German biblical criticism. In 1793 he published the first volume of his translation of Michaelis's (4th edition, 1788) *Introduction to the New Testament*, with notes from his own pen. This work introduced British scholars to German critical study of the New Testament. The remaining three volumes were published between 1793 and 1801. In vol. 3 appeared the 'Dissertation on the Origin and Composition of the First Three Gospels' with Marsh's own theory. This was heavily attacked in England and Marsh was accused of fostering scepticism. In 1807 Marsh was elected Lady Margaret's Professor of Divinity in Cambridge in spite of his progressive ideas, and he did something to promote the proper use of critical principles. But he was aware of the limits imposed by circumstances. See H. Marsh, *Lectures on the Criticism and Interpretation of the Bible* with two preliminary lectures on theological study and theological arrangement. New edition, Cambridge 1828, with two new lectures on the History of Biblical Interpretation.
21. Letter of Eichhorn to Geddes, in J. M. Good, *Memoirs of Dr Geddes*, p. 542.
22. J. M. Good, op. cit., p. 539. See also List of Unpublished Material, p. 164
23. Sir William Hamilton wrote: 'It is well known to all who know anything of modern divinity that the theological writings of Eichhorn, especially his *Introduction to the Old Testament*, concentrate in the highest degree all that is peculiar and most obnoxious in the German school of biblical criticism — of which in fact he was while living the genuine representative, and distinguished leader. Sir W. Hamilton, 'On the Right of Dissenters to Admission into the English Universities', in *Discussions on Philosophy and Literature, Education and University Reform*,

1852, p. 508. Reprinted from the *Edinburgh Review* October 1834.

24. See F. Schleiermacher, *A Critical Essay on the Gospel of St Luke*, translated with an Introduction by the Translator (Bishop Thirlwall), 1825, p. viii. Perhaps it goes without saying that the poor opinion which the British had of German theologians was heartily reciprocated by the latter! Professor Anton Hartmann of Rostock, after dismissing Italy as a land sunk in superstition from which nothing was to be expected, then turned on England, formerly 'the teacher of Germany' but now showing a deplorable inactivity in the field of biblical criticism which all the brilliant and liberal ideas emerging from Germany have hardly touched at all, let alone disturbed. A. T. Hartmann, *Historisch-kritische Forschungen über die Bildung, das Zeitalter und den Plan der fünf Bücher Mose's, nebst einer beurteilenden Einleitung und einer genauen Characteristik der hebräischen Sagen und Mythen,* Rostock und Güstrow, 1831, pp. 58-59.

25. Mark Pattison, 'The Present State of Theology in Germany', in *Essays* collected and arranged by Henry Nettleship, 1889, vol. 2, p. 210. Reprinted from the *Westminster Review,* 1857.

26. F. W. Farrar, *History of Interpretation,* 1886, pp. 421-22. Bishop Thirlwall in a footnote to his remarks quoted above, observed: 'The last warning voice against the infection of German divinity was raised by Mr Conybeare in the Bampton Lectures for 1824. The candour and earnestness displayed by the author increase our regret that his studies had not led him to feel the necessity of acquiring the German language before he undertook that work, and that he was snatched away before he had an opportunity of enlarging and correcting his views…It would almost seem as if at Oxford the knowledge of German subjected a divine to the same suspicion of heterodoxy which we know was attached some centuries back to the knowledge of Greek; as if it was thought there, that a German theologian is dangerous enough when he writes in Latin, but that when he argues in his own language there is no escaping his venom', op. cit., p. ix.

27. E. B. Pusey, *An Historical Enquiry into the Probable Causes of the Rationalist Character lately predominant in the Theology of Germany,* Part II, 1830, p. 68. Pusey, who had studied Oriental languages at Göttingen, was himself trained in critical method. He explained what he regarded as German excesses in terms of a use of the principles of historical interpretation to the exclusion of others equally necessary. But Pusey's energies and ability were soon to be turned in other directions and the early promise was not followed up.

28. Johann Ernesti, *Institutio Interpretis Novi Testamenti,* 1761; J. S. Semler, *Apparatus ad liberalem Veteris Testamenti interpretationem,* 1773. See Chapter 4, p. 65.

29. See also p. 153, note 20.

30. Cf. Chapter 5, p. 83; and see p. 147, note 2.

31. S. T. Coleridge, *Confessions of an Inquiring Spirit,* edited from the author's manuscript by Henry Nelson Coleridge, London, 1840. *Letters on Inspiration,* Letter III, p. 32.

32. Op. cit., Letter IV, p. 44.

33. Op. cit., p. 48.

34. Op. cit., Letter VI, p. 75.

35. Geddes and the scholars who shared his views clearly regarded the doctrine of absolute and universal inspiration as incompatible with the conclusions drawn from an unbiased study of the text. The doctrine made it impossible, as we have seen, to ascribe error in the text to the human author, without incurring the charge that one was imputing error to God the primary author. (See for example, the quotation from Dean Burgon given below in note 37.)

Unfortunately, many of these scholars contented themselves with disposing of the doctrine without seriously attempting to provide an adequate substitute. In short, they were regarded by many people as simply abolishing inspiration altogether; and this of course made the supporters of absolute and universal inspiration more determined than ever to retain it. Geddes seems to have attempted to reconcile the doctrine of divine inspiration of the Scriptures with the possibility of error in the text by interpreting the influx in such a way as to make it indistinguishable from the inspiration normally associated with poets and other gifted writers, cf. p. 42.

Geddes does not appear to have considered the possibility of an inspiration which, while remaining a genuine gift of the Spirit, *peculiar* to the sacred writer, nevertheless allowed not only for the characteristics, contemporary and personal, of the writers, but also for the defects in accuracy inseparable from human writings, always provided of course that the divine message remained intact. Perhaps Geddes would have offered a more extended treatment of the subject in the *General Preface* which he often spoke about but never published. Richard Simon had made a determined attempt (a century earlier) to provide a harmony between inspiration and criticism, see p. 141, note 59.

36. The volume contained contributions from seven members of the Church of England, of which one may notice, II. *Bunsen's Biblical Researches,* by Dr R. Williams, Vice-Principal of St David's College, Lampeter; V. *On the Mosaic Cosmogony,* by C. W. Goodwin; VI. *Tendencies of Religious Thought in England,* by Mark Pattison; VII. *On the Interpretation of Scripture,* by B. Jowett, professor of Greek at Oxford.

37. He wrote: 'The Bible is none other than *the Voice of Him that sitteth upon the Throne!* Every Book of it, — every Chapter of it, — every Verse of it, — every word of it, — every syllable of it, — (*where* are we to *stop?*) — every letter of it — is the direct utterance of the Most High! . . . The Bible is none other than *the Word of God:* not some part of it, more, some part of it, less; but all alike, the utterance of Him who sitteth upon the Throne; — absolute, — faultless, — unerring, — supreme!' John William Burgon, *Inspiration and Interpretation,* Sermons preached before the University of Oxford, with preliminary remarks being an answer to a volume entitled *Essays and Reviews,* 1861, p. 89.

38. John William Colenso, Bishop of Natal, *The Pentateuch and Book of Joshua critically examined,* Part I, London, 1862. 'I believe', wrote Colenso, 'that there are not a few among the more highly educated classes of society in England, and multitudes among the more intelligent operatives, who are in danger of drifting into irreligion and practical atheism, under this dim sense of the unsoundness of the popular view, combined with a feeling of distrust of their spiritual teachers, as if *these must* be either ignorant of facts which to themselves are patent, or at least insensible to the difficulties which those facts involve or else being aware of their existence, and feeling their importance, are consciously ignoring them', Colenso, op. cit., Part I, Preface, p. 18 (edition of 1865).

Colenso affirmed that it was not the clash with science that made him re-examine Scripture; one *could* explain the latter as myth where necessary. No—it was the barbarous commands ascribed to God. 'The fact that such commands. . . were here attributed to the Fountain of all goodness was painfully forced on my mind. . . I felt that it was absolutely impossible to believe this without abandoning all trust in a righteous and perfect Being', J. W. Colenso, *Lectures on the Pentateuch,* 1873, Lecture VII, p. 112.

39. Thirlwall endorsed his critical principles while Tait maintained his right to express them, as also to retain his bishopric.

40. A. Geddes, *Critical Remarks,* p. v, quoted in Colenso, op. cit., Part II, 1863, facing beginning of Preface.

41. Op. cit., Preface.

42. D. Moore, *The Divine Authority of the Pentateuch Vindicated,* 1863, p. vi.

43. See Chapter 5, p. 95.

44. Andrew Dickson White, *A History of the Warfare of Science with Theology in Christendom,* 1896, reprinted 1960, Introduction, p. v.

45. Samuel Rolles Driver, *An Introduction to the Literature of the Old Testament,* Edinburgh, 1891.

46. A. D. White, op. cit., vol. 2, p. 327.

47. *Dr Geddes's Address to the Public,* 1793, p. 1.

LISTS OF WORKS, ETC.

PUBLISHED WORKS OF DR ALEXANDER GEDDES

With an indication of libraries where copies may be found.

1774 *Letters on Usury and Interest.* Printed by J. P. Coghlan in Duke St., Grosvenor Sq., and sold by R. Snagg, Paternoster Row, and W. Drummond of Edinburgh. Being a series of letters originally published in the *Edinburgh Weekly Magazine* in reply to letters against taking interest written by an Irish Dominican called Albert Hope under the nom de plume of John Simple. Geddes wrote letters 5 and 7 under the nom de plume of Simon Sober. (Copies in SCA and St Mary's College, Blairs, Aberdeen.)

1779 *A Memorial to the Public in behalf of the Roman Catholics of Edinburgh and Glasgow.* Published by J. P. Coghlan, London, 1779.

Select Satires of Horace, translated into English verse and for the most part adapted to the present times and manners. Printed for the Author by Strahan and published by T. Cadell in the Strand. (Copies in British Museum, Nat. Library of Scotland and Scottish Catholic Archives.)

1781 *Linton, A Tweeddale Pastoral.* A Poem written on the occasion of the birth of a son and heir to Lord Traquaire. Published by C. Elliot of Edinburgh. (Copy in the SCA.)

1782 *Idea of a New English Edition of the Holy Bible for the Use of the Roman Catholics of Great Britain and Ireland.* Printed privately in London. (Copy in Ushaw College Library, Durham.)

1783 *Cursory Remarks on a Late Fanatical Publication entitled, 'A Full Detection of Popery',* and submitted to the candid perusal of the liberal minded or every denomination. London, printed for the Author and sold by Keating in Air St.; Faulder in New Bond St; Debrett in Piccadilly; Wilkie in St Paul's Churchyard &c. Price One Shilling. (Copies in Edinburgh University Library, British Museum.)

1786 *Prospectus of a New Translation of the Holy Bible from corrected Texts of the Originals, compared with the Ancient Versions, With Various Readings, Explanatory Notes and Critical Observations.* Printed for the Author and sold by R. Faulder, Bond St., London; by C. Eliot, Edinburgh; and —Cross, Dublin. (Copies in SCA: Nat. Library of Scotland; Ushaw College; Aberdeen University Library; Cambridge University Library; Bodleian Library, Oxford; Trinity College, Dublin, Oscott College, Sutton Coldfield, British Museum, Glasgow University Library.)

1787 *Rev Alexander Geddes LL.D. de Vulgarium Sacrae Scripturae Versionum vitiis, eorumque remediis libellus. Ex anglico vertit et notas quasdam adjecit Presbyter et Monachus Ordinis Benedicti.* Bambergae, ap. Vinc. Dederich. This is a translation of the *Prospectus* with additional notes. (Copy in the Staatl. Bibliothek, Bamberg. Xerox copy of this in Cambridge University Library.)

A Letter to the Right Reverend the Lord Bishop of London, containing Queries, Doubts and Difficulties relative to a Vernacular Version of the Holy Scriptures, being an Appendix to 'A Prospectus . . .'. London, printed by J. Davis for Robert Faulder, New Bond Street. (Copies in SCA; Cambridge University Library; Oscott College Library; British Museum; Bodleian Library, Oxford.)

A Letter to the Rev. Dr Priestley in which the Author attempts to prove by one prescriptive argument that the divinity of Jesus Christ was a primitive tenet of Christianity. London, printed for the Author and sold by R. Faulder, N. Bond St; J. Johnson, St Paul's Churchyard and C. Eliot in the Strand. (Copies in SCA, Nat. Library of Scotland, Ushaw College, Aberdeen University, Oscott College, British Museum, Trinity College, Dublin.)

1787 *A Letter to a Member of Parliament on the Case of the Protestant Dissenters and the Expediency of a General Repeal of all Penal Statutes that regard Religious Opinions.* London, R. Faulder in N. Bond St. (Copies in Ushaw College; Cambridge University Library; British Museum; Bodleian Library, Oxford.)

1788f. *Analytical Review.* Geddes published in this review articles on a variety of subjects and many book reviews. In 1788, 13; in 1789, 14; in 1790, 6; in 1791, 10; in 1792, 2; in 1793, 2. A complete list is printed in J. M. Good *Memoirs of Dr Alexander Geddes*, London, 1803, pp. 193-194. The Review was published by J. Johnson.

1788 July *Proposals for printing by subscription a New Translation of the Holy Bible* from corrected texts of the originals, with various readings, explanatory notes and critical observations; and with Specimens of the Work. London, printed for the author by J. Davis and sold by R. Faulder of Bond St and J. Johnson, St Paul's Churchyard.

Dec. A New Edition of the above 'with a specimen of the work', (i.e. some of the specimens of the first edition were omitted, only that from Genesis was included). (Copies in SCA, Aberdeen University, Cambridge University, Oscott College, British Museum, Glasgow University.)

1790 *An Answer to the Bishop of Comana's Pastoral Letter by a Protesting Catholic*. London, for R. Faulder and J. P. Coghlan. (Copies in Oscott College, British Museum, Cambridge University Library, Bodleian Library, Oxford.)

Dr Geddes's General Answer to the Queries, Counsils and Criticisms that have been communicated to him since the publication of his Proposals for printing a New Translation of the Bible. London, printed for the author by J. Davis, and sold by R. Faulder. . . and J. Johnson. (Copies in SCA, Aberdeen University, Cambridge University, Oscott College, British Museum, Glasgow University, Trinity College, Dublin, National Library of Scotland.)

1790 *A Letter to the RR. the Archbishops and Bishops of England*, pointing out the only sure means of preserving the Church from the Dangers that now threaten her. By an Upper Graduate. London, J. Johnson. (Copies in British Museum, Bodleian Library, Oxford.)

Carmen Saeculare pro Gallica Gente tyrannidi aristocraticae erepta. . . A Secular Ode on the French Revolution translated from the original Latin. Londinii, apud J. Johnson et Parisiis, apud Barois Juniorem. Composed in Horatian Sapphics. (Copies in SCA, Aber-

deen University, Cambridge University, Oscott College, British Museum, Glasgow University.)

1790 *Epistola Macaronica ad fratrem, de iis quae gesta sunt in Nupero Dissentientium Conventu*. Londini habito, apud J. Johnson ab aede Divi Pauli. 1790. Latin with Eng. tr. 1790. (Copies in Cambridge University, Oscott College.)

Epistola Macaronica. . ., with an English Version for the use of the ladies and country gentlemen. (Copies in SCA, Ushaw College, Aberdeen University, British Museum.)

A First Epistle of Simpkin to his dear Brother Simon in Wales. Smithfield, Feb. 29, 1790. (Copy in Oscott College.)

1791 *A Second Epistle of Simkin to his dear Brother Simon in Wales.* London, J. P. Coghlan. (Copy in Oscott College.)

Encyclical Letter of the Bishops of Rama, Acanthos and Centuriae to the Faithful Clergy and Laity of their respective Districts, with a continued Commentary for the Use of the Vulgar. London. Sold for the benefit of a poor clergyman. By J. Bell, Oxford St, opposite Bond St. (Copies in Birmingham Diocesan Archives, British Museum, National Library of Scotland.)

Considerations on the Present Situation of the English Catholics and on the best means of improving it. July 1791. (Copy in Essex County Record Office, Chelmsford. D/DP. F.187.

1792 *A Norfolk Tale, or a Journey from London to Norwich*, with a Prologue and an Epilogue, dedicated to one of the most amiable young ladies in Gt Britain by one of her greatest admirers. London, from J. Johnson and R. Faulder. (Copies in Oscott College, Glasgow University.)

The First Book of the Iliad of Homer, verbally rendered into English verse, being a specimen of a new translation of that poet: with critical annotations. London, Debrett. (Copy in the British Museum.)

The Holy Bible; or the Books accounted sacred by Jews and Christians; otherwise called the Books of the Old and New Covenants: faithfully translated from corrected texts of the originals, with various readings explanatory notes and critical remarks. Vol. I. Printed for the author by J. Davis and sold by R. Faulder and J. Johnson. Contains Genesis to Joshua inclusive. (Copies in Cambridge University Lib; Emmanuel College, Cambridge, Oscott College, National Library of Scotland, New College, Edinburgh, British Museum.)

1792 *Carmen Saeculare Alterum, pro anno libertatis quarto.* Eleutheropoli, 1792. 'Duci Dumouriero de Patria optime merito, hocce Carmen Saeculare dicat concivis auctor', Scripsi, pridie Id. Jul, 1792. (Copy in Oscott College.)

Three Scottish Poems with a previous Dissertation on the Scoto-Saxon dialect. Published in *Transactions of the Scottish Society of Antiquaries*, vol. 1, p.402.

Three Poems; Epistle to the President, The First Eklog of Virgil and The First Idyllion of Theokritus (all in Skottis verse!) published in the same volume as above. (Copies in Aberdeen University, Cambridge University; bound in W. Smellie, *Account of the Institutions and Progress of the Society of Scottish Antiquaries*.)

An Apology for Slavery, or six cogent arguments against immediate abolition of the Slave Trade. (an ironic work.) London, J. Johnson. (Copy in British Museum.)

L'Avocat du Diable. The Devil's Advocate or Satan versus Pictor Tried before the Court of Uncommon Pleas. In verse by A.G. London, J. Johnson. (Copy in British Museum.)

1793 *Carmina Saecularia Tria, pro tribus celeberrimis Libertatis Galliae Epochis.* (Includes the two earlier ones and adds a third. Mentioned by J. M. Good, *Memoirs of Dr Geddes*, and with translations, pp. 316f. But I have not been able to trace a copy.)

Ver-Vert or the Parrot of Nevers, a poem in four cantos, freely translated from the French of J. B. Gresset, by A. G. Oxford, for J. Cooke and sold by J. Bell and J. Johnson. Two editions. (Copies in SCA and Oscott College.)

1793 *Dr Geddes's Address to the Public*, on the publication of the first volume for his New Translation of the Bible. London, printed for J. Johnson, St Paul's Churchyard. (Copies in SCA, Cambridge Uni-

versity, Oscott College, British Museum, Trinity College, Dublin.)

1794 *Letter from the Rev. Alexander Geddes LL.D. to the Right Rev. John Douglass, Bishop of Centuriae and Vicar Apostolic of the London District.* London, printed for the author; and sold by R. Faulder, New Bond St; and J. Johnson St Paul's Churchyard. (Copies in SCA, Cambridge University, Oscott College, British Museum, Glasgow University.)

The Ordinances of the R.C. Bishops for the . . . General Fast.

1795 *Ode to the Hon. Thomas Pelham*, occasioned by his speech in the Irish House of Commons on the Catholic Bill. (Copy in Cambridge University Library.)

Ode Pindarico-Sapphico-Macaronica in Gulielmi Pitii &c Laudem. Translation of same. *Morning Chronicle*, Jan. 13th and 30th.

1796 *A Sermon preached before the University of Cambridge by H. W. C——t D.D., &c published by request; and now (for the sake of Freshmen and the Laity) by request translated into English Metre.* By H. H. Hopkins. London, A. M. Kearsley. (Copy in British Museum.)

1797 *The Holy Bible, or the Books accounted sacred by Jews and Christians: otherwise called the Books of the Old and New Covenants: faithfully translated from corrected texts of the originals with various readings, explanatory notes and critical remarks.* Volume II. London, R. Faulder. Includes Jud, Kgs, Chr, Ruth & Prayer of Manasseh.) (Copies in Cambridge University Library, National Library of Scotland, British Museum.)

Brother Burke to Brother Windham, in *Morning Chronicle*, Jan. 1797.

The Battle of B-ng-r or the Church's Triumph, a comic-heroic poem, in nine cantos. London, for J. Johnson, St Paul's Churchyard and J. Bell in Oxford St. (Copies in Oscott College, British Museum.)

1798 *A New Year's Gift to the good People of England*, a sermon, or something like a sermon, in Defence of the present War, preached on the Day of public Thanksgiving by Theomophilus Brown, Curate of P——n. (Copy in Cambridge University Library.)

1799 *A Sermon preached on the Day of the General Fast, Feb. 27th 1799* by Theomphilus Brown, formerly Curate, now Vicar of P——n.
The Abolition of Saints' Days, in *Morning Chronicle*, Mar 5th.
Epistle to Sir Walter Farquhar, Bart, in *Morning Chronicle*, Nov 11th.

1800 *Critical Remarks on the Hebrew Scriptures corresponding with a new translation of the Bible*, Vol. I, containing remarks on the Pentateuch, by the Rev. Alexander Geddes. London. Printed for the Author by David Wilks and Taylor: and sold by R. Faulder, New Bond St. and J. Johnson. St. Paul's Churchyard. (Copies in National Library of Scotland, Aberdeen University, Cambridge University, Oscott College, Glasgow University, British Museum.)
A Modest Apology for the Roman Catholic of Great Britain, addressed to all moderate Protestants, particularly to the members of both Houses of Parliament. London, printed for the author and sold by Davis, Taylor and Wilks, Chancery Lane. (Copies in Aberdeen University [with MS notes by Horne Tooke], Cambridge University, Oscott College, British Museum, National Library of Scotland.) Translated into German by H. E. G. Paulus (see letter, Geddes to Paulus, 15 July 1801, in Heidelberg Universitätsbibliothek).
Bardomachia; Poema Macaronico-Latinum. London, J. Johnson. (Copies in Cambridge University Library, British Museum.)
Bardomachia . . . translated into English verse.

1801 Poem. *In Obitum honestissimi, integerrimi, meique amicissimi Domini De Petre.* At the end of the poem is written: 'scribebam in lectulo, dolens et infirmus; Prid. Non. Jul. 1801'. Printed with English trans, in J. M. Good, *Memoirs of Dr Alexander Geddes* and in *Monthly Magazine*, Sept. 1801.
Ad Umbram Gilberti Wakefield Elegia, with an English trans.
Elegy on the Death of Gilbert Wakefield, published in the *Gentleman's Magazine*, Nov. 1801 under the signature of Musaeus Junior; also in J. M. Good, *Memoirs* . . ., pp. 510-518.
Paci feliciter reduci Ode Sapphica, auctore A. G. (translated into English by J. Ring); cf. J. M. Good, *Memoirs*. . ., p. 506 (See below).
'Fugitive Pieces' listed by J. M. Good, *Memoirs*. . ., p. 470, omitting only those already mentioned above, whose dates are known.
The Northern Hunt, or Brunswick Beagles.
The Blessings of a Free Press.
Trial by Jury.

'TRANSLATED' BY DR GEDDES

1785 *Mémoire de Mr Gordon, Principal du Collège des Ecossois à Paris, pour servir de réponse à l'invective de M.l'évêque Hay contre les supérieurs et les élèves du dit Collège.* (Copy in SCA, Edinburgh.) Later, Geddes claimed he only helped Gordon put it into French, and tried to moderate his language but without success.

POSTHUMOUS

1802 *Ode to Peace.* An English translation of *Paci feliciter.* . . made by J. Ring. (Copy in British Museum.)
1804 Letter of A. Geddes to G. Wakefield (see above, p. 149, note 54) written 14 April 1801, published in *Memoirs of the Life of Gilbert Wakefield*, 2nd ed., 1804, vol.I, p. 257.
1804 *A New Translation of the Psalms* (1-118) from corrected texts of the originals, with occasional annotations. Edited by John Disney D.D. and Charles Butler, who contribute a joint Foreword. London, J. Johnson. (Copies in the National Library of Scotland, Edinburgh, SCA. Cambridge University Library, Oscott College, The British Museum.) Psalms 1-118:11 were prepared by Geddes. Psalms 118:12-150 are by Bishop Wilson with some changes by Geddes.
1808 Letter of A. Geddes to Thomas Brand-Hollis, written 2 Oct. 1801, printed in Dr John Disney's *Memoir of Thomas Brand-Hollis*, 1808.
1963 *The Book of Zaknim* (i.e. The Book of Elders). A satirical account of a meeting in 1775 held by the Administrators of the Scottish Clergy Fund, written in the style of the Authorized Version. The

curious vocalising of the Hebrew word for elders (*zaknim*) is in accord with the system of Masclef, much in vogue in the early part of the 18th century, when the work of the Masoretes was widely held to be suspect, cf. François Masclef, *Grammatica hebraica a punctis aliisque inventis Massoreticis libera*, ed. 2da 1731. This essay of Geddes could not fail to annoy Bishop Hay, even though it remained in manuscript in his lifetime. The essay was printed in *The Innes Review*, 14 (1963), pp. 131-164 and edited by the Rev. W. J. Anderson M.A., Curator of the Scottish Catholic Archives.

UNPUBLISHED MANUSCRIPT MATERIAL

[Unless otherwise mentioned, all the material is preserved in the Scottish Catholic Archives, 16 Drummond Place, Edinburgh. There were no file or reference numbers at the Scottish Catholic Archives at the time this list was compiled. References to documents in other archives will be given as they occur. Those numbers indicated by an asterisk refer to Birmingham Diocesan Archives).

I. Letters Written by Dr A. Geddes

1767	Feb. 4	to Bishop George Hay	from Traquair
1770	Jan. 27	to Bishop James Grant	from Auchinhalrig
	Feb. 28	to Bishop James Grant	from Auchinhalrig
	Mar. 4	to Bishop James Grant	from Auchinhalrig
	Apr. 20	to Bishop James Grant	from Fochabers
	Aug. 31	to Henry Home, Lord Kames	From Fochabers
		(Abercairney Collection, Edinburgh Record Office)	
1771	Mar. 7	to Bishop James Grant	from Auchinhalrig
	Mar. 20	to Bishop James Grant	from Auchinhalrig
	Mar. 27	to Bishop James Grant	from Auchinhalrig
	Oct. 2	to Bishop James Grant	from Auchinhalrig
1772	Mar. 3	to John Reid at Preshome	from Auchinhalrig
	Oct. 23	to Charles Cruikshank	from Auchinhalrig
1773	Dec. 9	to Bishop George Hay	from Fochabers
	Feb. 7	to Bishop George Hay	from Fochabers
	Feb. 19	to Bishop George Hay	from Fochabers
	Mar. 14	to John Reid	from Fochabers
	Mar. 27	to Bishop George Hay	from Fochabers
1775	Sept. 27	to Bishop George Hay	from Fochabers
1777	Sept. 10	to Bishop George Hay	from Fochabers
	n.d.	to Bishop George Hay	from Fochabers
1779	Mar. 8	to John Reid	from Edinburgh
	Apr. 3	to John Reid	from London
	May 4	to John Reid	from London
	Sept. 22	to Bishop George Hay	from Auchinhalrig
	Oct. 16	to George Mathieson	from Edinburgh
	Nov. 2	to Bishop George Hay	from Edinburgh
	Nov. 14	to Bishop George Hay	from Edinburgh
	Dec. 4	to Bishop George Hay	from Edinburgh
	Dec. 15	to Bishop George Hay	from Edinburgh
1780	Jan. 2	to Bishop George Hay	from Edinburgh
	May 7	to Bishop George Hay	from Edinburgh
	May 12	to Bishop George Hay	from Edinburgh
	June 14	to Bishop George Hay	from Aberdeen
	June 22	to Bishop George Hay	from Aberdeen
	June 22	to Mr Mathieson	from Aberdeen
	June 24	to John Reid	from Aberdeen
	June 25	to J. Thomson	from Aberdeen
	July 10	to John Reid	from Aberdeen
	July 12	to Bishop George Hay	from Aberdeen
	July 22	to J. Thomson	from Dundee
	Aug. 4	to his father	from Edinburgh
	n.m.	to Bishop George Hay	from Blackfriars Wynd, Edinburgh
	Aug. 7	to ? ?	from Edinburgh

(re Mrs Inchbald [an actress] (British Museum Add. 28, 588).

Date	To	From
Aug. 29	to Bishop George Hay	from Traquair
Sept. 3	to John Reid	from Traquair
Oct. 10	to to John Reid	from Traquair
Nov. 27	to John Reid	from Traquair
Dec. ?	to John Reid	from Edinburgh
Dec./end	to John Reid	from Edinburgh
Dec. 20	to Bishop George Hay	from Edinburgh
1781 Jan. 3	to Bishop George Hay	from Edinburgh
Jan. 20	to John Reid	from Edinburgh
June 8	to John Reid	from London
June 5	to a 'friend'	from London
	(i.e. his cousin B'p J. Geddes)	
1782 July 23	to Bishop J. Geddes	from London
Jan. 26	to Bishop J. Geddes	from London
Feb. 12	to Bishop J. Geddes	from London
Apr. 10	to Bishop J. Geddes	from London
Apr. 22	to Bishop J. Geddes	from London
May 7	to Bishop J. Geddes	from London
Aug. 8	to Bishop J. Geddes	from London
Sept. 14	to Bishop J. Geddes	from London
Nov. 17	to Bishop J. Geddes	from London
Nov. 29	to John Reid	from London
Nov. 30	to Bishop J. Geddes	from London
Dec. 19	to Bishop J. Geddes	from London
1783 Jan. 9	to Bishop J. Geddes	from London
May 6	to Bishop J. Geddes	from London
July 18	to Bishop J. Geddes	from Manchester
Aug. 11	to Bishop J. Geddes	from Traquair
Aug. 25	to Bishop J. Geddes	from Glasgow
Oct. 22	to Bishop J. Geddes	from London
Dec. 25	to Bishop J. Geddes	from London
1784 Jan 9	to Bishop J. Geddes	from London
Feb. 16	to Bishop J. Geddes	from London
Feb. 25	to John Reid?	from London

Date	To	From
Feb. 27	to Bishop J. Geddes	from London
Mar. 6	to Bishop J. Geddes	from London
Mar. 20	to ?	from London
Mar. 20	to Bishop J. Geddes	from London
Mar. 29	to Bishop J. Geddes	from London
Mar./end	to Bishop George Hay	from London
Apr. 8	to Bishop J. Geddes	from London
Apr. 12	to Bishop George Hay	from London
Apr. 18	to Bishop George Hay	from London
Apr. 30	to Bishop J. Geddes	from London
May 14	to Bishop J. Geddes	from London
May 27	to John Reid	from London
May 28	to Bishop J. Geddes	from London
June 7	to John Reid	from London
June 8	to Bishop J. Geddes	from London
June 20	to Bishop J. Geddes	from near London
July 22	to Bishop J. Geddes	from London
Aug. 14	to Bishop J. Geddes	from London
Sept. 21	to Bishop J. Geddes	from London
Sept. 23	to John Reid	from London
Oct. 26	to Bishop J. Geddes	from London
Nov. 5	to John Reid	from London
Nov. 5	to Bishop J. Geddes	from London
Nov. 9	to Bishop J. Geddes	from London
Nov. 12	to Bishop J. Geddes	from London
Nov. 16	to Bishop J. Geddes	from London
Nov. 18	to Bishop J. Geddes	from London
Nov. 22	to Bishop J. Geddes	from London
Nov. 23	to a Bishop of the Episcopal Church	from London
Nov. 29	to John Reid	from London
Nov. 30	to Bishop J. Geddes	from London
Dec. 23	to John Reid	from London
Dec. 24	to Augustine Jenison	from London

Year	Date	To	From
1785	Dec. ?	to Lady Findlater	from London
	Mar. 3	to Bishop J. Geddes	from London
	Mar. 31	to Bishop J. Geddes	from London
	June 11	to Bishop J. Geddes	from London
	June 28	to Bishop J. Geddes	from London
	Oct. 5	to Bishop J. Geddes	from Glasgow
	Oct. 10	to Bishop J. Geddes	from Glasgow
	Oct. 23	to Bishop J. Geddes	from Glasgow
	Dec. 7	to Bishop J. Geddes	from Glasgow
1786	Jan. 9	to Bishop J. Geddes	from Glasgow
	Jan. 12	to Bishop J. Geddes	from Glasgow
	Jan. 18	to Bishop J. Geddes	from Glasgow
	Feb. 27	to Dr Kirk (*C.880)	from London
	Feb. 28	to Bishop J. Geddes	from London
	Mar. 18	to Bishop J. Geddes	from London
	Mar. 28	to John Reid	from London
	Apr. 25	to Bishop J. Geddes	from London
	Apr. 27	to Dr Kirk (*C.884)	from London
	May 1	to John Reid?	from London
	May 9	to John Reid?	from London
	June 17	to Dr Kirk (*C.886)	from London
	June 23	to John Reid?	from London
	June 26	to John Reid?	from London
	June 30	to Bishop J. Geddes	from London
	June 15	to Bishop J. Geddes	from London
	Aug. 22	to Bishop J. Geddes	from London
	Sept. 12	to Bishop J. Geddes	from London
	Oct. 2	to Dr Kirk (*C.893)	from London
	Nov. 1	to Dr Kirk (*C.896)	from London
	Nov. 29	to Dr Kirk (*C.897)	from London
	Dec. 4	to John Reid	from London
	Dec. 9	to Bishop J. Geddes	from London
1787	Jan. 12	to Dr Kirk (*C.897)	from London
	Jan. 29	to Dr Kirk (*C.900)	from London
	Feb. 15	to Bishop J. Geddes	from London
	Mar. 10	to Bishop J. Geddes	from London
	June 10	to Dr Kirk (*C.907)	from London
	Aug. 21	to Dr J. Kirk (*C.910)	from London
	Oct. 3	to abate Thomson? (Rome)	from London
	Dec. 6	to Dr Kirk (*C.913)	from London
1788	Jan. 28	to John Reid	from London
	Jan. 29	to the Rev. Mr Arthur	from London

(about the transcription of Wickliffe, by a certain James Telfer. The letter is attached to a receipt by J. Telfer for £3-2-0. Preserved in Glasgow Univ. Library, ref. no. 8959.)

Year	Date	To	From
	Apr. 15	to Bishop J. Geddes	from London
	May 19	to John Reid	from London
	June 16	to Bishop J. Geddes	from London
	Aug. 19	to Bishop J. Geddes	from London
	Sept. 12	to Bishop J. Geddes	from London
	Oct. 26	to Dr Kirk (*C.931)	from London
	Nov. 28	to Bishop John Geddes	from London
	n.m.?	to Dr Kirk (*C.933)	from London
1789	Jan. 17	to Bishop J. Geddes	from London
	May 23	to Rudolph Erich Raspe	from London

(*Nat. Lib. Edin.* S.N.P.G. Watson Autographs. Literary & Scientific, 912-1036 MS 584, fol. 1008.)

Year	Date	To	From
	n.m.	to Mr Woods	

(*Nat. Lib. Edin.* Autographs and Portraits, MS 967, fol. 184)

Year	Date	To	From
	Nov. 13	to Bishop J. Geddes	from London
	Nov. 20	to Bishop J. Geddes	from London
	Dec. 21	to Bishop J. Geddes	from London
1790	Jan. 18	to Bishop J. Geddes	from London
	Nov. 29	to Bishop J. Geddes	from London
1791	July 5	to Bishop J. Geddes	from London
	Nov. 30	to Bishop J. Geddes	from Thorndon
1792	n.m.	to Dr Kirk (*C.1124)	from London
	n.m.	to Dr Kirk (*C.1130)	from London
1793	Jan. 21	to Dr Kirk (*C.1259)	from London

Unpublished Manuscript Material

II. Other Papers Written by Dr A. Geddes

1. 1768. A 'Memorial' in the form of a letter to the Spanish Ambassador in London, written in French and drawn up by John and Alexander Geddes, concerning the recovery of the Scots College in Madrid. This Memorial is referred to in J. F. S. Gordon *Scotichronicon*, IV, p. 69, col. 1, and in M. Taylor, *The Scots College in Spain*, 1971, p. 53. It seems probable that John Geddes was mainly responsible for the contents of the document, while Alexander Geddes, newly returned from Paris, undertook the task of putting it into French.

2. 1778. *The Book of Zaknim*. A satirical account, written in the language of the Authorized Version of the Bible, of the meeting of the Administrators of the Scottish Clergy Fund. Printed for the first time in the *Innes Review* 14 (1963). The MS is in the Scottish Catholic Archives. (See also above in the list of Geddes's publications.)

3. 1785. *A short account of the Glasgow Octateuch*. A description filling ten octavo pages bound into the volume containing the MS. The MS (c. 1400–1450) contains the first eight books of the LXX. It is preserved in Glasgow University Library.

4. Two boxes of various writings, preserved in the Petre Archives, Essex County Record Office, Chelmsford, Essex. Box no. 1 contains papers on historical subjects and rough notes on biblical matters but nothing of importance. Box no. 2 contains a large number of poems very few of which have been printed. Among these are: An Epistle to the King, a poem in English iambics, written in 1799; poems in honour of the Duchess of Gordon; poems, often humorous about various acquaintances and a humorous poem about himself, his untidy habits and the efforts of his housekeeper to correct these. The Archive reference is: D/DP Z. 57.

Note. The Petre Archives at Ingatestone and Thorndon were transferred to the Essex County Record Office some years ago. M. D. Petre in her book *The Ninth Lord Petre* (1928) refers to biblical manuscripts of Dr Geddes preserved at Thorndon (p. 54). There are none there now; nor are they to be found in the Petre Archives at the Record Office.

| 1794 | May 5 | to Dr Kirk (*C.1297) | from London |
| 1798 | Dec. 6 | to Dr Kirk (*C.1512) | from London |

Letters undated but probably written in the 1790s
Preserved in Edinburgh University Library

n.y.	July 10	to Mr G. Dyer	from London
	n.d.	to J. Johnson	
	n.d.	to James Cumming (LA II 82/ 4)	
	n.d.	to J. Constable (LA IV 17)	

Twelve Letters to Miss Howard
Preserved in the National Library of Scotland, Edinburgh.
Classification number: MSS 10099, for this group

1792?	n.m.	
1792	Oct. 12	from Norwich
1793	Apr. 1	from London
	May 15	from Oxford
	July 16	
	Aug 22	from London

Also five letters or notes
undated probably sent in 1793

| 1800 | Oct. 24 | from London. |

Letters from Geddes to Prof. H. E. G. Paulus of Jena
Preserved in the Universitätsbibliothek, Heidelberg

1798	Sept. 14	(sent, 'favour of Mr Coleridge')	from London
1801	June 11		from London
	July 15		from London.

Reference: Heid. HS 855

III. *Letters and Documents about Dr A. Geddes*

1780　*Attested Account by Bishop George Hay* of the circumstances leading to the departure of Dr Geddes from Auchinhalrig. Preserved in the Scottish Catholic Archives among the 'Banff Affair' papers. There are also many letters from and to Hay concerning the same affair.

1781　Jan. 6. *Letter of Bishop George Hay to Bishop James Talbot, Vicar Apostolic of the London District*, written from Aberdeen, in which Hay gives a very long, detailed and somewhat slanted account of the Banff Affair which led to Geddes's departure for London. Preserved in Westminster Cathedral Archives, reference no. MS vol. XLVII, 1781-1789.

1782-83　*Lady Traquaire's Diary*, preserved in the Archives of Traquair House, Peebles, Scotland. Geddes had left Scotland in 1781 and corresponded frequently with Lady Traquaire for the first year or two. Then the Traquaires came south to London for a prolonged stay before finally leaving England for France and Spain.

1782ff.　*Sir John Throckmorton's Diaries. 1st Diary*, 1782-86 (Jan.); *2nd Diary*, 1786 (Feb.)-1792 (July). Also his *1st Common Place Book*, 1792 (July)-1798 (July); and *2nd Common Place Book*, 1798 (July)-1811. Contain mostly entries of dinner guests or places where he dined and journeys taken abroad. The entries referring to Dr Geddes are between the years 1786 and 1801. Preserved in the Archives at Coughton Court, Warwickshire.

1788　The *Reisejournal of Professor H. E. G. Paulus*, containing an account of his visit to England in 1788 (21st April-21st Oct.). The pages referring to Geddes, whom he visited many times during these months, are: vol. 2, pp. 23, 234, 237, 242, 253, 366f., 375, 377f. Preserved in the Universitätsbibliothek, Heidelberg.

1791　*Protestation of the English Catholics*. A Declaration of loyalty to the Crown and a denial of many beliefs and tenets commonly attributed to them, signed in 1791 by several thousand of the R.C. community in England. The last signature is that of Dr Geddes who took it the British Museum at the direction of the Catholic Committee, where it was lodged, against the express wishes of the Vicars Apostolic. It is still preserved there. The document, which is of great length, consists of parchment sheets sewn end to end. Ref. Add. MS 5416. B. 9.

1792ff.　*Bishop Douglass's Diary* (1792-1802), preserved in Westminster Cathedral Archives, Z. 1, contains various references to Bishop Douglass's dealings with Dr Geddes and in particular has an account of his death, see ch. 1, p. 1.

1802　March 19th. *Letter from Andrew John Geddes OSB* monk of the Scots Abbey in Würzburg (Herbipolis) and brother of Dr A. Geddes, to Professor H. E. G. Paulus informing him of Dr Geddes's death. Preserved in the Universitätsbibliothek, Heidelberg, ref. Heid. Hs. 855.

1803　Oct. 15th. *Account of the Death of the Rev. Alexander Geddes* written in French by the abbé de St Martin, and now preserved in the Archives of the 'Old Brotherhood', a purely honorary association of senior priests in England, successor to the 'Old Chapter' of the days before the restoration of the Hierarchy (1850). All the papers in these Archives are now available on microfilm. The abbé was the only priest to be admitted to Dr Geddes's bedside. Good's account in his *Memoirs of Dr Geddes* is very inaccurate, since Good knew no French and the abbé knew little English.

1804　*A Catalogue of the Entire, Extensive and Valuable Library of the late Alexander Geddes D.D.* (sic), *translator of the Bible; Author of the Critical Remarks of the Hebrew Scriptures, &c. &c.* which will be sold by auction by Leigh, Sotheby and Son, at their house in York Street, Covent Garden, on Monday, March 26th, 1804, and five following days (Sunday excepted), at 12 o'clock. To be viewed on Thursday, March 22 to the Time of Sale. Catalogues to be had of Mr. Cook, Oxford; Mr. Deighton, Cambridge, and at the place of sale. [Note. This Catalogue (as already stated) is preserved in the Bodleian Library, Oxford. It has a unique interest as an illustration of the range of books selected by an 18th century Roman Catholic biblical scholar, trained in Paris.]

IV. *Letters and Documents relating to the Roman Catholic Church in Scotland during and after Geddes's Ministry there*

The Church at this time was very largely dependent on funds supplied by the *Congregatio de Propaganda Fide* which was in charge of all missions (Scotland then being considered a 'mission territory'). The Congregation had (and still has) its headquarters in the Collegium Urbanum in Piazza di Spagna, Rome. In this College there is a fine Library and Archive, to consult which permission is readily granted. The volume relevant to our period is *SCOZIA 3, Scritture Referite nel Congresso del Em^{to} Prefetto* 1761–1797.

Bishop Hay, Vicar Apostolic of the Lowland District, (which included North-East Scotland, nearly as far as Inverness), was in frequent correspondence with 'Propaganda' on many matters. And in addition there was the joint annual letter of the Scottish Vicars Apostolic to Propaganda, sent from Scalan usually in August, to give an account of the Scottish 'mission' and especially how they had spent their money and what their future needs were.

1792, Feb. Report written in French, of a meeting at the Scots College, Paris, between John Geddes, George Hay, Alexander Gordon, in the presence of Bishop Colbert of Rodez and others. Hay complained of Gordon trying to dispose of the college property and to refound the college in another country, without any reference to the Vicars Apostolic of Scotland; John Geddes complained of the lack of contact between Gordon and the Vicars Apostolic; and Gordon complained of the lack of confidence in him on the part of the Vicars Apostolic. No result was reached. The meeting was in Dec. 1791.

SOME CONTEMPORARY PERIODICALS
British and German Containing Material on Geddes
(Book Reviews or Obituary)

Allgemeine Bibliothek der Biblischen Literatur.
(Ed. J. G. Eichhorn). 1788-1801 there appeared reviews of Geddes's biblical works.

Analytical Review.
1788-1793 many articles by Geddes appeared. These are listed in Good, *Memoirs of . . . Geddes*, pp. 192-94.

Annales Literarii (Helmstädt).
Reviewed several of Geddes's works, e.g. the *Prospectus and Letter to Dr Lowth*.

British Critic.
(Ed. W. Beloe and R. Nares). Between 1794 and 1802 reviewed *Bible*, vol. 1 and 2 and *Critical Remarks*. The reviewer was Bishop Samuel Horsley.

Critical Review.
(Ed. T. Smollett and P. Stockdale). Reviewed all Geddes's works between 1787 and 1802. Also reviewed Earle's reply.

Gentleman's Magazine.
(Ed. J. Nichols who assumed the name of Sylvanus Urban.) Reviewed Geddes's works between 1783 and 1792, but later confined itself to publishing letters in support of or attacking Geddes. In 1803 it published a review of Findlay's *The Inspiration of the Scriptures*.

Göttingische Bibliothek der neuesten theologischen Literatur.
(Ed. C. P. Ständlin.) In 1798 reviewed Geddes's *Bible*, vol. 2.

Monthly Magazine.
Reviews and obituary, 1798-1802.

Monthly Review.
Reviews of many of Geddes's works between 1790 and 1803, but without much detail.

Morning Chronicle.
  Published a number of poems and short prose pieces by Geddes between 1795 and 1799.
Neue Orientalische und Exegetische Bibliothek.
  (Ed. J. D. Michaelis.) 1787, 1790 reviews by J. D. M. of *Prospectus and Proposals.*
Neues Repertorium für Biblische und Morgenländische Literatur.
  (Ed. H. E. G. Paulus.)
Neuestes Theologisches Journal.
  (Ed. J. P. Gabler.) Between 1798 and 1802, reviews of Geddes's *Bible*, vol. 2, and *Critical Remarks*; and Obituary.
Scots Magazine.
  64 (1802). Obituary of Geddes, p. 276.

SELECT BIBLIOGRAPHY

Books referring to, or closely related to, Geddes and his work.

Adams, H. P., *The Life and Writings of Giambattista Vico*, London, 1935.

Addis, W. E., *The Documents of the Pentateuch*, translated and arranged in chronological order, with introduction and notes. In two volumes, London, 1892, 1898. Reference to Geddes on pp. xxxv-vi.

Aspinwall, Bernard. 'The Last Laugh of a Humane Faith', *New Blackfriars*, July 1977, p. 33.

——, 'Dr William Maxwell', *New Blackfriars*, Dec. 1978, pp. 565-69.

Banffshire Field Club, *Transactions*, 1906-37. Banff, 1907-37.

Bauer, G. L., *Hebräische Mythologie des Alten und des Neuen Testaments mit parallelen aus der Mythologie anderer Völker, vornehmlich der Griechen und Römer*. 2 Bde, Leipzig, 1802.

Bellesheim, A., *History of the Catholic Church of Scotland from the Introduction of Christianity to the Present Day*, tr. with notes by D. O. Hunter Blair. Edinburgh, 1887.

Benjoin, G., *The Integrity and Excellence of Scripture, a Vindication of the much controverted passages, Deut, vii, 2, 5; and xx, 16-17 whereby the justice of the commands they enjoin are incontrovertibly proved and consequently the objections of Thomas Paine and Dr Geddes completely refuted*. London, 1797.

Bossy, J., *The English Catholic Community, 1570-1850*, London, 1975

Bradner, L., *Musae Anglicanae; a history of Anglo-Latin poetry, 1500-1925*. (Reference to Geddes.) New York, 1940.

Bullough, O.P., Sebastian, 'Dr Alexander Geddes, 1737-1802', *Scripture Bulletin*, Winter 1984.

Butler, C., *Historical Memoirs of the English, Irish and Scottish Catholics since the Reformation*. 3rd edition, 4 volumes. London, 1822.

Chadwick, H., *Lessing's Theological Writings*. London, 1956.

Chambers' *Cyclopaedia of English Literature*, edited by R. Chambers, 2 volumes, Edinburgh, 1844. See vol. 2, pp. 798ff for Geddes.

Chambers' R., *Biographical Dictionary of Eminent Scotsmen*. See vol. 2, pp. 413-421 for Geddes. Glasgow, 1835.

Cheyne, T. K., *Founders of Old Testament Criticism.* London, 1893. See pp. 4-12 for Geddes.

Colenso, J. W., *The Pentateuch and Book of Joshua critically examined,* London, 1865.

Coleridge, Samuel Taylor, *Confessions of an Inquiring Spirit,* edited by H. N. Coleridge. London, 1840. (Includes the *Letters on Inspiration.*)

Cotton, H., *Rhemes and Doway* – an attempt to show what has been done by Roman Catholics for the diffusion of the Holy Scriptures in English. See pp. 62ff on Geddes. Oxford, 1855.

Creed, J., and Boys Smith, *Religious Thought in the Eighteenth Century, illustrated from writers of the period.* Cambridge, 1934.

Duffy, Eamon, 'Ecclesiastical Democracy Detected' (1779-1787). *Recusant History,* 10 (1970), pp. 193-209; ditto, (1787-1796), pp. 309-331.

Drummond, A. L., 'Alexander Geddes, 1737-1802, Roman Catholic Priest and Higher Critic in the Age of Reason', in *Historical Magazine of the Protestant Episcopal Church,* 35 (1966), pp. 73-85.

Earle, J., *Remarks on the Prefaces prefixed to the first and second volumes of a work entitled The Holy Bible. . . by the Rev. Alexander Geddes LL.D.,* in four letters addressed to him by the Rev. J. Earle. London, 1799.

Eichhorn, J. G., *Einleitung in das Alte Testament.* 1780-83, 3 Bde; 4 Ausgabe, 5 Bde, 1823, Leipzig.

Findlay, R., *The Divine Inspiration of the Jewish Scriptures or Old Testament,* asserted by St Paul, 2 Tim iii, 16 and Dr Geddes's Reasons against this sense of his words examined. London, 1803.

Gabler, J. P., *J. G. Eichhorn's Urgeschichte, herausg. mit Einleitung und Anmerkungen.* 3 vols. Altdorf, 1790-93.

Good, J. M., *Memoirs of the Life and Writings of the Reverend Alexander Geddes LL.D.* London, 1803.

Graham, H. G., *Scottish Men of Letters in the Eighteenth Century.* London, 1901.

Gray, John, *Near Eastern Mythology.* London, 1969.

Greenslade, S.L., (ed.), *The Cambridge History of the Bible,* Cambridge, 1963. For Geddes, see pp. 271-2, 290.

Gordon, J. F. S., *Scotichronicon, or the Ecclesiastical History of Scotland.* 4 vols. (the 4th entitled Journal and Appendix). Glasgow, 1867.

Harper, A., 'A Banffshire Poet Priest', in *Banffshire Field Club Transactions,* 20 Jan. 1905.

Hartlich, C., – Sachs, W., *Der Ursprung des Mythosbegriffes in der modernen Bibelwissenschaft.* Tübingen, 1952.

Horsley, S., *Animadversions on Dr Geddes's Critical Remarks on the Hebrew Scriptures.* Reprinted from the British Critic (1802). London, 1803.

Irving, D., *The Lives of the Scottish Poets.* 2 volumes, Edinburgh, 1804. A life of Geddes appears in vol. 2. pp. 353-410. This life was omitted in the second edition of 1839.

Jourdain, C. M., *Histoire de l'Université de Paris au XVIIe et XVIIIe Siècles.* Paris, 1862-66.

Kraus, H. J., *Geschichte der historisch-kritischen Erforschung des Alten Testaments.* 2nd edn., Neukirchen 1969. 3rd edn., Göttingen 1983.

Leith, W. Forbes, *Memoirs of Scottish Catholics during the XVIIth and XVIIIth Centuries.* Selected from hitherto inedited MSS. 2 vols. London, 1909.

Merk, Otto. *Methodische Probleme der biblischen Theologie des Neuen Testaments* (Studies of the work of J. P. Gabler and G. L. Bauer; in Marbürgische Theologische Studien. 9), Marburg, 1971.

Michaelis, the late Sir John David, *Commentaries on the Laws of Moses,* trans. from the German by Alexander Smith D.D., Minister of Chapel of Garioch, Aberdeenshire. London, 1814. Criticism of Geddes in the translator's Foreword.

McGregor, J. Geddes, *The Bible in the Making.* London, 1961. Ref. to Geddes on pp. 200-202.

Newcome, W., *An Historical View of the English Biblical Translations,* . . . to which is added a list of various editions. . . from the year 1526 to 1776. Ref. to Geddes on p.77. Dublin, 1792.

New Spalding Club, Publications. *Records of Marischal College and Uni-*

versity (Aberdeen), 1593-1860. Vol.2 (1898) entry on Geddes, p. 99. Aberdeen, 1898.

Paine, T., *The Age of Reason*, being an investigation of true and fabulous theology, London and Paris, 1794.

Petre, M. D., *The Ninth Lord Petre*. London, 1928.

Pope, Hugh, 'Alexander Geddes, Unhappy Biblical Scholar', *Irish Ecclesiastical Record*, 56 (1940), pp. 321-42.

Pope, H., *English Versions of the Bible*, revised & amplified by S. Bullough, O.P. Ref. to Geddes on pp. 379ff. St Lous, Mo., 1952.

Ramsay, John, *Letters of John Ramsay, 1799-1812*, Scottish Historical Society, Edinburgh, 1967.

Rees, Thomas, *Reminiscences of Literary London*. Ref. to Geddes on p. 79. London, 1896.

Reventlow, H. Graf, *Bibelautorität und Geist der Moderne*. Die Bedeutung des Bibelverständnisses für die geistesgeschichtliche und politische Entwicklung in England von der Reformation bis zur Aufklärung, Göttingen, 1980.

Reynolds, E., (ed.) *The Mawhood Diary*, (1764-1790). Catholic Records Society, London, 1956. Ref. to Geddes under 7th-8th May, 1786.

Rogerson, J. W., *Myth in Old Testament Interpretation*, London and New York, 1974.

——, *Old Testament Criticism in the Nineteenth Century: Germany and England*. London, 1984.

Schaffer, E. S., *Kubla Khan and the Fall of Jerusalem*. The Mythological School in Biblical Criticism & Secular Literature, 1770-1880. Cambridge 1975.

Sime, J., *Lessing, his Life and Writings*, 2 vols., London, 1877.

Smellie, W., *Transactions of the Society of Antiquaries of Scotland*. Edinburgh, 1792–. In vol. 1, pp. 402-468, poems and a dissertation by Geddes.

Smith, G. A., *Modern Criticism and the Preaching of the Old Testament*. London, 1901. Pp.25ff on Geddes.

Strauss, D. F., *The Life of Jesus critically examined*, trans. from the 4th German edn. by George Eliot. 3 vols. London, 1846. New edn. with

Intro. by Georg Pfleiderer.

Symington, J. L., 'The Rev. A. Geddes, an Early Scots Higher Critic', in *Records of the Scottish Church History Society*, vols. 9-10, 1945-50, pp. 19-36.

Vico, G., *Principii di Scienza Nuova*. Napoli, 1744.

Taylor, M., *The Scots College in Spain*. Valladolid, 1971.

Vater, J. S., *Commentar über den Pentateuch*, mit Einleitungen zu den einzelnen Abschnitten, der eingeschalteten Uebersetzung von Dr Alexander Geddes's merkwurdigeren, critischen und exegetischen Anmerkungen, und einer Abhandlung über Moses und die Verfasser des Pentateuchs. 3 Thle. Halle, 1802-05.

Wakefield, G., *Memoirs of the Life of Gilbert Wakefield B.A.*, formerly Fellow of Jesus College. Cambridge. Written by himself. 2 vols. ed. 2.1804. In vol.2, p. 257, a letter from Geddes to Wakefield.

Ward, B., *The Dawn of the Catholic Revival in England, 1781-1803*. 2 volumes. London, 1909.

Wette, W. M. L. de, *A Critical and Historical Introduction to the Canonical Scriptures of the Old Testament*. From the German of W. M. L. de Wette, translated and enlarged by Theo. Parker, Boston, 1843 (from the 5th ed.).

INDEX

ILLUSTRATIONS

Portrait (by an unknown hand)
said to be of Dr Alexander Geddes, c. 1770?

Scalan Seminary, at the foot of the Grampians

Scots College, Paris

The Tynet Chapel, on the Gordon Estate,
where Geddes officiated

Tynet Chapel interior

Traquair House, Peebles

Library, Traquair House

Robert Edward 9th Lord Petre

Thorndon Hall, Essex, 1883

I thank my very dear friend for two bottles
of good good—and I trust they will preserve me
in future from deluging my poor stomach
with laudanum—I send you all the
beans that appeared this morning fit
for use, and the first fruits of my few
appricots—I have also sent to your
care Mr Woodroffe's pomme unique:
for it seems to be nearly ripe, and
I am terrified lest some wicked hand
pull it.—In a day or two, I think it
will be a delicious morsel.—I ew shall
be with you at 5, and ever am &c
                                    M. Geddes

Letter to Miss Howard, c.1795

Dr Alexander Geddes, 1785
(by Sir George Chalmers)

His grave at St Mary's Churchyard,
Paddington, London